Elisabeth Bumiller

THE SECRETS
OF MARIKO

Elisabeth Bumiller is the author of *May You Be the Mother of a Hundred Sons: A Journey Among the Women of India*. She was born in 1956 in Aalborg, Denmark, grew up in Cincinnati, Ohio, and graduated from the Medill School of Journalism at Northwestern University and the Graduate School of Journalism of Columbia University. Starting in 1979, she worked for *The Washington Post* in Washington, New Delhi, Tokyo, and New York. She is now a reporter for *The New York Times*. She and her husband, Steven R. Weisman, live with their two children in Bronxville, New York.

ALSO BY *Elisabeth Bumiller*

May You Be the Mother of a Hundred Sons:
A Journey Among the Women of India

THE SECRETS
OF MARIKO

THE SECRETS
OF MARIKO

A Year in the Life of a Japanese Woman

and Her Family

Elisabeth Bumiller

VINTAGE BOOKS

A Division of Random House, Inc.

New York

FIRST VINTAGE BOOKS EDITION, NOVEMBER 1996

The Library of Congress has cataloged
the Times Books edition as follows:
Bumiller, Elisabeth.
The secrets of Mariko : a year in the life of
a Japanese woman and her family / Elisabeth Bumiller. — 1st ed.
p. cm.
ISBN 0-8129-2603-X
1. Women—Japan—Tokyo—Case studies.
2. Middle class women—Japan—Tokyo—Case studies.
3. Family—Japan—Tokyo—Case studies.
4. Middle class families—Japan—Tokyo—Case studies.
5. Japan—Social conditions—1945– I. Title.
HQ1765.T64B85 1995
305.4'0952'185—DC20 95-6930
VINTAGE ISBN: 0-679-77262-6

Random House Web address: http://www.randomhouse.com/

Printed in the United States of America
10 9 8

For my father

CONTENTS

The Principal Characters xi

1 · *From a Great Distance* 3

2 · *Memories of War* 31

3 · *"I Forget I'm a Housewife"* 65

4 · *The Festival of the Dead* 91

5 · *The Pleasures of Summer* 111

6 · *Back to School* 141

7 · *Neighborhood Politics* 179

8 · *Scenes from a Marriage* 199

9 · *The Gingko Trees* 223

10 · *Crisis* 253

11 · *Mariko's Secret* 285

12 · *A Japanese Life* 311

Acknowledgments 333

Selected Bibliography 335

Index 337

THE PRINCIPAL CHARACTERS

The Tanakas

Mariko, the energetic and overscheduled guiding force of the Tanaka family

Takeshi, Mariko's husband, a phlegmatic electrical engineer with a fondness for alcohol, distracted by a difficult year at work

Shunsuke, the sixteen-year-old son, eldest child and family hope

Chiaki, the Tanakas' moody and intelligent fifteen-year-old daughter

Ken-chan, the nine-year-old son, stubborn and cheerful

Saburo, Mariko's father, imprisoned in Australia during World War II, now devoted to the full-time care of his ailing wife

Ito, Saburo's bedridden wife and Mariko's mother

In the Community

Mr. Yukio Tanizaki, the unofficial mayor of Ichomachi

Mr. Hiroshi Mori, the priest of the Ichomachi shrine

Mrs. Yoko Mori, the wife of the shrine priest and the president of the Ichomachi Elementary School PTA

Mrs. Yumiko Sato, a neighborhood activist and tree advocate

Mr. Eiichi Kojima, Shunsuke Tanaka's world history teacher

THE SECRETS
OF MARIKO

1

FROM A GREAT DISTANCE

Mariko's living room

FEBRUARY

When I first heard the name Mariko, it sounded elegant and a little musical, nothing more. It could have been the name of any of the shy, wasp-waisted schoolgirls I saw on the subway, or perhaps of one of the self-possessed, sober-suited University of Tokyo graduates on her way up at the Ministry of Labor. But the Mariko I studied and interviewed and annoyed for more than a year was of another sort, though no less a part of Japan. She was stocky, earthy, and forty-four, overscheduled and sleep-deprived, a Tokyo woman of the middle class with three children, two part-time jobs, and one disengaged husband. She relaxed at the end of each day with a bath, a beer, a cigarette, and a videotape of her favorite lunchtime gab show; once she told me that she looked forward to the mindless, inefficient proceedings of PTA meetings because they gave her two hours to sit still. She was vigorous, positive, a person who thrived on busyness—indeed, her enthusiasm tended to grate on her husband, a phlegmatic electrical engineer, and her three children, one of whom once commented with an air of resigned amusement, "I think my father has been overwhelmed by my mother's cheerfulness." Mariko made homemade pickled cabbage year-round and every December supervised the family's preparation of rice cakes, a New Year's delicacy that most people simply ordered from neighborhood shops. Mariko also took lessons on the samisen, a three-stringed banjo-like instrument introduced to Japan from China in the sixteenth century, which is so difficult to play that studying it requires more seriousness of purpose than learning how to arrange flowers or perform a tea ceremony, hugely popular cultural pursuits for stay-at-home Japanese wives. Mariko was an equally serious nag of her three children, and although she was no "education mama," as the Japanese say with a mixture of derision and pride of the women obsessed with getting their children into the right schools, she did pester her three to do their homework, get off the phone, and, in the case of her plump fourth-grade son, not snack so much.

Hers was in fact such an ordinary existence that in the beginning I never imagined there could be a thread of poetry running through it, but there was: In Japanese, the characters that make up Mariko's name mean "from a great distance." Her father, an Imperial Army soldier in World War II, had been captured in the New Guinea jungle and imprisoned for three years in Australia. Mariko was conceived shortly after his return, and her name was a moving remembrance of his long journey home. The name also had a resonance in my own relationship with Mariko. I felt that we had met across a great geographic divide and then together traveled a long emotional distance, deepening our understanding of each other and our cultures along the way.

This book is a chronicle of one year in the life of Mariko and her family—the story of an ordinary Japanese woman at the close of the twentieth century in one of the richest nations on earth. It is about the interior lives of a handful of individuals in what at first seems to be a nation of maddening conformists—about their singular and complicated joys, ambitions, insecurities, disappointments, resentments, misgivings, and mixed feelings. It is also a story of postwar Japan, where economic triumph has been nourished by a measure of social coercion, a flawed education system, and often corrupt politics. It is about the burdens shouldered disproportionately by women, and why the Japanese self-image of a harmonious, classless society is partly myth. Woven into the history of Mariko's family are the ghosts of Japan's past—a legacy of war and defeat—and the demons in its troubled, neurotic relationship with the United States today. Above all, Mariko's story is a reminder that certain universal themes transcend borders. Like all of us, Mariko struggled to balance her own needs with those of her family. She also understood the euphoria and risks of emotional intimacy and the loneliness and safety of distance from others.

From February 1991 through April 1992, I talked extensively with Mariko, her husband, her children, her parents, her neighbors, her friends. I went to her children's schools and her husband's office. I visited the hospital when her father had an operation. I attended PTA meetings, community board hearings, and neighborhood festivals. I went to her samisen lessons and concerts, and to a live performance of one of her favorite television shows. In that year alone, Mariko's family bumped its way through quarrels, depressions, illnesses, drinking binges, and exam anxieties, as well as holiday celebrations and other highs. In the beginning, Mariko said I could use the family's real name, but as the year wore on and our conversations became more intimate, we both agreed I had to be more protective of her privacy. So I will call Mariko's family Tanaka, her neighborhood Ichomachi, and her husband's company Nippon Electric. I have also changed the names of a community leader, a community activist, and the neighborhood priest and his wife.

No one is really "typical," but Mariko did have much in common with the majority of women in her country. She believed, as do most Japanese women, that a woman's primary duty is to be at home with her children, and that motherhood is a vital job in her society. Only as I got to know her did I discover some of the emotional layers underneath the cheerful surface. In the beginning she told me she had a good, satisfying marriage, but later she said it felt sometimes like "putting one foot in the grave." Mariko also told me at first that she could not make sense of the talk about fulfillment in the workplace by leaders of Japan's small and fragmented women's movement. But after a family illness forced her to stay home for two months later in the year, she became depressed and said she realized she was much happier when she worked. She accepted the view that Japan's success rests on a complete division of labor between the sexes—that while the Japanese woman is wholly responsible for running the household and overseeing the education of the all-important next generation, the Japanese husband is free to pursue his work. And yet she later told me that there had been a bleak moment when she imagined, in a way that frightened her, what it would be like to walk out the door. "It would have been like throwing my whole history away—my parents, my children, my husband, my life," she said, recalling the fantasy. "All my memories would have been gone." Above all, Mariko was human.

Although the structure of my book is a chronology of the Tanaka family's year, along the way I found myself digressing into other aspects of Japan, much as I discovered them myself. After I went to classes with the Tanaka children, I talked to educators about the Japanese school system. I went with Mariko to a famous shrine festival much favored and well attended by Japan's *yakuza*, or mafia, and returned later to speak to the police and the gangsters themselves.

Before I went with Mariko to the set of the television show, I interviewed the star, one of the most popular comedians in Japan. I pursued what interested me, trying to let my curiosity be my guide.

It made particular sense to me to explore Japanese society through the experience of one family. More than most countries, Japan likes to think of itself as one large family, united by a unique, inscrutable Japaneseness. For most of history, the islands of Japan have been geographically and linguistically isolated from the rest of the world; as a result the racially homogeneous Japanese are self-conscious in their dealings with outsiders, feeling both inferior and superior to foreigners, particularly Westerners. A soaring economy during my time in Japan seemed to bring out the feelings of superiority, until the recession of the 1990s forced another period of collective self-doubt. At the height of national self-confidence, for example, the Tanaka family, like everyone else in Japan, was caught up by the international furor prompted by the comments of Prime Minister Kiichi Miyazawa in the Japanese Diet, or Parliament, to the effect that American businessmen "lack a work ethic." Since it seemed that he was talking about Americans in general, most Japanese publicly recoiled with embarrassment. But I was able to understand from the reaction in Mariko's family that most Japanese *do* have a low opinion of American work habits, though they keep it to themselves. The view of the Tanaka household, at least, was not that the prime minister had said something incorrect, but that he was too blunt. "He thought he was speaking just to the Japanese—to us, to the family," Mariko's husband, Takeshi, said.

Some Americans may think that a nation that values the family as much as Japan does would therefore be made up of tight-knit households more fulfilled and happier than our own. But in the course of my year with the Tanakas, I learned that Japanese families experience the same tensions and conflicts as American families do and seem no more "happy" than those in the United States. Indeed, below the surface of the "stable" Japanese family there is often an overworked, hard-drinking father who is gone eighteen hours a day. He is a visitor in his own home, sometimes seeing his children only on Sundays, only vaguely aware of their teachers, schedules, and friends. It often struck me that such families—that is, the majority of Japanese families—would be considered dysfunctional by American standards. But Japanese expect far less from marriage than Americans do, and while they may not be individually happier, their families are on average far less apt to break down. In America, where one of every two marriages fails, the per capita divorce rate is almost four times that of Japan. For Japanese, at least, happy families may not be as important to a nation's health as stable ones.

I met Mariko in February 1991, when I had been living in Japan for almost two years. I had spent that time studying Japanese, finishing a book about India, and writing feature stories for *The Washington Post*. In January 1990, my first child, Madeleine, was born in a Tokyo maternity hospital. Giving birth is perhaps the most intense event of a woman's life. In Japan it was also, for me, the most intense cultural experience I had ever had. I could not believe that at the height of labor, on my walk from the labor room to the delivery room, ten minutes before Madeleine emerged, I was asked to change from a pair of pink slippers, the labor room set, to a pair of green slippers for the delivery room; afterward, the hospital held compulsory group breast-feeding classes. There was a definite feeling of kinship among the women in that class. But like most Americans and other foreigners in one of the world's most closed societies, even those who spoke fluent Japanese, I always felt like an outsider in Japan. With the help of a cost-of-living subsidy from my husband's newspaper, we lived in a small, Western-style house in an affluent Tokyo suburb, home to some of the city's establishment families, business people mostly, who in recent years had watched with a mixture of pride and alarm as the neighborhood became a sought-after haven for Japanese baseball stars, ruling-party politicians, and new real estate money. I spoke enough Japanese to engage in polite conversations about the weather, the quantities of food our large dog ate, and how much I liked the beautiful wildflowers when my family went hiking in the Japan Alps. But I could not understand the television news or read best-sellers by the trendy young novelists. Most of my interviews for *The Washington Post*—with Japanese art dealers, a Kabuki actor, two upmarket geisha, the inventors of the Sony Handycam, and the first woman (a Japanese) to climb Mount Everest, to name some of the most interesting—were conducted through an interpreter. In two years, my husband and I had been invited to only a handful of Japanese homes, which was not unusual, given that the Japanese in Tokyo rarely extend such invitations to one another. (Once, when I went to dinner at a Japanese friend's house, she told me it was the first time she had ever had guests over for a meal.) And yet I was not so bothered by the lack of conventional hospitality as I might have been, perhaps because I had expected so little from Japan in the first place. I had been brought to Japan by circumstance, in March 1989, when my husband became the Tokyo bureau chief of *The New York Times*. Initially I had little enthusiasm about going; India, where we had lived for three and a half years, remained my real love. But after a few months in Japan, I happily realized I was again in a wholly alien culture, more foreign even than India.

Japan is deceiving at first. Americans who come for a week on business often note that it seems disappointingly Westernized, like New York without the glamour. And it is true, Tokyo at first impression is one of the world's most characterless cities, a big gray dud where the restaurants close at nine P.M. and movie theaters schedule the late show at seven. The nightclubs and bars are open into the small hours, but by midnight an army of Japanese office workers,

the "salarimen," are dragging themselves home under the glaring
fluorescent lights of the last train, heads slumped forward on their
chests, mouths open in uneven snores, exhausted from work and
the compulsory drinking with colleagues. Eventually I came to see
that underneath the dreary façade was a city with a rich history and
distinctive neighborhoods, from the traditional crafts of the old
downtown area of Asakusa, to the secondhand book shops of Jimbo-
cho, to the live sex shows of Kabuki-cho, to the expensive boutiques
of Ginza. More than that, Japan is a country where American
assumptions about behaving in society and functioning in life are
often useless, a country where "yes" means "yes" but sometimes
means "no." In the United States, one expects consumer groups to
be on the side of the consumer. In Japan, consumer groups oppose
cheaper imported rice because imports will hurt the nation's heavily subsidized farmers. In the United States, one expects labor
unions to be in conflict with management. In Japan, labor unions
cooperate closely with management and worry about how they can
contribute to the company's bottom line. In a larger sense, the Japanese always seem to put their country before themselves. The
longer I was in Japan, the more foreign it seemed to me, and therefore the more I liked it. Certainly the late eighties and early nineties
were an extraordinary time to live in Tokyo. Those were the days
when the Japanese were buying Rockefeller Center, Columbia Pictures, and Renoirs in bulk and telling Americans to be encouraged
because the United States trade deficit with Japan had fallen to a
mere $49 billion, which of course represented almost no progress at
all. Americans were gobbling up Japanese cars, Handycams, and
microchips, while the Japanese disdained as shoddy and inferior
most of what Americans made and sold. In the evenings I used to
walk past the flashing neon billboards on the main streets in Ginza,
gazing at the bright lights and immaculate sidewalks and bustling
crowds, and think I had come to the electrifying, frightening center
of the world. Never had I felt so humbled as an American.

At the start of 1991, I was ready to write another book. As a feature writer, my subject had always been the private lives behind public figures, and to me the truth behind the image of the model Japanese family presented tantalizing possibilities. Of course many good books on Japan already existed, including some excellent studies in English on family life. Among them were Ezra Vogel's *Japan's New Middle Class*, about Tokyo families in the 1960s, and *Haruko's World*, a 1983 book about a Japanese farm woman and her community by Gail Lee Bernstein, a professor at the University of Arizona. But I wanted to see what a journalist could add to the outside world's understanding of families in Tokyo now. Most of the recent books on Japan by foreigners seemed to me to fall into two categories. First were those that marshaled facts in support of a thesis as to how outsiders should think about Japan. The best of these in recent years has been Karel van Wolferen's *The Enigma of Japanese Power*, which rejects the old view that Japan is a place of harmony and cooperation and sees it instead as a mighty juggernaut run by power elites unaccountable to the people. Van Wolferen, along with a handful of other influential writers known as revisionists (or, depending on your point of view, Japan-bashers), are callers-to-arms, demanding that Americans wake up to see Japan as a society fundamentally different from ours, one that will never relent in its challenge to the United States. The novelist Michael Crichton learned at the knee of the revisionists and acknowledges his debt to them in *Rising Sun*, his best-selling thriller.

An entirely different category of book has been produced by Westerners focusing on their own adventures in Japan. These books, while absorbing, usually concentrate on the author's personal experiences and impressions in encountering the country. Among them is a new genre—the story of the rite of passage of young men teaching English or working in a Japanese company. What was missing from the canon, I thought, was a book about the Japanese as individuals—a book about a few Japanese rather than "the Japanese," a book that looked closely at how people lived their lives.

In starting my pursuit of the ideal family, I had visions of having to interview countless prospects before deciding who might be the best subject. One of the first friends I called for help was Sachiko Kamazuka, an interpreter who had done some work for me for *The Washington Post*. I told her I wanted the family to be fairly middle-of-the-road: solidly middle class, not affluent, with two or more children, at least one of whom had gone to one of the proliferating private cram schools, known as *juku*, that teach students how to pass the grueling entrance exams for private junior highs, high schools, and colleges, and for the best public schools as well. I also wanted a mother who had a part-time job; most Japanese women return to the workforce, usually in part-time jobs, when their children are in school all day. Most important, the family had to be willing to put up with me for a year. Sachiko called back a few days later and said she had a promising subject—Mariko, a casual friend who lived in her neighborhood. Sachiko's son and Mariko's son were in fourth grade at the same school.

Sachiko arranged a meeting for the following Thursday morning, February 14, a gray and depressing St. Valentine's Day. I remember the holiday well because all over Tokyo young secretaries, called office ladies, or O.L.s, were giving their bosses and boyfriends chocolates in its honor. The weather was not the only sodden feature of life in Japan at the time. The nation's economic boom was beginning to slump, and there was political infighting among would-be prime ministers. The only news anyone was following with intensity was the embarrassing search for a bride by Naruhito, Japan's thirty-one-year-old crown prince and heir to the throne. So far no one would have him.

Sachiko instructed me to take the train from my house to the Ichomachi station, and when I got there she was waiting for me in a gleaming red RX-7 sports car. Sachiko was married to a former racing-car champion and was one of the few Japanese I knew who took the subways and trains only out of dire necessity. She didn't like the crowds, and seeing all the burned-out, identically dressed businessmen depressed her. She much preferred dealing with Tokyo, even at rush hour, from the comforts of her bucket seat while listening to George Michael on her car CD. In a nation of sheep, Sachiko often stood out like some exotic hybrid. Opinionated, outspoken, and elegant, she was in her late thirties (I never got a straight story from her on her age) and had a weakness for beautifully tailored suits created by a dressmaker. She had first learned English on a three-month Rockefeller Foundation fellowship that began at California State University in Long Beach, continued with a bus trip across the United States, and ended with a stay with a family in Tarrytown, N.Y. Later she studied at UCLA. In Japan, a country that has never been famous for its sense of humor, Sachiko was a saving breath of irreverence. When she met a Bangladeshi journalist, a friend of my husband's, who was visiting Tokyo from Dacca, she told him (we were all having tea at Mariko's) that the problem with his overpopulated country was that people had too much sex. We were all laughing, and our friend from Bangladesh was not so much offended as astonished. He went home and used Sachiko's comment as the lead anecdote in his newspaper column.

Mariko's house was a five-minute drive from the station. Ichomachi seemed at first to be identical to so many other neighborhoods I had seen, as monotonous as the road out of town. Before World War II, it had been a farmland of rice paddies and dirt roads, but prosperity had changed it to a helter-skelter jumble of low ferro-concrete apartment buildings jammed alongside boxy new homes of stucco, brick, or what looked like bathroom tile. Telephone wires, electric power lines, and television aerials crisscrossed the skies, adding to the functional, make-do feeling, as if everything had been slapped together by someone in a tremendous hurry. Of course much of Tokyo had been built in exactly that way after the Great Kanto Earthquake of 1923 destroyed half the city, and again after the American firebomb attacks during World War II. The specter of war is gone, but calamitous earthquakes strike Tokyo every sixty years or so, and the city lives in fatalistic anticipation of the big one that is long overdue. Permanence has never been a part of Japanese architecture. The Japanese often like to point out that the most important edifices in the Shinto religion, the shrines at Ise, have by tradition been torn down and reconstructed out of cypress wood every twenty years, almost without interruption, since A.D. 690.

And yet Ichomachi had its charms. Off the main thoroughfare was a maze of winding, narrow back streets bordered by camellia hedges, noodle shops, and a few traditional Japanese homes with big wooden beams and sliding paper-screen doors, their entrances graced by azaleas and pines. The alleys were empty on this particular morning, but by afternoon school would be out and those too young for cram classes would be playing ball or accompanying their mothers on their daily trips to buy fish and vegetables in the small storefront markets. There, enormous white radishes called daikon were piled neatly alongside lotus roots, eggplants, and fat Chinese cabbages. By early evening, the pungent smell of yellow-tail frying in oil would waft from kitchen windows. Soon spring would arrive, Ichomachi's most glorious season, when clouds of cherry blossoms burst over walkways in the center of the streets, following the course of the old stream that had been there when Mariko was a child. In the blazing heat of late summer, people shaded their porches with chick blinds and watched the old-fashioned bush clover meander over their fences and bloom in a profusion of pink. In autumn, the Japanese maples turned a deep red and the fan-shaped leaves of the gingko trees a glowing, flamboyant yellow.

Sachiko turned onto a quiet side street and pulled up in front of Mariko's house. It was an unremarkable two-story building, vaguely Western in style, covered with cream-colored aluminum siding. It sat about five feet back from the street, partially hidden by a thick bamboo hedge. A spindly tree with naked branches grew in the patch of dirt in front of the house; later I discovered that it was a prized persimmon tree that bore delectable bright orange fruit in the fall. Sachiko and I opened the front gate and walked over the stepping-stones along the side of the house, past bicycles and umbrellas, to a big sliding door. Sachiko opened it and called a polite good morning—"Ohayo gozaimasu"—into the darkness inside.

Mariko came to the entrance. She was smiling and was dressed in a big turtleneck sweater over an old pair of jeans. "Ohayo gozai-masu," she said. She had a ruddy, round face, thick, healthy hair cropped short and close, a full but compact body. There was none of the frail delicacy sometimes associated with Japanese women; Mariko exuded energy, competence, and control. She led us through the dark, cold entrance hall to what served as the family's main living area, a cluttered, cozy room covered with a traditional woven floor mat, or tatami, made from dried Japanese reeds, and asked us to have seats at a low rectangular table, which had a smooth wooden top about a foot and a half from the floor and a thick quilted skirt. Mariko called the contraption a *kotatsu*, and as I sat down and stuck my legs inside I discovered with great enthu-siasm that it was toasty warm underneath, thanks to a built-in heater. In Mariko's chilly house (there was no central heating, as is the case in many Japanese homes), I soon came to love the *kotatsu*. So did Sachiko, who lived in a modern, warm apartment. Once dur-ing the New Year's holidays, when Mariko had prepared more food than could fit in her tiny refrigerator, she simply stored the over-flow in her freezing entrance hall. I was amused but Sachiko was sardonic. "This whole house is a refrigerator," she observed.

Mariko had green Japanese tea waiting for us. She sat down at the head of the table, with me on her left side and Sachiko opposite me on her right, and as she pulled out a cigarette, I took a quick look around the room. It was a mix of Japanese tradition and modern consumer electronics. A big television, a VCR, and an electric heater dominated one corner; up above was a big shelf of videocassettes. A wooden breakfront against a wall was filled with a mismatched collection of china, sake cups, and souvenirs. Next to it was a low rattan table with a black rotary-dial telephone, a virtual antique, and above, thumbtacked to the wall, was a calendar and a jumble of papers announcing school events and schedules. Mariko always put her younger son's lunch menus here, sent home each month by his elementary school. (Some weeks later, I learned how meticulous Japanese schools can be. The school reported on one day that the students would be having sushi, milk, Japanese clear soup, and fruit, for a total of 593 calories; on another day, they were served a hamburger, spaghetti, butter and roll, milk, salad, and fruit, at 722 calories.) On the opposite side of the room was a sliding door that led to Mariko and her husband's bedroom, a small room with some large closets for clothes. Mariko and her husband pulled out futons, or mattresses, to sleep on at night. Another sliding door at the far end of the living area opened to the patch of mud and the persimmon tree in front. Even in the winter, Mariko often left this door open so that the cat, a skinny, chronically dusty white beast named Kiri-chan, could come and go as she pleased. This of course brought further blasts of Tokyo cold into the room.

As Mariko sat at the head of the table, smoking her cigarette, her legs curled under her, I explained to her through Sachiko that I wanted to write a book about a Japanese family. I assumed this would be the first of dozens of preliminary interviews with potential subjects, and that it would take months to settle on the right family. Actually, I guessed I would never be back. Certainly what Mariko at first told me about her family did not add up to anything especially interesting. The house we were in was actually her parents' home, where she had been raised; four years ago, she and her husband and children had moved there from their own small but more modern and comfortable house a few streets away to be with her parents in their final years. Mariko's three children were sixteen, fifteen, and nine. Her husband, an electrical engineer, designed and supervised the installation of wiring in small apartment buildings, which the Japanese call mansions, all over Tokyo. I remember being disappointed that he didn't work on, say, the Honda assembly line, or at least at a big, well-known Japanese company. I was equally unimpressed when Mariko told me that her main part-time job was as a water-meter reader, and that she also made extra money working one week a month as a clerk at the Japan Travel Bureau, where she kept the books on Air France tickets. It was possible, I reflected, to find an ordinary family that was a bit too ordinary.

I was thinking in stereotypes, of course. Most Japanese work for small and medium-sized companies, not the giants like Mitsubishi, Mitsui, and Sumitomo in the nation's industrial oligarchy. In that way, the Tanakas were quite typical. So was their combined annual family income of $60,000, which, with three children, put them slightly below the average Japanese household income. Mariko and her husband, however, had more security than their earnings reflected. Unlike most Tokyo residents, they owned their home— the house they had left when they went to live with Mariko's parents. The house, I later learned, still had most of its furniture and even a few plants, ready for the day when Mariko's parents died and she and her family could move back in. Takeshi had inherited the property, about two thousand square feet, from his father, and he and Mariko had built their home on part of it, with the help of an eighteen-year loan taken out against the value of the land. At the hyperinflated Tokyo real estate prices of the early 1990s, the two thousand square feet was worth $1 million; in today's recession it is worth probably half of that. Either way, the Tanakas had money only on paper. Each month, faced with the astronomical cost of living in Tokyo, Mariko had to juggle and scrape to make ends meet.

At this point in our conversation Mariko said two interesting things. The first was that her husband was unhappy in his job—"He doesn't like electric work," she said simply—and the second was that while she had great hopes that her sixteen-year-old son, Shunsuke, would go to Waseda University, one of Japan's most prestigious institutions, she was so mentally and physically exhausted from getting him through cram school that she had given up similar ambitions for her nine-year-old son. "When our kids are young, we have dreams," she said. "But when they get older, we see the reality. We know they can't go to certain schools, and we realize there are other alternatives. A mother begins to enjoy herself."

Neither of these was a startling revelation, but they surprised me. It was a little unusual for a Japanese woman to tell a stranger that her husband didn't like his job, particularly in a nation where work was often considered more important to a man than his family. The standard response would have been that her husband was exhausted and depressed by his long hours and the terrible demands made on him by the company—with the implication, of course, that he was an important person at the office. But to say flatly that he did not like his work, which had supported the family for twenty years and was his reason for being? In my view that spoke of uncommon honesty.

It was also unusual for a Japanese woman to admit so quickly that she had pushed one child and not another. Most everyone did, of course; first children in Japan were as much a repository of their parents' dreams and ambitions as those in the United States. Here again, Mariko was uncommonly frank, but I was more impressed with her eloquence—"When our kids are young, we have dreams. . . ." Mariko also said the biggest headache among her three children was her fifteen-year-old daughter, Chiaki, who had evolved into a moody, rebellious teenager. "She is very difficult," she said. "The problems began when she was nine years old. That's when all the conflict started. We don't communicate very well."

I thought about Mariko as I took the train back home. She was open and talkative, and I liked her. Most important, she had told me as I left that she was enthusiastic about the idea of my book. At the time, I wasn't sure why. Who would want a reporter nosing around for a year? But Mariko had said she was involved in community work, so I assumed she saw me as her personal project in internationalization, or *kokusai-ka*, the word of the year as the government urged its citizens to become more aware of the world beyond the isolated shores of Japan. Mariko had neither traveled outside of Japan nor met an American before, and here I was, a bit of exotica from the West, dropped into her life. Her curiosity about another culture, like my curiosity about hers, would help keep the project going through the inevitable troughs. My gut instincts told me she was the right one.

I have to admit there were also practical advantages in not having to interview another twenty-five families. Then, too, Mariko lived only minutes from me, door to door. In Tokyo, two-hour, one-way commutes from home to office are commonplace, and I had dreaded that my search for the perfect family might end on the outer reaches of the metropolitan area. Mariko's location was a godsend. For once in my life, I decided to make something easier for myself rather than harder. The next day I called Sachiko to tell her that if Mariko was really willing, so was I. This, then, was how I conducted my extensive, scientific research to find the perfect Japanese family.

There was a delicate question of money—Japanese reporters often pay for interviews. Mariko never brought it up, but Sachiko did. Would I be paying Mariko, she wanted to know, for the huge amounts of time involved? (I had told Mariko I wanted to sit down with her for a long interview at least once a week, and also to spend time with other family members, at her children's schools, and in the neighborhood.) I told Sachiko that although this book was not part of any work I was doing for *The Washington Post*, I still felt bound by *Post* ethics, and my own, not to pay for interviews.

Instead, I said, I would give the family a large present at the end of the year, perhaps something they needed for the house. Of course I paid Sachiko the standard rate for interpreters. That settled, Mariko went through the charade of asking her husband's permission. ("I try to let him think he's number one—that puts a man in a good mood," she told me months later.) Mariko's husband gave his approval, which I know he later regretted. I think he suspected, correctly, that Mariko was sitting around with Sachiko and me complaining about him. He was also mystified why his wife, of all people, was so interesting to me.

At any rate, for the next year Mariko, Sachiko, and I were an oddball threesome with a chemistry that somehow, miraculously, worked. Obviously, my presence changed the course of the year in subtle ways, and I know my questions forced Mariko to think and talk about her life more decisively. And yet, no reporter has any sway over the daily disasters and powerful emotions that roil through a family. My interviews with Mariko, interpreted by Sachiko, were never formal exchanges but rather three-way conversations in two languages. I continued to take Japanese lessons, and by the end of the year with Mariko, I understood many things she said, not least because I had come to know her well. Mariko had studied English in school for six years, the minimum required, but like most Japanese she could hardly speak a word. Or so I thought. By the end of the year, I discovered that she understood much of what I said too, and occasionally she would even answer me in tentative English. Often the three of us, sitting on the floor in Mariko's house, drinking endless cups of tea and eating Japanese junk food, would get into long discussions about marriage, children, work, husbands, cooking. Other times, Mariko and Sachiko, both strong-minded and opinionated, would get into disagreements as I waited for the dust to settle.

I remember one especially heated exchange about cram schools, a major concern for Tokyo families torn between the desire to give their children every educational advantage and the worry that such intense studying would snuff out a childhood. Sachiko, with some misgivings, was sending her fourth-grade son to *juku*, but Mariko refused on principle to send Ken-chan, her nine-year-old.

"I am against *juku* during elementary school," Mariko said, "because I hope that during those six years, children play and learn about friendship."

"I really disagree with you," Sachiko retorted, irritated. "There are things that some kids can learn at *juku*, like self-control."

"The kids are threatened by the teacher," Mariko shot back. "That's why they're self-controlled."

Sachiko, infuriated, turned to me. "She's so stupid," she spit out in English, knowing full well that Mariko understood.

Other times, Sachiko smoothed the rough edges. Once when I asked Chiaki, Mariko's fifteen-year-old daughter, if she wanted to have a career in business after she finished school, she sat there silently, too shy to answer the question. Sachiko brought her out by saying, "You know—good suits, good attaché case, high heels." Chiaki immediately said yes with great enthusiasm. Of course this was not quite the question I had asked, but it broke the ice. By this time, I realized that even if I had spoken perfect Japanese, or even if Mariko had spoken fluent English, Sachiko, with her gifts of intimacy and humor, was a crucial part of what made it all work. And yet Sachiko and Mariko could not have been more different; there were actually times when I felt I was more like Mariko than Sachiko was. But if Mariko saw Sachiko as extravagantly stylish, I knew she also admired her for her skills in English and the career she had made for herself through talent and drive. And if Sachiko sometimes thought Mariko was just another housewife, she often told me how much she respected her intelligence, hard work, and spirit.

But, obviously, my great disadvantage in not speaking Japanese well was that I missed the subtleties in some of our conversations.

Japanese is one of the world's most difficult languages, frustrating in its many levels of politeness, so bafflingly nuanced that the Japanese seem to understand more through instinct than through words. Also, practically speaking, everything took twice as long to say. And yet, there was one clear advantage. As a complete outsider, writing in English for a distant land, I posed no threat. There were many things Mariko did not want the neighbors to know—a feeling that is particularly strong in a nation as concerned with appearances as Japan. She insisted, for example, that nothing about her family ever be published in Japanese. But what did it matter if she told me? I hesitate to say this because it sounds self-serving, but I think that if I had spoken fluent Japanese and lived full-time with the family, I would have been less of a safe harbor. True, I might have heard for myself precisely how rude Chiaki was when she talked back to her mother, but I am not sure Mariko would have been as open with me about the things that were really important to her.

"For me, this is a good opportunity to look back at the old days—and to look forward to the future," she told me two weeks after our first meeting, and then explained why she had really agreed to the project. "It doesn't happen very often that you can open yourself to people like this. I can't say this to anybody else—there are so many things you try to hide here. Sometimes you just want to bring them out, all these things that are stuck inside. I feel very happy to bring all those things out that I have hidden for so long. This is a tremendous opportunity for me to think about myself, and my life."

Gradually, with Mariko as my focus, I came to appreciate the subtleties and mysteries of the society around her. I often associate that learning process with the time, about halfway through the year, when I found out about a beautiful grove of thirty gingko trees that had been cut down for a parking lot at the neighborhood's Shinto shrine. Gingkos, native to China, are venerable and respected trees at shrines across Japan and are said to be home to sacred spirits. The chopping down of the gingkos at the Ichomachi shrine spread anger through the neighborhood, and as my year with Mariko progressed, I tried to find out who was behind what seemed like an avaricious and shortsighted decision. In the course of investigating, I discovered that the trees had become a focal point for the interest groups of Ichomachi, and also a subtext that altered the politics of the ward council and the PTA, sometimes chaotically, as if the tree spirits had been made homeless by the chain saw and were now up to mischief. The issue kept coming up again and again in my conversations with Mariko and my reporting, as I discovered how many Ichomachi lives intersected at the trees. Although I never learned exactly how the gingkos came to be cut down, I did learn more about the sometimes mysterious workings of Japan. By the end of the year, the fallen trees were to me a metaphor not only for the secrets of Ichomachi, but also for the secrets of Japanese lives behind public façades, and of course for Mariko herself.

Like all Japanese, the Tanakas lived in the shadow of a powerful social history that shaped the way their family functioned in modern-day Tokyo. I came to learn it was impossible to understand Mariko—and her relationships with her children, her husband, and her parents—without understanding a bit of the past. Certainly for centuries, and perhaps for millennia, the family has been the essential building block of Japanese society. As recently as one hundred twenty-five years ago, for example, during the military reign of the powerful Tokugawa Shogunate, the individual was not even recognized by law. Rights and privileges were instead extended to the family, and one's place within the family determined one's place in society.

Significantly, Japan never had a Renaissance that celebrated humanism and the capacity of men and women to shape their own destinies. Japanese thinking has never included a belief in the sanctity of the individual, or much faith in the notion that one person can make a difference. Japanese society was instead shaped by the powerful force of Confucianism, the ancient ethical system of filial piety borrowed from China. The Japanese government later extended Confucianism to include total obedience to Japan's great patriarch, the emperor, the symbol of government power. But at its core, Confucianism centered on the importance of the family and the hierarchy within the family as the source of political strength.

The story begins in primitive Japan, which historians say was probably matrilineal—meaning that the line of descent, though not necessarily of authority, was traced through women. Very little is known about the early tribes of Japan, and the racial origins of the Japanese are in some dispute. Scholars believe that the Japanese archipelago may have been inhabited two hundred thousand years ago, but that modern Japanese are more likely descended from a mixture of other Asian peoples, including seafarers from the South Sea islands, who migrated there after the last Ice Age.

Not until about seventeen hundred years ago did a sophisticated rice-cultivating people organize themselves into tribes, whose wars culminated in the victory and supremacy of the Yamato clan about A.D. 400. The Yamato chieftains led a society based on what the historian John Whitney Hall calls "family or simulated family connections," with themselves at the top as supposed descendants of the sun goddess, Amaterasu. The Sun line continues today as the world's oldest dynasty, and Emperor Akihito, the son of the wartime emperor, Hirohito, still worships Amaterasu as his mythical ancestor. In truth the succession was highly irregular, but the myth remains powerful and many Japanese speak reverentially about its importance.

The next great phase of Japanese history came when the Japanese, inspired by the splendors of the T'ang Dynasty in China, built new capitals on the Chinese model at Nara in the eighth century, and later at Heian-kyo, the present-day Kyoto. The Heian Era, a magnificent age of classical Japanese culture, also marked the rise of the Fujiwara family, which wielded immense power behind the throne. Again, as the historian Sir George Sansom has observed, Japan was ruled by a system whose "dominance came from family solidarity rather than from the merit of individuals."

As the Fujiwara family's power slipped in the thirteenth century, a newly armed military aristocracy arose in the countryside—the samurai, who alternately banded together and warred with one another for the next six hundred years. Japan's great feudal age was a time of battles among families and clans that still resonate in Japanese literature, drama, music, movies, and television serials. The Gempei War, a struggle between two great samurai factions at the end of the twelfth century, for example, is celebrated by a lilting theme Mariko played on the samisen.

In the seventeenth century, the wars among the feudal lords, or daimyo, subsided with the rise of Ieyasu Tokugawa, the general who unified Japan, ruled as shogun, and initiated the closing of Japan to the West, a policy that remained in effect for two hundred fifty years. The Tokugawa Shogunate also ushered in a crucial period in the development of the Japanese family, instituting a rigid class system and establishing the *ie* (pronounced ee-eh), a three-generation property-owning household, as the basic unit of society. The idea that every individual had a predetermined place in a natural hierarchy of classes reached its zenith, and the government achieved an astonishing level of social control, which many sociologists say continues to exert an influence in contemporary Japan.

The *ie*, for example, was the center of Tokugawa society, and it included those brought in through marriage and adoption, as well as servants. The head of the *ie* had broad legal rights over them all, since it was the *ie*, not the individuals within it, that owned property and paid taxes. Under the law, in fact, a person was recognized only as the head of a family, son, second daughter, wife, and so on. Today, the *ie* lives on most obviously in the many Japanese companies that operate like surrogate families for their employees.

In 1868, the Tokugawa Shogunate was overthrown by a rebel group of samurai, which led to the "restoration" of the emperor, who became known as Meiji, and the supposed abolition of Japan's feudal class system. Public education was made available to all. And yet the Meiji oligarchy not only continued the *ie* but wrote it into the new civil code, institutionalizing it nationwide. Heads of households had absolute legal authority to rule on the marriages of dependents, and primogeniture, inheritance by the eldest son, became the law of the land. By the 1920s, the increasingly militarist and nationalist government extended the concept of the *ie* to the nation itself, using it as a vehicle to command obedience for Japan's imperialist ambitions in Asia. "The nation came to be conceived of ideologically as one large *ie*, a 'family state' headed by an emperor father," writes the anthropologist Susan Orpett Long.

During World War II, Japanese society remained a mystery to the outside world, particularly to the U.S. State Department, which tried to solve the riddle by commissioning Ruth Benedict, a cultural anthropologist, to write a study explaining the mind of the enemy to Americans. In her classic work *The Chrysanthemum and the Sword*, Benedict described Japanese society in a way that is as true as ever today: "Every Japanese learns the habit of hierarchy first in the bosom of his family and what he learns there he applies in wider fields of economic life and government. He learns that a person gives all deference to those who outrank him in assigned 'proper place,' no matter whether or not they are the really dominant persons in the group."

After the war, the American Occupation authorities introduced sweeping changes, imposing a constitution and effectively abolishing the *ie* as the foundation of society. Implicitly, the individual became the primary social unit. All children were to inherit equally and were free to choose their marriage partners. Women had equal rights. Naïvely, the Americans thought they could change Japanese society simply by writing new laws into the books.

In the last half century, the Japanese family has undergone enormous stress from industrialization, urbanization, and the postwar economic miracle, but family lives have not necessarily improved. Exploding real estate prices have forced families to find homes far from the center of Tokyo, and fathers are at home less now than their own fathers were in the prewar days. The Japanese birthrate has dropped to an all-time low as more and more women have entered the workforce or declined to raise children with virtual absentee fathers. All these changes have eroded the strength of the family in ways that could never have been envisioned a few decades ago. Once the most powerful unit of Japanese society, the family is now at a turning point that could determine the character of the nation itself in the years ahead.

Mariko spent the rest of that first day I met her, February 14, 1991, exhausted from the wear and tear of her life. I later found out it was her forty-fourth birthday, but she had not mentioned this to me and, typically, the family had no plans to do anything special. As usual, Mariko had been up at 6:50 A.M. to prepare breakfast and to pack lunches, known as *bento*, in small plastic boxes for her husband and three children. Each *bento* included two sticky rice balls wrapped with seaweed, called *onigiri*, plus grilled fish or chicken and steamed vegetables. Ordinarily Ken-chan, the youngest, ate the lunch served at his elementary school, but the school kitchen had been under renovation for six months, so Mariko had to pack his lunch, too. Making lunch was a serious duty. No self-respecting

Japanese housewife would let her charges go out into the world without proper *bento*. Not only that, the lunches had to meet certain standards. The teachers at Ken-chan's school lectured the mothers in parents' meetings about making good *bento* and complained that many had actually given their children too much food. "Some *bento* weighed three hundred eighty grams, but some weighed nine hundred sixty," one ever-vigilant teacher informed a group of mothers that year. "I tried to get rid of all the extra calories in the *bento* with exercise. The children must not become fat."

After her husband and children left for the day, Mariko cleaned the house, saw me in the late morning, then left for her meter-reading job shortly before one in the afternoon. She was home by five, when she pulled out the futon in her bedroom and lay down for an uncharacteristic nap. As she told me later, "Ordinary life is more difficult than extraordinary life. Right now, I can't think only of myself. I have to think of everyone else in the family. If I do just what I want to do, the whole family will collapse." But today was her birthday and she felt entitled. Chiaki was graduating from junior high the next month, and Mariko—an inveterate joiner, I would later find out—was on the school's graduation committee, and the round of meetings had left her exhausted. On this day, she found it hard to think about preparing dinner yet again for her husband and children. The family almost never went out. The cost of a meal for five people at an ordinary neighborhood restaurant was astronomical. Enough sushi to feed everyone would have cost four hundred dollars, and even ordering in pizza cost nearly one hundred dollars. I calculated that in twenty years of marriage, Mariko had made dinner close to seven thousand times.

Mariko was still horizontal when her husband arrived home at six-thirty. This was early for a Japanese husband; many if not most men kept longer hours. On the other hand, Mariko had to put up with her husband's drinking binges, some four or five a year, when he did not come home at all. On such occasions he never called, but he always turned up after work the following evening, hung over, silent, and contrite. Mariko had decided she was no longer going to worry about him unless she heard from the police.

"Happy birthday," Takeshi said to his wife, seeing her on the futon. He was a trim and lean man of forty-four, with close-cropped hair and a handsome face. Mariko had known him since high school, when he had been just a friend, but one with a remoteness and a mysteriousness that interested her. She had called him a nihilist back then. "He brought out my maternal instincts," she once told me. Today, she noticed he had not brought her flowers for her birthday as he usually did.

"Why don't *you* make dinner tonight?" she asked, knowing she was making a radical request. Japanese men of Mariko's husband's generation are virtually incapable of cooking for themselves, let alone for others. The Japanese press currently makes much of the "new" Japanese father in his thirties who actually prepares meals, cleans, and spends time with his children, but on the basis of my experience listening to complaints from Japanese women friends, I decided there are only seventeen such creatures in Japan and they all happen to have been interviewed by the same women's magazines. Certainly the "new" father remains a very small minority. My favorite Japanese survey is the one that reported that Japanese married men spend an average of eight minutes per week on household chores.

In any case, Mariko's husband was in an acquiescent mood. Perhaps he was feeling guilty for forgetting the flowers. He called the kids, and together they all made fried rice. Mariko went back to sleep, thinking that her birthday had brought some satisfaction after all.

2

MEMORIES OF WAR

Mariko, age one, and her family, 1947

MARCH AND APRIL

The morning of Chiaki Tanaka's junior high school graduation dawned breezy and cool, one of those muddy days at the end of March that hold promise of the annual cherry blossom ritual of renewal and carousing a few weeks later. The blossoms usually burst into bloom by the first week in April, coinciding with such mundane events in the rhythm of Japanese life as the end of the school and fiscal years and the spring campaign for wage hikes by the labor unions. Then the Japanese engage in their yearly metaphysical musings about the tragic, beautiful blossoms, blown away, sometimes the moment they arrive, by the first warm winds and rain. The flowers are such a part of the Japanese ethos that the kamikaze pilots who crashed into American battleships during World War II were always compared to cherry blossoms, struck down in their prime.

For ordinary Japanese, the blossom season was a time to reflect on the transient nature of pleasure and love, and to wallow in depressed thoughts. Mariko, typically, said she always had a bittersweet feeling when she walked beneath the blossoming trees along the winding paths in her neighborhood. Of course not all cherry blossom rituals were quite so poetic. As the morning news shows broadcast their color-coded maps indicating the progression of the blossom-opening from south to north, office staffs planned *hanami*, the compulsory employee picnics beneath the flowering branches, where the men got extravagantly drunk, sang soulful songs, and pawed the O.L.'s.

Here in the gym at Ichomachi Junior High School, on Wednesday, March 20, Chiaki and eighty-two other ninth-grade graduates were nervously wedged onto folding chairs. Chiaki was a slender, solemn young woman with long, dark hair and bangs framing a serious face; Mariko pointed her out to me in the crowd. Everything seemed in order, but there was an underlying tension. I did not know it at the time, but two weeks earlier, on March 7, a minor scandal had occurred at the school, caused by an event more common than outsiders in Japan might expect. Four of Ichomachi's third-year girls, all about fifteen years old, had summoned two second-year girls to a neighborhood cemetery and then attacked them and kicked them. One girl was smacked so hard on the side of her head that her eardrum was hurt, and she had to be taken to a hospital.

To me the episode seemed bizarre behavior for middle-class girls from the suburbs, but it was not so very unusual. By the early 1990s, bullying—what the Japanese call *ijime*—and violence in general had become alarming problems in the nation's schools. There was no particular explanation for what happened in Chiaki's school, but Japanese educators are alarmed about what they say is a growing problem in public junior highs, where those who have failed the exams for private school often end up feeling like losers. During Chiaki's last year in junior high, from April 1990 to March 1991, five students were killed in Japanese schools nationwide, the Education Ministry reported. The next year at least six were killed, including one fourteen-year-old boy who was brutally beaten to death by classmates in Okinawa. The episodes may seem few and far between compared with similar events in the United States, where some inner-city schools explode with gunfire and gang fights. But it is a surprising number for a middle-class society that has no serious poverty or major racial and ethnic divisions. Bullying first became a big issue in Japan in 1985, when several well-publicized incidents, some of them reported in the Western news media, led the Ministry of Education to begin keeping statistics. By the late 1980s and early 1990s, the campaign against bullying seemed to have been successful, because the number of reported incidents decreased. But even Education Ministry officials were skeptical of their own statistics and suspected that the number of reported incidents was down because schools, fearing for their reputations, simply did not report what really went on.

If the numbers were in dispute, the causes of bullying were not. Japanese educators all agreed that increasingly difficult entrance exams and an ever more demanding curriculum put unusual stress on students who cannot keep up. The Japanese call these students dropouts, but unlike those in the United States, they are really psychological dropouts, who are physically in school but have abandoned any hope of learning at the pace of the rest of the class. In their boredom, frustration, and self-loathing, they resort to violence against those they deem different. Dropouts in the United States may get a second chance, or may become successful in other ways, but that is rare in Japan, where a student who fails to make the grade knows that his chances of success are slim. This was the underside of an education system that prided itself on promoting proficiency and harmony.

Chiaki's school was taking no chances that anything untoward would happen at the morning's graduation. The school had held a series of meetings about the incident, and the day before, Mariko and the other mothers on the graduation committee had been assigned the responsibility of keeping a close watch on the students during the ceremony. Mariko took her task seriously. Even though nineteen other mothers had similar duties, she was nervous. What if she missed something? What if she let the other mothers down?

As the ceremony began, Chiaki, characteristically, completely ignored her mother and the further embarrassment of Sachiko and me. The three of us boring *obasan*, or middle-aged women, were over in the parents' section, which was in fact the mothers' section, where everyone was dressed in a gray or blue version of the same boxy suit. Predictably, there was not a father in sight. But then, no one expected the men to take off even a few hours from work, particularly for something as minor as a graduation. (Some years earlier, the Japanese were appalled when an American on a Japanese baseball team took time off to attend his son's high school graduation in Virginia just as he was about to reach a home-run record. His decision elicited much commentary in the sports pages about lazy Americans.)

The graduates soon filed one by one up to the stage, which was decorated with a spray of gladioli and a large banner that proclaimed CONGRATULATIONS. The girls wore their blue sailor uniforms, the boys the severe black suits with high collars that were introduced after the Meiji Restoration and were modeled on nineteenth-century German student uniforms. Each student came up to the principal, who was dressed in a morning coat for the occasion, bowed deeply, received the diploma, then bowed again. The girls with long hair bowed by letting it flip dramatically forward, the kind of self-conscious adolescent gesture that apparently spans the Pacific. Soon one boy appeared on the stage, and Mariko tapped my shoulder. "Chiaki-no-boyfriendo"—"Chiaki's boyfriend"—she whispered conspiratorially. Mariko had pieced this information together on her own, since Chiaki viewed her mother as an unconscionable snoop and would never have let her in on something so interesting.

The principal was now at the podium, dispensing stern wisdom to the sea of faces beneath. "Whether you develop well or not depends on your efforts," he said. "Effort is the most important thing." Indeed. Not for nothing do the Japanese refer to their society as the effort culture. All Japanese are taught from their earliest days that talent is not as important as effort, and almost anything—even admission to Tokyo University, the Valhalla of higher education, a kind of Harvard, Yale, and Stanford all rolled into one—can be accomplished by applying yourself.

Next up at the speaker's podium was the PTA president. "Don't be afraid to make mistakes," she told the students, and then launched into admonitions that they should be grateful they had such fine parents. She also thanked the local politicians who had sent congratulatory telegrams. Mariko was not impressed. "That's because the election is so soon," she muttered in my ear.

Finally a graduate came up to the podium to give a kind of valedictory address. This, I hoped, would at last be interesting, but it turned out that his speech, like so much else at the graduation, was filled with the platitudes necessary for all public occasions everywhere.

"So much has happened in the past three years," the graduate began. "We were praised and criticized by our teachers, but we really have made a lot of progress because of your help." He then talked about the class trips to Kyoto and Nara, the two ancient capitals of Japan. "We didn't enjoy the shrines so much, but we did enjoy having fun in the inn after the lights were off. The hardest time was the third year, when we were so uncertain about what direction to go in. But finally, under the teachers' warm and strict guidance, we made decisions."

The ceremony closed with "Hotaru no Hikari," or "Light of the Firefly," a staple of Japanese graduations that is sung to the tune of "Auld Lang Syne." (It is also played over loudspeakers at the nightly closings of the pinball gambling dens, called pachinko parlors.) As the graduates filed out, Mariko sniffled. Even if it had been a less than perfect ceremony, she was overwhelmed by seeing her only daughter grow up so fast.

When I went to see Mariko a week later, the tears had passed. "Frankly, I wasn't that impressed," she said over tea. Chiaki's new uniform, for Ichomachi High School, was hanging on a hook behind her. Mariko then told me how worried she had been at the ceremony because of the bullying incident, though it was never clear to me what exactly she feared might happen. "My main concern was to watch the kids," she said. "And I didn't think the graduates were celebrated that much by the rest of the students." When the ceremony was over, she said, her main emotion was relief.

During April, I got to know Mariko's parents. They lived in the large corner room of the house, down a hallway that was cut off from the comings and goings of Mariko, her husband, and the three children. Mariko's mother, Ito, who was seventy-five, had suffered a stroke twenty years earlier and had been bedridden ever since; her father, Saburo, who was seventy-eight and at one time had been a heavy drinker, now devoted himself soberly to his wife's considerable care. Within the family, the two were called *Obaachan* and *Ojiichan*, for Grandmother and Grandfather. What was striking to me was how disconnected their lives were from those of the two younger generations. Rather than being a tight-knit three-generation household, the Tanaka grandparents, parents, and children maintained separate existences. Saburo and Ito ate their meals in their room, away from the rest of the family, and watched their own television set. The children and Takeshi rarely spoke to them. Mariko, as the only one in the family who spoke regularly to everyone, served as the principal link between generations. Even so, she did not get along particularly well with her parents, and over the years her relationship with her own mother had been as difficult as her present relationship with Chiaki was. "My mother did whatever she wanted, she said whatever she wanted, and when it came to me, she really ordered me around," Mariko complained, with an air of resignation underscored by her knowledge that Chiaki had the same grievances against her. Mariko also had unpleasant childhood memories of her father, who often came home drunk. "He was working for the lumber company, and he used to drink sake with the carpenters," she said. "He devoted his life to his work and never paid attention to his family. I don't remember my father ever taking me anywhere." She recalled one episode when he got drunk and sang loudly while riding a bicycle at a streetcorner near her house. "I was so embarrassed," Mariko said.

And yet in 1987 Mariko had felt compelled by duty and tradition to move in with her ailing parents. Living with elderly parents is not uncommon in Japan, but three-generation families living under the same roof are not the norm they once were. Mariko saw no other recourse. Heavily burdened with the care of his ailing wife, her father needed help. Her mother spent her days confined to bed, napping and watching television, and might benefit from more family contact, however distant. They were not perfect parents, it was true, and her father now nattered on, always repeating himself, about how much money he had to spend on taxis and groceries. Often he would gleefully call out to Mariko whenever his wife managed a bowel movement. Mariko just rolled her eyes. She was equally exasperated by her mother, who she felt had been indulged over the years. Ito was only partially paralyzed from her stroke, and Mariko sometimes thought her mother might have tried harder to perform simple tasks like combing her hair. After all, effort was everything. Once I asked if she was mad at Ito. "Always," Mariko sighed.

But nonetheless they were her parents, they had raised her, and she felt a powerful loyalty to them. It was her responsibility to see them through their old age for as long as she could; given the poor quality, expense, and inadequate number of nursing homes in the country, any son or daughter in Japan would do the same. "Otherwise, you'll regret it later," Mariko said. Aggravating the situation was Mariko's elder brother, who by tradition, as first son, should have taken on the care of Saburo and Ito himself. But he had, years before, gone to live near his wife's family in the bordering prefecture, on the outer limits of the metropolitan area, and saw his parents only twice a year—and then would complain that he thought Mariko talked too roughly to her father. For her part, Mariko viewed her brother as a shirker who had neglected his own parents to be closer to his socially superior in-laws. But she claimed, not convincingly, that after many years she no longer resented him.

In any case, Mariko's parents were to me a rich mine of the past—the family's, and Japan's. Understanding them would also help me in understanding the present. When I asked Mariko about them, she said I should talk to them quickly because her mother did not have much time left and was more and more forgetful. So the next week, one mild day in April, Sachiko and I sat ourselves down on folding chairs by Ito's bed, with Saburo alongside, and asked a few questions about how the two had met. Ito spoke slowly, with slurred words. She was propped up in a hospital bed and had a smooth, white face and a vacant look in her soft, wet eyes. She looked a lot like Mariko, or what Mariko might look like in another quarter century. Saburo was lean and wiry, with a gray stubble on rough cheeks and a mischievous smile. Like all family stories, theirs led to other stories and soon evolved into the long saga of an ordinary couple in an extraordinary time.

The two were married in 1940, in an era of seething nationalism, and their first child, a son, was born just weeks before Saburo headed off to World War II. For the next five years, Saburo's path across the Pacific was determined by Japanese triumphs and then defeats as the nation pursued its disastrous dream of extending its control throughout Asia. He came home to a nation that lay in ruins. The United States won World War II and moved on, but Japan has never fully faced up to its legacy and remains chained to the past. To a surprising degree, the war remains a topic of newspaper editorials and intellectual debate today. The year 1991 marked the fiftieth anniversary of the Pearl Harbor attack, but while historians, academics, and journalists argued the broad principles—Should Japan apologize for its aggression? Was Japan at all justified in going to war?—I learned from Mariko's family just how much the war would change the lives of individual Japanese for generations to come.

Ito, Mariko's mother, was born in 1916 near the town of Oyama at the foot of Mount Fuji. The countryside was farmland back then and still is today; the region, some fifty miles southwest of Tokyo in central Japan, is known for the fine Japanese horseradish, wasabi, that grows on the edges of streams. Ito, the daughter of a horse trader, was the youngest of seven girls and three boys. The family was poor, and four of the children died when she was quite small; Mariko's mother never knew why, but such things happened often in those days. It was the beginning of the reign of the Emperor Taisho, the son of the Meiji emperor "restored" in 1868, fifteen years after Commodore Matthew C. Perry arrived in his black ships and forced Japan to open itself to the West. The Taisho Era was a time of limited self-government and rapid industrialization. By siding with Britain in World War I, Japan profited handsomely from munitions sales and also picked up some of Germany's Asian colonies, establishing them as thriving new markets for exports. In this period, Mitsui, Mitsubishi, Sumitomo, and other cartels synonymous with the economic development of Japan expanded into heavy industry, banking, and shipping. Tokyo's population grew to nearly two million, drawing people from the countryside, where life remained backward and half of Japan's farmers had little more than an acre of land. Mariko's mother grew up surrounded by a patchwork of small rice paddies.

When she was seven, Ito's life changed for the worse when her father died of a heart attack, leaving her mother to support the family as a day laborer in the fields. There was never enough money, especially for a young girl's education, so after seven years of schooling, at the age of fourteen, Ito began work at a handloom factory weaving cotton for kimono. She stayed there until she was twenty, when she found work in the growing metropolis of Tokyo as a live-in maid for the family of a businessman, a Mr. Nakaminami, who ran a pharmaceutical company. Like other men of the new professional classes, he brought in girls from the countryside as servants.

Japan had changed mightily in the two decades since Ito's birth. Rightists and an increasingly aggressive military were transforming the nation into an ultranationalist state obsessed with its lack of natural resources and reliable markets for its goods. Japanese leaders especially were resentful that the Americans, British, Chinese, and Dutch—the A-B-C-D powers—seemed to be blocking Japan's proper role as the paramount imperial power in Asia. In 1931 Japan invaded Manchuria and six years later was involved in a full-scale war with China. The conflict was costly, forcing the government to look toward Indochina and the Pacific for the oil, rubber, and other natural resources it needed to continue the fight.

In this turbulent climate, in the fall of 1939, Ito's marriage was hastily arranged. Everyone knew Japan would soon be fighting a great battle in the Pacific, most likely with the United States, and young men all over the country were trying to find wives before the arrival of their draft notices. Ito had already turned down three proposals of marriage when a fourth prospect, considered quite promising, materialized that October. The man worked as a driver for a lumberyard; he had been drafted once already, at the age of twenty, for the war against China, and had spent 1933 in Beijing. Now he was twenty-seven and eager to be married before the government sent him off once again.

A lumberyard worker who happened to be a cousin of Ito's employer, Mr. Nakaminami, was the one who came up with the idea of matching his colleague with Mr. Nakaminami's servant. And so in October 1939 they were formally introduced at the home of the cousin and his wife, over tea. In the Japan of the time, prosperous families who employed country women as maids commonly assumed the responsibility not only for arranging their marriages but for paying for the weddings as well. The maids were like family members but were on call twenty-four hours a day, with no days off and no chances for socializing.

The tea went well. The prospective groom, of course, was Saburo, and as he told me fifty years later, he was in such a hurry that virtually any woman would have sufficed. "She passed," he told me of Ito. "She didn't have to be very beautiful, but I didn't want her to be ugly. As long as she was normal, she was all right." Arranged marriages were the norm at the time, and Saburo's matter-of-fact tone as he recounted the meeting to me didn't seem to bother Ito, who was listening closely. After all, it was an arranged marriage, not a romance. Love would come later. Besides, it was an unusual time and one could dispense with certain niceties of life; Ito even went so far as to ignore a fortune-teller who advised her against the match. Saburo impressed her as serious and diligent and she quickly said yes. As was the custom, she did not see him again until their marriage celebration four months later, on February 2, 1940, when some forty people came for lunch at a large Tokyo wedding hall, a rambling place with traditional tatami rooms built to accommodate numerous wedding parties at once. Her parents, who never could have afforded a Tokyo wedding, were happy simply to attend. Ito wore a black wedding kimono with a flower print, a gift from the wife of Mr. Nakaminami's cousin, purchased at Takashimaya, the already famous Ginza department store. Afterward, she and her husband went to their first new home, a rented room, but soon moved to a rented house in a residential area south of the center of Tokyo. "Nobody went on honeymoons then," Ito recalled. "We had a honeymoon at home." Like all good brides, Ito quit her job. Saburo continued at the lumberyard, and later that year, using wood given him by his employer, built a house in an outlying area called Ichomachi. Saburo thought he might live in the house one day, but until then he would rent it out. It was in this house that we were speaking, in the big corner room, down the hall from Mariko.

Japan, meanwhile, was mobilizing for all-out war. The summer after Saburo and Ito's marriage, Germany's occupation of Paris was complete, and Japan moved easily into French-controlled Indochina. Under the newly installed war minister, Hideki Tojo, the government capitalized on the nation's patriotic fervor and moved to control the populace through neighborhood groups that spread propaganda and collected cash and gold for the war effort. As the United States and its allies imposed an oil embargo and tough economic sanctions on Japan, Japanese leaders increasingly viewed Washington as the principal threat to its destiny.

Ito had other things on her mind. In the midst of Japan's growing hysteria, on September 28, 1941, she gave birth to her first child, a boy, at a hospital in Ebisu. Her husband scarcely had time to admire his new son. Five days after the birth, on October 3, the long-awaited draft notice finally arrived. Saburo was ordered to report to a nearby training center, and fifteen days later, on October 18, 1941, the same day that General Tojo became the nation's prime minister, he left his wife and three-week-old son for the seaport of Haiphong in Japanese-occupied Vietnam. For Saburo, it was the first leg of his five-year journey across the Pacific. He was a transport soldier ferrying ammunition and supplies, always a month behind the front, hearing of, but not experiencing, the army's successes and failures.

Today, at a time when Japanese leaders still debate whether to apologize to the United States and other Asian nations for Japan's role in the war, I found Saburo ambivalent about the part he played. Most Japanese prefer to see themselves as victims rather than as perpetrators of the conflict, unknowing innocents dragged into battle by a power-mad military. Since school textbooks continue to whitewash the history of the war, much to the rage of China and South Korea, Japan's next generation will probably feel much the same. Certainly Saburo's mixture of regret and self-justification was part of the longtime legacy. "We should not have gotten involved in that war," he told me. "But I didn't have any option—I was just a soldier. I had no opinion at the time. I didn't want to go, but I had no choice." He felt Japan was justified in occupying Manchuria and seemed annoyed that his country had been singled out as an aggressor, especially by others with equally imperialistic ambitions. "Every country tries to occupy other countries," he said. "Japan is no exception." Like most Japanese, he could not—or would not—see the conflict in moral terms and instead viewed it as a colossal mistake to have entered a war Japan was bound to lose. "When we started the war with China, we should have stopped at that point," Saburo said. "Our resources were finished at that stage."

From Haiphong Saburo quickly moved to Songkhla, a seaport on the southeast coast of the Malay Peninsula. He arrived on December 8, 1941 (December 7 in the United States), as bombs fell on Pearl Harbor. Japan's grand scheme for a swift, decisive war with the United States was finally under way, beginning with its plan to wipe out the Pacific Fleet and quickly capture the oil supplies of the Dutch East Indies before the U.S. Navy could recover. The ultimate dream was the establishment of a "Greater East Asia Co-Prosperity Sphere" extending from the border with Russia in the north to the islands of the Pacific and west to India.

In the Malay Peninsula seaport of Songkhla, Saburo transported artillery shells by truck to a storage base as Japanese forces sped toward Singapore. He then moved south and was in Johor Baharu, across the narrow strait from Singapore Island, when the Japanese overran Singapore in one of the biggest military disasters in British history. A month later, Saburo was transferred 150 miles north, to Kuala Lumpur, where he helped transport rubber from the Malaysian plantations back to Japan.

After the triumph in Singapore, newspapers back in Tokyo exulted in victory, declaring that the war was virtually over. But as early as the spring of 1942, the tide began to turn. Japan had expected that Pearl Harbor would demoralize the Americans. Instead it galvanized them into a determination to fight back, inflicting losses on Japan in the Battle of the Coral Sea.

Still Japan pushed south, hoping to attack from its remaining positions in New Guinea. But General Douglas MacArthur, the Supreme Commander of the Southwest Pacific, had other plans in mind. He decided to defend Australia with a counterattack against the Japanese-held villages in New Guinea, a move his staff considered far too dangerous. New Guinea was a nightmarish jungle, and MacArthur's forces were meager. But the battle for New Guinea was critical, not only to save Australia, but also because it could serve as a stepping-stone toward MacArthur's cherished target, the Philippines. The warfare in the New Guinea jungle turned out to be some of the most brutal for both sides. Years later, in his memoirs, Lieutenant General Robert Eichelberger—who had been ordered by MacArthur to take the village of Buna "or not come back alive"—recalled that the jungle was more frightening to his men than the fighting itself.

To this uninviting battleground came Saburo, from Kuala Lumpur via the island of Palau, in October 1943. He was based in relative safety, or so he thought, four hundred miles up the coast from the Japanese front lines, and drove one of the trucks that transported fuel for airplanes. It was a job he could only vaguely remember a half century later; much more vivid were his memories of the bombs dropped during the daily American air raids in January 1944. The Japanese were losing the war and were less and less able to defend themselves. Soon the Americans would begin their systematic firebombing of Tokyo and other major cities on the home islands, killing hundreds of thousands of civilians.

For Saburo, his time in New Guinea was terrifying, and he and the other soldiers were soon taking shelter from the daily bombs in the island's natural caves. "It was very hard even to fix rice," he recalled. "It was the worst time for me during the war." Along with the Japanese military leadership, Saburo assumed that the Americans would battle their way slowly up through the jungles of the northern New Guinea coast, fighting village after village. Indeed, by the spring of 1944, MacArthur's staff felt the obvious move was to hit the Japanese at their front lines in Wewak.

But, in a fateful moment for Saburo, MacArthur decided instead to surprise the Japanese by carrying out a daring attack behind the front lines at an ill-defended spot known as Hollandia, where Saburo was cowering in his cave to escape the American bombs. On April 22, 1944, a hot and humid Saturday morning, two U.S. infantry divisions landed at Humboldt and Tanahmerah Bays, on either side of Hollandia. The Japanese were stunned and fled into the jungle, Saburo among them. Fifty years later, Saburo told me he suspected that MacArthur was somewhere off the coast just before the attack, and indeed MacArthur was watching the bombardment of Humboldt Bay that morning from the bridge of the light cruiser *Nashville.* At eleven A.M., about four hours after the first wave of infantrymen had hit the island, MacArthur went ashore with his top command and promptly took off on a brisk three-hour inspection hike of the beachhead. The Japanese had run so quickly that they had left behind weapons and equipment, and rice still boiling in pots.

In his memoirs, Eichelberger recalls how U.S. troops were sent into the jungle to flush out the fleeing Japanese. "It was the job of the doughboys to hunt them out and kill them," he wrote.

Through ambushes and roadblocks, thousands were killed or captured in the following weeks. On his way deep into the jungle, Saburo could hear the sounds of the American gunfire coming closer. Very quickly, he and three friends caught up with another group of fleeing Japanese soldiers. Some were injured; almost all were unarmed. But Saburo and his two friends had guns, and so they were placed at the front and back of the group, some two hundred strong, to watch for the Allies. Saburo was at the front but somehow got separated from the group. Suddenly he found himself alone, lost in the New Guinea jungle.

For the next six days, he wandered, exhausted and hungry, drinking water that had collected in the trunks of trees. A half century later, Saburo found his jungle ordeal too horrible to remember in detail. But William Manchester, in *American Caesar*, his biography of MacArthur, describes a New Guinea terrain of "steep slippery root-tangled trails" and "waist-deep slop," a jungle where the "air reeked with vile odors—the stench of rotting undergrowth and of stink lilies." This was "the setting of the green war: the green of slime and vegetation, the green of gangrene and dysentery, and the green-clad enemy." Bugs were everywhere, and at night "enormous insects" would "land on a sleeping man and, like vampires, suck his body fluids. . . . Pythons and crocodiles lurked in the bogs and sloughs, waiting for a man to stumble from the mucky trail. At night a soldier would rip away blood-gutted leeches from his genitals and his rectum."

Saburo had no watch and had to judge time by the sun. One day, almost spent, he reached a mountainous area, with small trees and scrub. He shot his gun into the air, and only silence came back. He grew more feeble, and the thought that he would probably die of starvation made him feel oddly relaxed. But it was at this point, when he had given up all hope, that another Japanese soldier suddenly appeared. The man had some rice and dried eggs, which he and Saburo agreed to share. Soon they had made a meal over a fire they started with a page from a Japanese-English dictionary that the man was carrying.

After eating, the two went down to a river and climbed on top of a large boulder, only to find it littered with dead Japanese soldiers, all apparently victims of starvation. Saburo and the officer decided to head for the sea. Before leaving, an exhausted Saburo threw his heavy gun into the river and replaced it with a small pistol he removed from the body of a Japanese soldier. He apologized to the dead man, then bowed.

The river flowed to the sea, and in a few days Saburo and the officer could see the water from a distance. They could also make out men swimming, but through the jungle it was impossible to tell who they were. Up close, unfortunately, they turned out to be Australians. One came out of the water, grabbed his gun, and crouched, naked. Saburo looked back at his fellow soldier, who had taken off his shorts and was holding them up for surrender. The Australian put a gun in Saburo's back, and led both men away. Later he asked if they wanted coffee or milk. "Milk," Saburo said. They chained him together with five other Japanese prisoners; his soldier friend, the one with the dictionary, was used as an interpreter. "They treated me very nicely," Saburo recalled. It was early May 1944.

Three weeks later Saburo was a prisoner of war at Cowra, a small town in the Australian outback, home to a prison camp that was soon to have its own place in history. It was from here that 1,100 Japanese soldiers tried to escape, an attempt that ended in bloody disaster when some 230 of them were killed. In trying to put down the uprising, the Australians lost four men, who were stabbed or bludgeoned to death. The few hundred Japanese who did manage to escape later surrendered or were captured—among them Saburo, who fifty years later said he thought the prison break was a bad idea carried out by hotheads.

The prison lay 150 miles west of Sydney on a dry, scrubby red-clay plain of sheep pastures and wheat fields. The sprawling facility was split into four quadrants, each made up of twenty bungalow-type huts. Each quadrant held 1,000 men. Quadrants A and C housed Italians, D had Japanese officers, and B, where Saburo apparently was held, was for Japanese privates and noncommis-sioned officers, and for Formosans and Koreans. Charlotte Carr-Gregg, in her book *Japanese Prisoners of War in Revolt*, writes that although the Australians got along well with the Italians, the atmosphere at the prison took a bad turn when the Japanese started arriving in 1943. They were ravaged by their long months in the Pacific jungles, and they also felt great shame at having been cap-tured; their military code held that they should have committed suicide instead. Harry Gordon, in *Die Like the Carp*, his account of the Cowra break, writes that the captured Japanese were "arro-gant" and a "moody, brooding lot" who were all "deeply conscious of the fact that they were dishonouring the Emperor and their ser-vice by just remaining alive."

As the Japanese military position worsened throughout 1944, more and more Japanese POWs flooded the Cowra camp. To lessen the strains of overcrowding, the Australians decided to separate the privates from the officers, whom they viewed as agitators. But the impending move so angered the officers that it became the impetus for a riot, which began before the separation could be carried out.

Saburo was in a room with some twenty others. The officers in the group, he remembered, "had an aggressive military spirit, not like me. These young officers couldn't stay quiet." On the night of August 4, 1944, he and the other men were ordered to set fire to their mattresses. Then around two in the morning, according to the account of Carr-Gregg, a single Japanese soldier climbed over an inner fence and ran toward an outer gate, weeping and fright-ened. Before the guards could stop him, the Japanese shouted, "Banzai!" and a large group, Saburo among them, rushed toward the fences. Saburo, who like many of the others used a blanket to protect himself from the barbed wire, was still on the fence when bullets started coming at him from all directions. "I said to myself," he recalled, " 'This is the last time. This is the end. I will be killed.' " Saburo managed to get over the fence and outside to freedom, but the bullets were still coming so close and so fast that once again he gave up and began walking slowly. He assumed he would be shot, but miraculously he was able to continue walking unimpeded into the outback, where he quickly realized the futility of trying to get away. "It was impossible to really escape," he said. "I was in a foreign country." With no map and no knowledge of the area, he knew that even if he reached the town of Cowra he would immediately be captured or killed. "So I returned to the camp," he said. "The whole idea behind the riot had been to make trouble for the enemy—not to escape. I didn't agree with the riot anyway. I thought it was useless." In all, 334 prisoners escaped that night, but within nine days of the outbreak, 25 of them had been killed and the rest were recaptured.

After the outbreak, Saburo was transferred to another Australian prison about 180 miles to the west; he remembered playing baseball, mah-jongg, and the Japanese game of *go* there, in a lazy, even pleasant, atmosphere. The food wasn't bad—mostly rice and fish—and the men were allowed to go for walks. "Unless you thought of the future, it was a very relaxed life," Saburo recalled.

Meanwhile, the Allied forces pushed from the Philippines and other Pacific islands to converge on Okinawa, where the Americans lost more than 12,000 men in three months of battle. Fearing that casualties in taking the remaining Japanese islands might soar into the hundreds of thousands, the United States decided to end the fighting with the atom bomb. On August 6, 1945, Hiroshima was destroyed in a nuclear blast, and Nagasaki three days later. On August 15, Japan surrendered, its dreams of an Asian empire in ruins.

Eight months later, in April 1946, Saburo finally came home. It was hardly a hero's welcome. When his boat docked south of Tokyo, Saburo was inspected for disease by officials of the Ministry of Health and Welfare, issued an identification card and a set of khaki clothes, then perfunctorily released into the chaos of postwar Tokyo.

The city was a smoldering wreck, reduced to rubble and cinders. More than 30 percent of the Japanese had lost their homes, and the entire nation faced starvation. Women sold their kimono for food, and even rich families bartered heirlooms for rice. MacArthur had arrived in the city shortly after the surrender, riding into the capital from Yokohama like a conquering emperor, and would later observe in his memoirs that "never in history had a nation and its people been more completely crushed than were the Japanese at the end of the war." As Supreme Commander for the Allied Powers, MacArthur took charge of the Occupation, setting up army kitchens and cabling Washington for food immediately. When the Congress questioned why he was feeding the former enemy, MacArthur cabled back that cutting off relief "would cause starvation to countless Japanese—and starvation breeds mass unrest, disorder and violence. Give me bread or give me bullets."

Saburo, meanwhile, tried to find his way to the family house in his old neighborhood near the center of the city. He was not at all sure that Ito would be there. He had not been able to write her from prison, and the last of his letters that reached her were from Singapore in 1942, four years earlier. "I didn't know where she was," he recalled. "I returned to our old neighborhood, but all of Tokyo had been burned. From the old train station, I tried to walk to the house, but there was so much vacant land. I couldn't find anybody I knew. The people there could not believe I was really from the neighborhood. They thought I was a stranger. If my family had been there, they would have known. But no one knew who I was. The lumber shop was gone—nothing. My home was gone.

Then I found some neighbors who had a house, and I stayed one night there. Finally, somebody told me my wife was in Oyama"—Ito's childhood home in the countryside. "But before I went to see her, I tried to find a job. Of course there was no hope to find a good job at the time."

Ito had lost track of Saburo after his last letters from Singapore. At the start of the war, when the mails were more regular, she had heard from him often and had saved everything he had written. (Fifty years later, she found one of his old, yellowed postcards for me, undated and with no indication of its origin, as the military required, but still evocative of the time. "I received your letters dated April 29 and May 19 today," Saburo wrote. "I am very happy to know that everyone is in good health. Since I came to Blank Blank Island"—these were Saburo's actual words, as required by the military censors—"blank blank months and blank blank years have passed. While our ship was sailing, it was attacked by enemy submarines. We were bombed from the sky but we finally landed. We have survived so many dangerous war incidents. . . .")

During the war, Ito had taken her young son back to Oyama, where she rented a room near her brother's house. The countryside was far safer than Tokyo under the terror of the firebombs, even though some days her son could see the American B-29s making their turns around Mount Fuji. Ito could support herself by working in the fields or as a maid to the farmers, and when she needed extra money she took in sewing. Like so many other women, she had no idea where her husband was and could only take solace in what a fortune-teller had told her, which was that Saburo was on a big island and would come home after the war.

Back in Tokyo, meanwhile, Saburo was not only unable to get a good job, he could find no work at all. Dejected, he went to the train station penniless, told the clerk his troubles, and said he had to see his wife. The clerk was sympathetic and gave Saburo a free ticket. Later that evening Saburo was at last in Oyama, where he found the home of Ito's brother, opened the sliding wooden door, and said hello. His brother-in-law looked up, astonished. "Saburo is back!" he shouted. The brother-in-law immediately sent his daughter to fetch Ito and her son. Saburo, hoping to clean off the dirt of the journey before his wife arrived, quickly headed for the bath.

Ito came running toward the house, breathless and weeping. With her five-year-old son in tow, she went straight to the bath, and there she saw her husband outside the old wooden tub. He had all his clothes off and was sitting down and scrubbing himself before getting in for a soaking. Saburo stopped and looked at her and the son he had last seen as a three-week-old infant. He stood up, speechless. Ito stared back at this naked stranger, this husband. There was no hug, no embrace, no kiss. This was Japan, 1946. Ito, still crying, simply bowed.

"Welcome home," she said.

Ten months later, on February 14, 1947, a daughter was born. Ito and Saburo named her Mariko. She had been conceived in the weeks after Saburo's return, and her name had been chosen with care. During Saburo's first active duty overseas, in China in 1933, he had visited the Great Wall. The Japanese call the Great Wall Banri no Chojo, but the ideograms that make up *banri*—and mean "from a great distance"—can also be read as *mari*. The suffix *-ko* is often added to girls' names in Japan. Saburo decided right then, in 1933, that if he married and had a daughter he would name her Mariko. Now, fourteen years later, he was home at last from a second horrible war, and the name for his baby girl was more poignant and apt than he had ever imagined.

Mariko did not learn the story of the events leading up to her birth until after she graduated from high school, and then she was not impressed. One night at home she asked her father exactly when he had returned from the war, and when he told her, she counted the months. It became clear she had been conceived almost immediately after his return. "That's disgusting," she told her mother, conjuring up an image of her libidinous parents celebrating an end to their long separation. "It's not disgusting," her mother replied. "It was a wonderful thing." Mariko, of course, eventually grew up to be pleased and amused by the circumstances of her birth and realized soon enough that she was not alone—Japan's first postwar baby boom occurred from 1946 to 1948. Two of Mariko's children were born in the second baby boom, of the early 1970s, when the children of the first boom gave birth.

By the time Mariko was born, the family had moved back to Tokyo, to the house in Ichomachi that Saburo had built and rented out before the war. Mariko was born in the main room of the house, the area where Saburo and Ito would live much later. Saburo, fortunately, had finally found work, at another lumberyard, and if he frequently came home drunk—Mariko remembers her mother just stepping over him once when he fell down in the hall—he was, like all of Japan, attempting as best he could to reconstruct a life for himself and his family. The United States Occupation under General MacArthur was in full force, introducing dramatic social and economic change. The Japanese war machine was dismantled. Seven military leaders, including General Tojo, were sent to the gallows in 1948. MacArthur and his team wrote and imposed the new constitution, establishing a parliamentary democracy that was a mix of the British and American systems. The emperor was reduced to a non-divine symbol who could not even vote. Land reform drastically reduced the holdings of the old feudal lords, antimonopoly laws were passed in an attempt to break up the giant business cartels, and an education system based on the American model began.

Historians have only recently begun to examine the Occupation in a thorough way, but the consensus is that it was successful and benevolent. Indeed, one of the powerful questions that historians address is why the Japanese so quickly and enthusiastically turned around to embrace their former enemy. Two factors are usually cited: First, the Japanese public immediately ascribed the guilt and responsibility for the war to the military leaders, not themselves; and second, the Japanese—who as a group have always been known more for pragmatism than for high-minded ideals—decided that if they had been so soundly defeated by democracy, then democracy as practiced in the West must be superior after all. The more significant question in recent years has been how much change the Occupation really represented. The myth once promoted by both the United States and Japan had conceived of Japan as a warlike country that overreached, was conquered, and then rose from the ashes with the help of the U.S. Occupation to emerge as a peace-loving and democratic nation. Few hold so simplistic a view today. Some historians argue that democracy was not entirely grafted onto Japan by the outsiders but had some roots in Japanese history, particularly in the 1920s, when there was a functioning parliament. Challenging this view, later historians argue that Japan had no such democratic roots, and that it never became as pure a democracy after the war as the myth suggested. The nation may have democratic institutions—a court system, a parliament, a more or less free press—but modern historians, particularly the revisionists, argue that these are not the same as the democratic institutions of the West, and that they have remained in the hands of the political-industrial elite to fuel the engine of economic growth.

The Occupation ended in 1952, when Mariko was five. Like so many others at the time, her family struggled to make ends meet, but no more than the neighbors, and certainly Mariko never looked back on her childhood as one of deprivation. Ichomachi in those days was still largely countryside and rice paddies, far from the center of Tokyo, a perfect setting for a young girl's games. It snowed more then, and in the winters Mariko and her friends went sledding down the big hill of the Ichomachi shrine. Mariko also played hide-and-seek in the graveyard of the beautiful Buddhist temple, climbed trees, splashed in the nearby stream, and shot marbles outside her house in the street, just dirt in those days. It was always a dusty mess, and the mud was fun when it rained.

Mariko's younger brother was born in 1948, just eighteen months after she was. "He was such an adorable boy," she remembered. "Everybody loved him. Girls loved him a lot." She was never as close to her elder brother, who was six when she was born, but she adored her younger brother and doted on him like a little mother throughout her childhood. All five in the family slept in the same room; the rest of the house was rented out to as many as six boarders at a time, usually boys who went to college nearby.

By 1960, when Mariko was in junior high, Japan was booming. Even the massive student demonstrations that year against the new defense arrangements in a security treaty between Japan and the United States—which forced the cancellation of a trip by President Dwight Eisenhower—could not stop the giant cranes and earthmovers that were all over Tokyo. New buildings, roads, subways, and bridges seemed to be changing the face of the city overnight. Even though the West still dismissed much of what was produced in Japan as little more than paper umbrellas and cheap trinkets, Japan had the highest growth rate of any nation in the world. Sony, an upstart young Japanese company, had just shrunk the transistor, invented at Bell Labs in the United States, to create the world's smallest transistor radio, an immediate hit. It was the company's first success at the kind of miniaturization and adaptation that would make it famous—and eventually help Sony and its Japanese competitors to wipe out the consumer electronics industry in the United States.

In Mariko's life, too, important things were occurring. Chief among them was an accident her younger brother had in a corridor at his junior high school. He collided with someone or something —Mariko could not remember exactly what—and fell down and lost consciousness for a short time. Mariko was a year ahead of him in the same school and so was called to his side. When he woke up a little later, she always remembered, his first words were "Oh, my sister." At the time Mariko assumed that he was fine. She could not remember if anyone sent him to the doctor, but in any case, no one took the accident seriously.

Yet over the years, the accident came to be seen in the family as a kind of watershed event. After the fall, Mariko's brother became obsessed by it, at least in the opinion of the family, and blamed it for his frequent mood swings and irritability. Whenever he had a problem, the family listened while he ranted about how the accident had caused it. For whatever reasons, the sweet little brother of Mariko's childhood did seem to be undergoing a personality change. In high school he began to drink heavily, just at the time when Saburo, who was getting older and even less able to hold his liquor, was finally slowing down. Father and son would have terrible fights. Mariko, meanwhile, was rebelling against what she saw as the outrageous control of her mother, who had refused to allow her to play sports in junior high school and had made her go to after-school classes in math and English instead.

Mariko's high school friends remember the household differently. If it wasn't the most modern of houses, and if other families in the neighborhood had some of the new luxuries—like phonographs for listening to 45-rpm Beatles records—it was still the best house to visit after school. "I remember that Mariko's family always had lots of friends around," Hiroko, one of Mariko's high school classmates, told me. "I really looked forward to going over there." The college-student boarders were always amusing and taught Mariko and her friends to play mah-jongg. Mariko's friends knew that she and her mother often argued, but to them Ito was just a bustling, bighearted woman, a mother to everyone, who kept a tight hand on the household. Meals were ample and noisy, and in the evenings everyone would relax by watching a fuzzy picture on their black-and-white television. The one thing the friends did not see was that Mariko's younger brother was becoming increasingly violent. He was drinking more and more, and sometimes in an especially nasty drunk he would hit Mariko. "I was very afraid," Mariko recalled years later.

But Mariko loved high school and was part of the school's most popular group. "From the first year, Mariko stood out," her friend Hiroko remembered. Mariko did well academically, worked for the school newspaper, and had a supporting role in a production of *The Bamboo Cutter and the Moon Maiden,* a famous Japanese folktale about a princess from the moon who brings happiness to a country village. By 1964, Mariko's last year in high school, the Beatles were wildly popular, and Mariko listened to them, as well as Simon & Garfunkel and Joan Baez, on Radio Kanto all the time. She went to both American and Japanese movies in nearby Shibuya, and if a film was especially good, she and her friends went early on Sunday and sat through it twice. She loved James Dean in *East of Eden* and Clark Gable in *Gone With the Wind.*

Takeshi Tanaka, the man who would become her husband, was on the fringes of Mariko's high school group. In an old black-and-white photograph in Mariko's graduation album, the two are captured together in a group of eight friends, separated from each other by a single boy. "*Smah-to tatchi, ii tatchi,*" the caption underneath says, summing up the group: "Smart feeling, good feeling." Mariko had first met Takeshi in junior high, when he wore glasses and was very short and quiet. "I felt nothing toward him," she remembered. By high school he had changed. He was clever, finished his tests before everyone else, and seemed adult and aloof. "He was very popular with girls because he was mysterious," Mariko's friend Hiroko remembered. Although Mariko quietly pined after another boy in high school, she did find Takeshi attractive. "He was the type who didn't have an umbrella on a rainy day, or never hurried, even if he was late," Mariko said. "He wasn't proper. He was the kind of man who women like to mother. But I never thought I'd fall in love with him." Sometimes the bus they both took would arrive late at school, and the other students would leap off and run to class. Takeshi just walked, and Mariko remembers pulling him along to get him there in time. He hated it. "He was so weak that he really brought out my maternal instincts," she said, realizing that the pattern had remained through their marriage. "As a result, we are doing the same things now."

Mariko graduated from high school in March 1965. Her parents told her they could not afford to send her to college, and in any case she did not pass her university entrance exams. Her failure did not produce the kind of crisis it would today in Japan's high-pressure education system; in the mid-1960s, when the country's rapidly expanding industries were eager to hire workers for production plants, not everyone had to go to college. Mariko lived at home and got an office job at a small company that sold golf course memberships, then switched the next year to the Japan Travel Bureau, or JTB, where she handled train trips, hotel stays, and other domestic vacation plans for Japanese clients. Takeshi, her future husband, had entered college but had come down with tuberculosis and was hospitalized for six months. Mariko visited her old high school friend in the hospital, at first as often as three times a week, because she could see it cheered him up. But as she got more involved in her new job at JTB and her own life, she went less and less frequently and felt terribly guilty. Takeshi recovered, and soon after, in 1967, there was a high school reunion. Mariko and Takeshi had drinks together on the way home and late that evening stopped at a park. They kissed each other. It was Takeshi's first kiss, or at least that is what Mariko told me years later; she herself had already kissed a boy in high school. In any event the kiss sealed a promise to marry in the future. Years later, Mariko looked back on the promise as the impulsive, careless whim of two naïve twenty-year-olds, and certainly, for the four years following their kiss, the two busily went their separate ways. Takeshi was getting himself through a technical college, and Mariko was involved in her job and the travel and social life that came with it—skiing, mountain climbing, and casual dates with other men. The two hardly paid attention to each other, let alone to the student riots—against the Vietnam War, the U.S. and Japanese governments, and student regulations in general—that were ripping apart Tokyo college campuses in the late 1960s.

In March 1971 Takeshi graduated from college and the next month started work at Nippon Electric. By August he and Mariko, who had seen each about once a year since their kiss, were engaged. Years later Mariko tried to explain their decision. "It was never a burning love," she said. "But he was hospitalized because of his TB. I promised I would see him every day at the hospital, and I didn't. I think it caused some setbacks. I felt I owed him something." Takeshi, too, felt obligated. "Since I'd said, 'Let's get married,' when we were twenty, I thought she was waiting for me," he told me. Then too, it was high time they both settled down. At the advanced age of twenty-four, Mariko was almost a spinster in Japanese society; in another year she would have been considered too old to be married at all. Takeshi, fresh out of college and new on the job, was in dire need of a wife to manage his life and help him assume his proper place in the world. In the Japan of the time—and to a great extent now—everyone had to get married. "I was so busy, and I didn't have time to get to know other girls at all," he said. Fortunately, Mariko was still available. "It seemed she didn't have any boyfriend," he said. "I'd known her since junior high, and I didn't have to have a pose with her. I could talk to her very casually, as a friend rather than as a woman." Arranged marriages had been the norm before the war, and although modern Japan was rapidly changing, the head rather than the heart still ruled many unions.

The other unspoken factor in the decision was Mariko's younger brother. His drinking had not stopped, and his life was continuing on its downward spiral. In 1966, he entered Meiji University in Tokyo, but during his third year his girlfriend became pregnant and the two decided to get married. Mariko, who was still living at home, was vehemently against it, but her parents gave the couple their blessing, allowed them to live in their home, and supported them financially. (Mariko's elder brother had already married and was living elsewhere with his wife.) But the younger brother continued drinking and sometimes became so violent that he threatened Mariko with a knife. Mariko was terrified, and she found living in the house unbearable. When Takeshi began coming around in that spring of 1971, he suddenly seemed like a ticket out. Mariko was grateful, too, for the way he handled her brother. "My husband was the first man to deal with my brother as a human being," Mariko recalled. "He treated him very nicely—like a normal person."

In December 1971 Takeshi and Mariko were married. They took a small apartment, and Mariko continued at the Japan Travel Bureau until her first child, Shunsuke, was born in 1974. Mariko took a year off from work and dreaded returning—"I hated the thought of leaving my baby," she said—but she did not have to face the separation because Chiaki was born within twelve months of Shunsuke. After that, Mariko never went back to work full-time. Ken-chan came six years later, when Mariko was such an old hand at childbirth that she simply walked to the hospital when her labor began.

Meanwhile Mariko's younger brother's wife had walked out on the marriage, taking the couple's two-year-old daughter and leaving Mariko's brother in the family home. After the divorce his drinking and violence grew worse, culminating in one terrifying incident in 1977 when, in the middle of a fight, he attacked his father with a knife. Saburo's hand was cut slightly; a police car came, but no arrests were made. Mariko told no one outside the family of the incident; she had long been so embarrassed by her brother's drinking that she had confided in no one, even though she assumed the neighbors knew. Over the next few years, her brother spent time in mental institutions and had ups and downs with jobs. "Whenever he got work, he didn't show up," Mariko said. "Once he started to drink, he would drink for a whole week."

Finally, in 1985, the inevitable occurred. "One day he came downstairs and said, 'I feel sick—will you please call an ambulance?'" Mariko recalled. In the hospital, as he rapidly deteriorated, he told Mariko over and over, "Gomen-nasai, gomen-nasai, gomen-nasai"—"I am so sorry, so sorry, so sorry." Finally, two hours after speaking these words for the last time, on April 29, 1985, at the age of thirty-seven, he was dead. Mariko said the cause of death was simply a burst pancreas, a colloquialism for what doctors have told me could have been a ruptured or bleeding pancreas—a common, often fatal, disorder brought on by long-term alcohol abuse.

For Mariko, the most haunting memory of the adorable little brother she had so loved as a child was that reiterated "Gomen-nasai" just before his death.

Mariko was crying. We were all sitting around her *kotatsu*, our tea cold, listening as she finished the long stories of her childhood. "It was only at his death that my brother regretted what he had done," she said, still sobbing, stabbing at her eyes with a tissue. It was a cold day in March 1991, nearly six years later, but his death seemed as painful as ever to her. "My brother really affects my life a lot still," Mariko said. The next month, she added, the family would be marking the seventh anniversary of his death (the Japanese count the end of the first year as the second anniversary) with a special ceremony called a *nanakaiki*. With some hesitation, I asked Mariko if I could observe it. She quickly said yes, and Sachiko and I made arrangements to go.

Monday, April 29, turned out to be gray and rainy, a suitably
ressing day. At eleven-thirty that morning, Sachiko and I met
with Mariko and sixteen other members of her family on the
ounds of a nearby cemetery. We assembled inside an old wooden
ilding, standing uncomfortably and making awkward conversation. Mariko's husband and children were there, and her elder
brother and his wife, and Ito's older sister and the sister's son, and
Saburo's younger brother and the younger brother's wife, and
Saburo's older brother's daughter, and on and on. All the women
were dressed from head to toe in black. A few had on a single strand
of pearls, to represent tears, the only jewelry acceptable at funerals.
The men were in solid black suits, black ties, and white shirts. When
everyone had arrived, we went out in single file under umbrellas,
stepping carefully between the gravestones. Like most cemeteries in
urban Tokyo, this one had no grass or trees, just headstones packed
side by side, wedged into a little parcel of congested land; in death as
in life, I thought, thinking of the Tokyo subways at rush hour or the
camping spots in the Japan Alps, where people pitch their tents in
one little section, leaving whole tracts unoccupied. Mariko's brother,
like every deceased person in Japan, had been cremated, and the urn
containing his ashes was buried beneath the headstone. Mariko
placed a handful of chrysanthemums in a holder near her brother's
grave, and then, one by one, each member of the family came forward to pour cleansing water from a wooden ladle over the headstone. In a few minutes, the ritual was over. It had been six years, so
the mood was somber but hardly tragic.

Afterward, we all went to the private upstairs room of a neighborhood restaurant for lunch. The food was delicious—sushi, miso
soup, a Japanese custard called *chawanmushi*, and grilled fish and
vegetables, all presented in exquisite little dishes. I sat at a far end
of the table with Sachiko, across from Ito's older sister. Mariko had
told everyone who I was and why I was there, but I still felt awkward. And yet there was little talk of Mariko's brother; the mood

was festive and friendly. Everyone assured me I had picked a good family to study. "They are very typical," one of the relatives proudly told me. "We hardly ever see each other," another one said, "so this is a great way to get together. It's a very good Japanese custom." Toward the end of the lunch, Takeshi stood up and made a quick speech. "I didn't think the years would pass so quickly," he said. "I'm very happy so many people could get together. I'm very happy to see every one of you."

From there the party headed back to Mariko's. Ito, of course, had been unable to attend the lunch. Now her bed was cranked up so she could visit with the family. Sachiko and I had gone home from the restaurant, but Mariko told me afterward that everyone stayed in Ito's room and talked for two hours. If the relatives rarely saw each other, and if, like many relatives, they had little in common, this was nonetheless a return to their roots and was a source of comfort. The next day, everyone would feel much better for having been there.

3

"I FORGET I'M A HOUSEWIFE"

The Sanja Matsuri festival

MAY

Mariko left her house early on Sunday, May 19, knowing full well she would face a sulking husband when she got back. It would be a small price to pay, she had decided, for some hours of freedom. For today was the day of the annual Sanja Matsuri, the biggest, noisiest—and raunchiest—religious festival in all of Tokyo. Mariko, the decorous housewife from the suburbs, was going to wedge in with the gangsters and drunken construction workers and join in the frenzy of carrying a *mikoshi,* or portable Shinto shrine, through the streets. The central, primal idea of the Sanja Matsuri was that the soul of an eminent, if childlike, local god was temporarily transferred to the *mikoshi* from its home within a larger, permanent shrine. Now the god was to be transported by *mikoshi* on a wild, circular joyride through the community, the more turbulent the better. He

en to be brought home to the main shrine so superbly amused
so the community hoped—that he would bestow good fortune
e people for the rest of the year. Mariko was to help carry the
shi for one of the most important festival gods, but there would
ne hundred *mikoshi* at the Sanja Matsuri in all, one for trans-
ting each little neighborhood deity. Scores of separate *mikoshi*-
arrying throngs would be bouncing through the narrow streets,
creating clusters of bedlam. Other towns and villages across Japan
had their own deities; most would be entertained with similar
mikoshi processions at the thousands of annual festivals at different
times of the year, bringing distinctive splashes of color, life, and tradition to the countryside. The celebrations were of course religious
in background, but most were in fact excellent occasions to have fun
and get drunk. The gods, it was said, looked favorably upon exuber-
ant young men intoxicated with sake.

For the past decade, Mariko had helped carry the small *mikoshi*
at her own neighborhood festival, but in the last two years she had
branched out, through a *mikoshi*-carrying club, to bigger produc-
tions like the Sanja Matsuri. The festival attracted one and a half
million people over three days to Asakusa (pronounced Ah-socks-a),
the old neighborhood of narrow streets and old-fashioned shops that
sold an appealing array of modern junk and traditional Japanese
goods. Asakusa lay in the northern, low-lying part of the city, almost
one hour by train from Mariko's house, a distance that Mariko's
husband viewed as excessive—particularly since she was traveling to
jostle a shrine around with a lot of drunken men, in varying states of
festival dress and undress, whom he had never met. Takeshi felt her
shrine-carrying hobby had gotten out of control. "She's addicted,"
he said. Worse, the festival seemed another symptom of her growing, and alarming, independence. Who would serve his meals when
she was gone all of Sunday? And what was a forty-four-year-old
mother of three doing amid the debauchery of the Sanja Matsuri
anyway? Although more and more women had been carrying

mikoshi in recent years, most were young and single. A woman like Mariko was an oddity. I did not understand exactly how odd—or liberated—until I saw the festival for myself that day.

Sachiko and I met up with Mariko early that afternoon in a back alley of Asakusa, near street vendors selling the skewers of delicious charcoal-grilled chicken called yakitori. The aroma of sizzling chicken slathered with yakitori sauce, a mix of sugar, soy sauce, and the sweet Japanese liquor called *mirin*, was irresistible; when it mingled with the ubiquitous fragrance of icy cold beer from the street stalls, I always found it impossible not to stop and wolf down a few skewerfuls on the spot. Asakusa was the best known of Tokyo's old traditional neighborhoods and clung proudly to the Shitamachi, or "downtown," culture that had been such a part of its history. Its geographic isolation, far north of the center of town, had colored its rich past. The Tokugawa Shogunate banished the brothels to Asakusa in 1657 and the popular Kabuki theater in 1841, hoping that distance might keep desire at bay. All the move did was ensure that Asakusa became the city's number-one entertainment district. The fun continued into the Meiji Era, and for a century, until about 1940, Asakusa reigned as the center of a brilliant common people's culture, a bawdy pleasure quarters that had prostitutes, theater, opera, movies, restaurants, and bars for the tens of thousands who jammed the neighborhood's narrow streets. Badly damaged during World War II, it was rebuilt but was never the same. Asakusa declined to a minor stop on the city's train lines as postwar Tokyo looked for entertainment and nightlife to the new districts of Shinjuku, Roppongi, Shibuya, and Harajuku.

Of course the twentieth century had come to Asakusa too, and in the 1990s the neighborhood's modern office buildings and new hotels had more claim to being the "real" Japan than the handful of picturesque side streets. But Asakusa still took much of its character from the sluggish, malodorous Sumida River that flowed along its eastern edge; it remained worlds away from the European boutiques and French restaurants of Ginza. Shopkeepers on the old, narrow streets sold anything from entertaining junk—I remember little windup plastic dolphins that leaped from tubs of water—to exquisite traditional Japanese dolls, fans, kimono, one-toed "tabi" socks, pickles, sweets, and roasted eel. Sachiko always viewed a trip to Asakusa as an important opportunity to shop, and we usually came home laden with traditional cotton robes for our children or freshly roasted rice crackers from the best shop in the city.

When I saw Mariko, I could tell she was in a good mood. "Kon-nichiwa—hello!" she said happily. It was hard to tell whether her spirits were due to the festival, her day of freedom, or the Asahi Super Dry, Japan's trendiest beer, that she was knocking back. She was dressed in a traditional festival outfit issued by her club—a pair of tight-fitting, dark blue cotton pants called *momohiki* and a short, indigo-blue, kimono-like jacket with the name of her club in Chinese characters on the lapels. The jacket was cinched around her hips with a narrow cotton belt. On her bare feet were straw sandals. For the final touch, she had casually draped a deep purple cotton towel, called a *tenugui*, around her neck. The clothes were inspired by the uniform of firemen during the Edo period, some three hundred years before, but Mariko's look, identical to that of waiters in any of Tokyo's noisy *robata-yaki* grilling restaurants, had held up over the centuries and was young, stylish, and hip.

"This is my friend," she said, introducing us to a woman simi-larly attired, an old pal from Ichomachi who had known Mariko since their sons were together in nursery school. I had brought my husband, Steve, and my eighteen-month-old daughter, Madeleine, with me, and after we had all bowed and said how honored we were to meet each other, Mariko and her friend swooped down on Madeleine to feed her some strands of *yakisoba*, which were deli-cious fried noodles she had bought from a street vendor. On a nearby corner were the men of Mariko's *mikoshi*-carrying club, a mostly unsavory bunch, sitting cross-legged, snacking on street food, and reeking of beer. They were all unshaven and were so outgoing toward us that I could tell they had been drinking all day. Standing on the curb, Steve, Sachiko, and I each had a beer and waited for something to happen.

The festival had loftier origins than our surroundings suggested—modern life in Japan rarely lives up to the exotic past. Legend has it that in the seventh century a golden statue of Kannon, the goddess of mercy in Buddhism, was hauled from the Sumida River by two fishermen. A huge temple, the Asakusa Kannon, was built in her honor; it was bombed during World War II and has been reconstructed. Today it is surrounded by throngs of worshipers, pigeons, and street vendors. The original statue of Kannon, said to be inside, is never shown in public. A nearby Shinto shrine, the Asakusa Jinja, was built in the seventeenth century and dedicated to the two brothers who fished the Kannon statue out of the river, and to their village chief. The statues of the two fishermen and the village chief are said to be behind the shrine's closed lacquer doors. No one has seen them, either, but they are the lords of the festival that was just then getting under way.

By three in the afternoon it was time. Mariko got up with the men from the *mikoshi* club and followed them around the corner. Sachiko, Steve, Madeleine, and I followed her. We soon came to one of Asakusa's broad thoroughfares and were face-to-face with an enormous, writhing, nearly out-of-control mob. Coming toward us, borne on wooden beams that were digging into the bruised, bleeding shoulders of its carriers, was the *mikoshi* itself, a glittering gold-and-brass-plated palanquin about the size of a compact car, which could be seen above the crowd and seemed to be on a rampage of its own. First it would violently shake, then it would lurch drunkenly backward, then slowly and rhythmically undulate forward again. This *mikoshi* was called the Ichinomiya and weighed one ton. Five magnificent phoenixlike golden birds crowned its black lacquer roof, and plump, deep purple braids were entwined along its sides. Inside, hidden from view in a plain wooden box, was the soul of one of the fishermen. As far as I could tell, it was having a good time.

The shrine moved closer to us, Mariko and her club members scrambled to trade places with the exhausted carriers under the beams, and the wild dance started again. Hundreds of sweating, drunken men began moving the shrine forward with rhythmic pelvic thrusts, all the while chanting together in loud, animalistic grunts—*uh UH, uh UH, uh UH, uh UH!* Now I understood Takeshi's objections: this was one of the most public, unapologetic displays of the male sexual drive I had ever seen. At this point, several muscular men, dressed only in *fundoshi*, a kind of traditional Japanese loincloth, clambered to the top of the shrine, precariously balancing themselves as they showed off taut chests, thighs, and buttocks covered in tattoos of tigers and dragons. They were *yakuza*, or Japanese mobsters, and for the local *yakuza* gangs in Asakusa the Sanja Matsuri was the biggest event of the year. What was Mariko, the nice housewife from the suburbs, doing in a place like this? The police shouted through loudspeakers for the tattooed men to climb back down, but their appeals were futile.

As Koiichi Kikuchi, the head of the biggest *yakuza* gang in Asakusa, told me later, the Sanja Matsuri was like the Super Bowl to him. "It's our number-one event," he said. His gang, the Takahashi-gumi, kept scrapbooks of each Sanja Matsuri, and every year other *yakuza* gangs from all over Tokyo sent them beer, sake, and $40,000 in cash as tribute in recognition of the Takahashi-gumi's big event. The *yakuza*'s enthusiasm for the festival made the Asakusa business establishment that organized the event deeply unhappy, particularly since television news crews invariably filmed the *yakuza* exhibitionists climbing all over the *mikoshi*—vivid, entertaining footage that always made the Tokyo evening news shows and inaccurately promoted the festival, the organizers complained, as a celebration of gangsters. In fact, many ordinary people participated;

organizers claimed some twenty thousand people carried the one hundred different *mikoshi*, and the police said only seven hundred of them in recent years were *yakuza*. But gangs did come from all over Japan to take part, and their presence was so conspicuous that the Asakusa police had been forced to respond by making a nonaggression pact with them: The *yakuza* could participate unharassed by the police as long as there was no violence. The agreement seemed to work. "When it comes to this festival, it's as if they have the hearts of children," the Asakusa police chief, Yoshihiro Okada, told me afterward. "They really want to participate. They are very obedient about this festival." Japanese *yakuza* have traditionally made money by extortion, gambling, prostitution, and drugs, and have in many places coexisted with the authorities as a kind of shadow police force that kept peace in the neighborhoods. *Yakuza* movies, a popular genre much loved by the *yakuza* themselves, glamorized the gangs as the Robin Hoods of Japanese society. But in recent years, as reports surfaced of *yakuza* payoffs, shakedown operations, and money laundering involving Japan's most elite companies and senior politicians, the Japanese have grown less tolerant of them.

Along with other members of her club, Mariko now had her shoulder under one of the beams of the *mikoshi* and was inching forward in the chaos. I was in my own crush on the sidelines, but I could see her, sweating and red-faced, her expression intent. "*Uh uh, uh uh, uh UH!*" went the mob. Mariko kept pace, jostling with the men, reeling with the *mikoshi* as it suddenly lurched backward. Frequently I would lose sight of Mariko in the mob, then I would find her, then lose her again. This went on for fifteen minutes. Finally, after moving the *mikoshi* perhaps three hundred yards forward, Mariko's club switched off in a scramble with another waiting group. The *mikoshi* lunged ahead. Mariko, spent, wiped her brow, then followed the *mikoshi* as it staggered through the streets toward the Asakusa Jinja. Around eight that evening she finally left, vaguely disappointed. The Sanja Matsuri had not been as much fun as she expected. It was too big, too disorganized, too chaotic. She realized she much preferred her own neighborhood festival in Ichomachi.

By nine-thirty that night she was home. Takeshi, as predicted, was in a sullen mood, hardly placated by the dinner she had left. It was curry rice, a staple of the Japanese housewife, a dish of rice slathered with stew that bore no resemblance to any Indian curry. It would do in a pinch, and Mariko threw it together whenever she had to go out at night. She dissolved a bouillon cube for the gravy, added beef or pork, and potatoes, onions, butter, and salt. All the family had to do was heat it up.

Mariko tried to tell the family about the Sanja Matsuri, but her husband cut her off. "We're not interested in hearing about it," he snapped. She retreated, exhausted.

A few days later, I asked Mariko the question that had formed so often in my mind as I watched her carry the *mikoshi:* What was a nice housewife from the suburbs doing in a place like that?

"But I forget I'm a housewife," she said, smiling. I smiled too. Whatever its shortcomings, the Sanja Matsuri filled a vital need for something strange and exotic in her ordinary world. "When I carry the *o-mikoshi,*" she said, adding the honorific *o,* as women often do, "I feel liberated. It feels like I'm going to a discotheque. I can relax. I can be myself."

Mariko was hardly a feminist in the conventional sense, but anyone could see that her participation in the Sanja Matsuri was a small rebellion in a life that, in other respects too, was becoming more and more independent from that of her husband. Like so many of her friends, she and her husband had long led separate existences, and now that her children were older, she was freer than she had been in years to pursue her own hobbies and friends. While American feminists might view this stage in Mariko's life as the inevitable empty and trapped period in the life of a woman who had spent her most productive years sacrificing for her family, Japanese women would see it as a natural evolution toward greater freedom. I never agreed with the view that Japanese women grow more "liberated" as they age, but I did learn how hard it is to apply American standards of independence to their condition. In the strictest sense of feminism as practiced in the West, Mariko was an oppressed person belonging to to an aggrieved, exploited group. I shared that attitude to some extent, though Mariko of course rejected it entirely. She eventually helped me see that the situation is far more complicated.

The lives of Japanese women have improved dramatically since World War II. Sixty years ago, one out of eight Japanese women went to high school; most, like Mariko's mother, were married off in matches that were arranged for them. Today, Japanese women are among the best educated in the world; 95 percent graduate from high school and more than a third go on to higher education. Japanese women marry for the first time at an average age of 25.8, later than women in the United States and other advanced countries. More than half of Japanese women work outside the home, and in recent years they have moved in small but increasing numbers into management positions at some companies. New laws prohibit sexual discrimination on the job and require that women be given maternity leave. Meanwhile, sexual harassment at the office has emerged as an issue in the courts and the mainstream press.

But these statistics—always included in any of the countless "Changing Japanese Women" articles that proliferate in the Western and Japanese press—do not tell the whole story. If one holds Japan to the standards of a rich and highly literate industrial democracy, the story, I think, is how slow and superficial the change has been. True, Japanese women work outside the home, but the vast majority are in part-time and low-paying clerical jobs. (Almost all are required to serve tea, the great symbol of a woman's servility in Japan.) Most of the women who seek higher education go only to junior college; in 1989, Japanese women accounted for barely more than a quarter of four-year university students, whereas women represent about half of the graduates at four-year colleges in the United States. Some women may be moving into management positions, but their numbers are minuscule: the Labor Ministry found in 1989 that women accounted for only 1.2 percent of department heads. Similarly, a 1991 poll of 1,500 Tokyo companies by a major job-placement firm found that while most companies said they wanted their women employees to stay with them longer, only one in four had a system set up for women to advance to higher responsibilities. The rest hired women solely as "office ladies." Not surprisingly, 87 percent said that women should serve tea, and 70 percent said women should be the ones to wipe the tables and desks.

In the late 1980s there was much talk in Japan about women advancing in politics, not least because the Japanese wanted to show they were keeping up with developments in the West. The focus of much of the excitement was the woman recently chosen to head the opposition Socialist Party, Takako Doi. In 1989—heralded by the Japanese press as the "Year of the Woman"—she led the Socialists to an extraordinary victory in the upper house of Parliament. Prime Minister Toshiki Kaifu responded to the voters' rebuff by selecting Mayumi Moriyama as the first woman to serve as chief cabinet secretary. But it soon became clear that the "Year of the Woman" was a lot of hype and wishful thinking. In the next election, the Socialists failed to oust Kaifu and the ruling party in the lower house, and Takako Doi was blamed for not capitalizing on Kaifu's dismal record of scandals and economic problems. Perhaps more embarrassing, she had tried unsuccessfully to persuade her own male-dominated Socialist leadership to run more than a handful of women as party candidates. Soon she too was ousted. The final humiliation for women came when the victorious Kaifu chose his new cabinet, unceremoniously dumping Moriyama from her cabinet post after he no longer needed any female window-dressing. Since then, a succession of Japanese cabinets and parliaments have had mostly token representation by women.

At the close of the twentieth century, the lives of most Japanese women are, like Mariko's, still defined by their families. Today, although women now work for some years after college or high school, the vast majority quit when they marry or give birth to their first child. Like Mariko, they usually do not return to work until their children are older. Surveys also show that most women feel they should work only if a job does not conflict with their responsibilities at home. Admittedly, younger women's attitudes are changing. A 1990 government survey found, for instance, that only 4.2 percent of women in their twenties thought that a woman's chief happiness was in the home. But I was more struck by the finding in the same poll that only a third of the women in their twenties felt there was no reason to marry if the right person did not come along. To me, this showed that *two thirds* of women in their twenties still think there is a reason to marry even if there is no Mr. Right. The desire for economic security, status, and children obviously remains foremost in their minds.

The Japanese love statistics and poll results. I found a 1989 survey of seven thousand women, most in their twenties, especially interesting. In questionnaires distributed by *More,* a respected Japanese women's magazine, the women were asked to select a response to the question "Why did you get married?" "Because I loved him" got the highest rating, 37 percent—barely more than a third. Other answers included "Because I liked him" (15 percent), "Because I believed he would make me happy" (15 percent), and "Because he met my terms and conditions" (10 percent)—that is, he was "high" in three specific areas: income, education, and height. Marriage was still the paramount goal among three quarters of the single women surveyed.

The numbers told me what was obvious: Like Mariko, most Japanese women are mothers first and workers second, and the home remains a woman's number-one priority. This is true for many American working women too, but the statistics show something more subtle at work in Japan, where a mother's role in running the home is much more widely accepted as one of the most fulfilling things a woman can do. Even the kind of emotional closeness with a spouse that Americans strive for is secondary to overall domestic life. Although women may harbor hopes of romance in the year or two after their wedding, most settle down, like Mariko, to marriages in which they expect no excitement or passion. I once asked a university lecturer I knew, Namiko Suzuki, how she put up with a husband who worked such long hours that she saw him only on weekends. "After we got married, I felt lonely for a few years," she admitted. "But after ten years, I feel my life is much easier without him. When we stop expecting things from our husbands, we become liberated."

The great paradox of Japanese women is that most of them, married middle-aged women especially, see their lives as more fulfilled and far richer than those of their husbands. Mariko, at forty-four, perfectly reflected this sensibility, as I learned one day when I asked her if the typical pattern of a Japanese woman's life—work, babies, then part-time work—wasn't unfair, compared with the steady career paths of most men. "It's not a matter of fair or unfair," she replied. "Men and women have different characters. If you change your point of view, men *just* work. They can't spend beautiful time with their children. I didn't choose this pattern, but by having this pattern, a woman can be exposed to many experiences. Through your children, you meet lots of people who have different environments. It's not a meaningless life. So I myself don't think that my life is fair or unfair when compared with a man's. If you limit your point of view and say, 'There are only a few woman politicians,' well, that is true, and it seems very unfair. But if you change your point of view, then you see that women, through this kind of living, can really learn about life. On the contrary, men have a burden. Regardless of whether a man likes his job or not, he has a huge burden to feed his family through work. As a result, men get immature. They don't have wide social contacts. For example, in my husband's case—he goes to the construction place. He draws designs. That's it."

How could I argue with her? Her words were eloquent, and within the confines of her life, of course, she was right. Few Japanese women envied the overworked, overstressed, single-minded Japanese salariman of the late twentieth century, a man who had sacrificed himself to the nation's economic machine. Japanese women did not want to work full-time over the course of their lives, as the inevitable polls on the subject showed. From this perspective, it was the men who were enslaved.

This is in fact the central theme in *The Japanese Woman*, a provocative and to me irritating book by Sumiko Iwao, a top adviser to the Japanese government and a prominent professor of psychology at the prestigious Keio University. Iwao was one of the few women to be part of Tokyo's male-dominated power establishment. Her book was published only in the United States, in 1993, and it was frankly aimed at countering what she considered a stereotyped image among Americans of the kimono-clad, tea-serving Japanese woman. Frustrated that the West still views Japan as socially backward, Iwao writes of American acquaintances who exclaim that "they cannot understand how Japanese women tolerate the blatant sexual discrimination evident in their society."

In Iwao's view, real Japanese women do not need Western sympathy. Even though professionally they lag far behind women in other advanced countries, she asserts, educated Japanese women have in recent years undergone a "quiet revolution" of attitudes that has enabled them to lead lives of their own liking. While Japanese women admire American women for demanding equal rights, she writes, they have come to realize that the American ideal of trying to play all roles—wife, mother, professional, community member—is a losing battle and, in its own way, oppressive. When I interviewed Iwao briefly in Japan, she sounded this theme and seemed puzzled as to why Americans insist on living their lives by abstract principle, even though doing so might make them unhappy. Japanese men, she went on, are to be pitied rather than emulated; they are "chained" to the corporate ladder, whereas women can choose any combination of motherhood, work, hobbies, and community service they desire. To my mind, her argument would imply that American feminists should look back on the 1950s not as a period of frustration and oppression but as a Renaissance made possible by the advent of dishwashers, vacuum cleaners, TV dinners, and other labor-saving devices.

There are problems with Professor Iwao's view. It turned out, for instance, that her glorification of the abundant choices available to Japanese women was a little premature. As the recession of the 1990s settled on the country, women were the first to be laid off. They had been hired, of course, not because of some "quiet revolution" of feminist beliefs sweeping Japan's corporate halls, but because the nation's economic growth over the past two decades had created huge numbers of unskilled and low-paying jobs. Were it not for Japan's resistance to immigration, these jobs might well have gone to foreigners. Instead, women were the principal ones to gain. Then, in the economic slump, the marginal last hired became the first fired. Companies laid off whole groups of women, and "career track" jobs for women at large companies dried up.

Japan does have a handful of what I would call traditional feminists, who are critical of the status quo celebrated by Professor Iwao and considered so fulfilling by Mariko. I found them instructive to talk to. One of the most thoughtful, acerbic, and famous of the feminists, Chizuko Ueno, a woman in her forties, is a professor at Tokyo University who writes in both academic journals and the general press, and whose hugely popular books have such titles as *The Theater Beneath the Skirt* and *The Pleasures of Being a Woman.* Trying to tell women they're repressed when they don't think they are is obviously a major challenge, and I asked Ueno why so many Japanese housewives say they have such wonderful lives. "Every woman tries to seek a justifying ideology for her own status quo," she told me. "But I'm sure if you go into depth, and start talking with them, they'll start speaking out." In fact, that was the process I was seeing with Mariko, who was starting to speak out herself in small ways. But in feminist terms, she had a long way to go.

Perhaps the best illustration of the feminist critique of the status of Japanese women is the issue of money and income. In Japan, I often heard people say that Japanese women have enormous control over the household purse strings because their husbands turn over their paychecks to them. The wife then doles out an "allowance" to her husband as if to a child. One government survey found that 40 percent of full-time stay-at-home Japanese housewives thought of themselves as economically independent. (Mariko was unusual in that her husband gave *her* an allowance, which she supplemented from her own earnings. Her husband never told her how much he made, but she found out from foraging through the payroll statements he tried to stash away.) It seemed to me, of course, that the common "wife controls the purse strings" arrangement overlooked the essential truth: The husband makes the money, and his wife is dependent on him.

Feminism has never really been a mass movement in Japan, although women's-rights activists in the early twentieth century worked for suffrage, equal rights, and birth control. It was not until the 1970s that a splintered feminist movement, in part inspired by examples in the United States and Europe, sprang up in the big cities. Like their American counterparts, many college-age Japanese feminists had been active in the left-wing student riots in the late 1960s and had come to feel betrayed by their male colleagues. The men, it turned out, were as sexist as the members of the old order they were trying to tear down. Chizuko Ueno, herself a veteran of these wars, dismissively recalled that women activists at Kyoto University were either "free love" types who slept with the men or support staff who bandaged wounds and prepared meals.

There were significant obstacles to feminism in its early stages. In the first place, Japanese women are raised to avoid confrontation. Furthermore, the number of women enrolled in universities in the 1970s was small. In the United States, feminists enjoyed generally sympathetic press coverage, particularly from women reporters. But in Japan there were no prominent figures like Betty Friedan and Gloria Steinem. The largely male media never took seriously the work of Mitsu Tanaka, the founder of a women's shelter and organization called the Shinjuku Lib Center, and they laughed at the antics of Misako Enoki, a pharmacist and the leader of Chupiren, a band of pink-helmeted women who raided the offices of unfaithful husbands and worked to lift the ban against the birth-control pill. (One example of their failure is that the birth-control pill remains banned in Japan on the grounds that it may have harmful side effects. Women often use abortion as a means of birth control.)

For many Japanese outside the movement, the pink helmets of the 1960s are a vivid image frozen in time, like bra-burning in the United States. Mariko often thought of the pink helmets when she heard the word "feminist," and to her they were all strident and silly. Today Misako Enoki has vanished from public sight, and Mitsu Tanaka is an acupuncturist who has given up on changing women through mass movements. And although some present feminist groups working against sexual harassment have had victories in the courtroom, most Japanese feminists of the 1990s continue to operate on the margins of society.

The fact remains that compared with women in other modern industrialized societies, Japanese women have almost no significant choice when it comes to work versus home. Yumiko Jansson Yanagisawa, a well-known Tokyo feminist active in the issue of reproductive rights, once summed it up succinctly in a conversation I had with her. "The ideal of a woman's life is so conservative—work, babies, work," she said. "All the social reforms are based on this standard." Japanese women can enter the management tracks of male-dominated professions and perhaps achieve real authority in the workplace. Or they can have children. But statistics show that very, very few women in Japan can ever do both. Combining family and career is difficult enough for women in the United States. It is almost impossible in Japan.

The main obstacle is that Japanese social customs force a woman, whether she works or not, to operate as a virtual single parent. With her husband gone from seven in the morning until midnight many days, she alone is responsible for all child care and household chores. It is the nature of Japanese society that women find it extremely distasteful to incur any uncomfortable obligations—for example, asking a neighbor, friend, mother, or mother-in-law to pick up a child at the day care center, assuming there is one nearby. It used to be common among well-to-do Japanese families to bring an outsider into the home to help with children, but today it is almost unheard of. Live-in maids, such as Mariko's mother was a generation ago, have also disappeared. Even a mother who can afford in-home care has a difficult time in an increasingly affluent society finding a Japanese woman willing to work in her house and look after her children. There are some Filipino women in Tokyo who look after the children of European and American families, but most Japanese are reluctant to hire foreigners, particularly other Asians, whom they often look down on, to work in their homes. Perhaps the most subtle deterrent is that a mother with any kind of in-home child care risks criticism from the neighbors for putting on airs and neglecting her children. Even hiring a Japanese teenager for a few hours on a Saturday night so a stay-at-home mother can go to the movies with her husband is an unheard-of, wholly American proposition.

When I asked Japanese women who could easily afford it why they didn't at least hire baby-sitters, I always got the same responses as I got from Mariko. First, Japanese teenagers are too busy studying for the entrance exams to have time to baby-sit. Second, if you have an outsider in the house—even a sloppy teenager—you have to clean, and this is a big nuisance. Third, what if something terrible happened while you were away? And fourth, Japanese husbands and wives of Mariko's generation seldom go out socially together anyway. The assumption behind these responses was obvious: the belief that a Japanese woman's primary job is at home with her children. Reiko Morikawa, one of the handful of women members on Mariko's local ward council, put it this way: "Japanese women feel guilty if they use a baby-sitter so that they can play tennis or go to aerobics class. But in the case of going to a funeral, no." Mariko never hired baby-sitters, but in the past she and her husband had occasionally left the children sleeping alone in the house for two hours while they slipped out to relax over a drink and some karaoke—singing to recorded background music—at a neighborhood bar five minutes away. This was at the time when the family lived on its own, in the more modern house, away from Ito and Saburo. Ken-chan was one year old, Chiaki was seven, and Shunsuke was eight. I knew of other suburban Japanese parents who left sleeping kids alone in the house, and I think they felt they could do so in part because Japanese parents never worried about crime and break-ins. They did, of course, worry about the risk of emergencies like fire, or simply that a child might awake and suddenly need a parent. Years later, Mariko still felt guilty about having left her children alone. "I think I was a bad mother," she told me.

Not all women in Japan fit the mold of Mariko, of course, and there were in her generation some extraordinary, highly successful exceptions to the rule. I was curious about how those few women managed to maintain demanding careers, and so I sought out six— two managing directors at major companies, three government officials, one prominent lawyer—and learned a great deal about the problems facing all women in Japan. Born in the 1930s and 1940s, the six women I talked to had several crucial things in common. All had been among the first women admitted to Tokyo University, the essential passport to success in government and the top Japanese companies. All were from professional middle- and upper-middle-class families, the postwar ruling class of Japan. One, Ayuchi Takita of Japan Air Lines, had not married; the five others, who had children, had unusual husbands who either supported their careers or at least did not object. Of those five women, four had mothers or mothers-in-law who had moved in with them and raised the children. The other, Mayumi Moriyama, the first woman to be a career bureaucrat in the Japanese government and the chief cabinet secretary during the "Year of the Woman," had a live-in Japanese staff—and a husband who encouraged her by pointing out that she had every advantage. "In those days we had good help," she told me. "It was not easy, but I knew I was the first woman to pioneer the way. Sometimes when all three of my children were sick, and I had to go far from Tokyo to do my work, in such cases I sometimes said to my husband, 'Maybe it would be better for me to stay at home with the children. Maybe I should take some years off.' But my husband said to me, 'If you can't continue your career—and you have healthy children, a very good husband, very good help, and rewarding work—who else can do it?' " Each time she agreed to continue working for a few more months, and in that way she went on for thirty years.

The career women I interviewed got ahead by thinking in the long term, making compromises, serving and holding their tongues. As Takita, sixty years old, the managing director of the JAL Foundation and the highest-ranking woman at Japan Air Lines, explained: "One of my doctrines is, whatever job you are given, never complain. Just become the best at that job. And if you do that job well, then you are given another job." Many women, she feels, have been too shortsighted, "like two-hundred-meter runners and not like marathon runners. . . . If you feel a job is not suitable for you, why don't you just wait for three or four years. And then maybe you'll be transferred." As she worked her way up in executive positions at JAL, she never let the requirement to serve tea stand in her way, and even found a comforting rationale for the exercise. "I took these things from the positive side," she said. "If someone comes to your home, you serve tea. Tea softens the atmosphere. And at the office—why not? In those days, if a strong man had served tea, the guests would not feel as much at home. So it was part of the job, and I took it that way." These days, she still serves tea occasionally. The issue is not as big among women in the workplace as one might expect, although there was a rebellion among a group of office ladies in the 1950s and 1960s in Kyoto. As recounted by the Japan scholar Susan Pharr, now of Harvard University, the movement fizzled out, but it suggested that there would be ongoing dissatisfaction among women over their subordinate status.

Over the years, all of the six women I talked to had had to watch while men were promoted ahead of them. Today, in most government ministries, women are more and more likely to be promoted on an equal basis with men, but they remain largely shut out of the upper levels at the powerful Finance and Foreign Ministries and at MITI, the Ministry of International Trade and Industry. (The few women who hold high positions are invariably in jobs in which they come in contact with foreigners, to show the world how advanced Japan is theoretically becoming.) "Top successful women can still not reach the same level as top successful men," said Mariko Bando, who had worked her way up through the prime minister's secretariat and is now the deputy governor of Saitama Prefecture. "If I had been a man," she said, "my level would be the same, but I would be in a more important job. This is a very elegant job—but not so hard and a little dull."

Another of the women, Harumi Sakamoto, was also a case in point. In 1962, she was the first woman to become a career bureaucrat at the Ministry of International Trade and Industry. Two years later, she married a fellow bureaucrat who had entered the ministry at the same time she did. Over the years the Sakamotos had three children and advanced up the ladder. Both left the house each morning at eight. The difference was that Mrs. Sakamoto returned around eight at night, the earliest she could, whereas her husband came home at midnight, as part of the ritual of Japanese male bureaucrats and office workers. He was able to form the bonds and contacts that she did not, and he advanced much faster.

Like most married working couples everywhere, the Sakamotos followed a traditional pattern in their division of labor at home. She had the main responsibility for the domestic chores. "I worked hard at the office, and as soon as I got home, I worked hard at home," she said, adding that she regretted not demanding more help from her husband and children.

For the younger generation of working mothers, life is not much easier. Megumi Tanaka is a full-time editor at *Lee*, a women's magazine, and she has had to hire five college students, one for each working day, to pick up her elementary school son and care for him until she gets home at seven. Working full-time has been highly stressful, she admits, recalling that her son was once taunted at school for not having a real mother. "It was very hard for me to hear that," she said.

. . .

Thursday, May 23, dawned clear, sunny, and hot, a scorcher. As usual, the cherry blossoms had been blown away by the April rains, and spring had vanished as soon as it arrived. Late that morning, Sachiko and I met Mariko at her weekly samisen lesson, the class she had been attending for almost three decades. Mariko had dabbled in flower-arranging lessons and tea-ceremony classes before she was married, but the samisen had held her interest. "In terms of depth, samisen is the best," she said. "You can never achieve it. There is no end. You always have to keep learning." The samisen is the instrument of the finely trained geisha and is the musical backbone of Kabuki, the traditional Japanese theater. Although Mariko had hated having to study samisen at first, back in the days when her mother forced her to begin lessons under a family relative at the age of sixteen, the instrument, after twenty-eight years, had become an important part of her life. Fortunately her husband did not disapprove of this hobby as much as her *mikoshi*-carrying, but the twanging, mournful *plink, plink, plink* of her practicing bothered him and she did not do it while he was home. Her deference to him was well known even among her fellow students. ("Mariko's husband is a little more feudalistic than most," one of the women in her class informed me.) Mariko was especially careful to keep from her husband the total cost of her lessons and the concert fees she herself had to pay, which added up to some twenty-five hundred dollars a year. Cynical Japanese pointed out that the multitude of schools for samisen, the tea ceremony, and flower arranging were big moneymakers and exploited the Japanese housewife's insecurity and cultural longings for something uplifting to do with her time. Mariko, for example, felt compelled at least every three years to buy a new silk kimono suitable for her concerts. That expense came to another twenty-five hundred dollars, which she scrounged by scrimping and saving and spending less money on her regular clothes. She kept her husband in the dark about this extravagance, too. "I try to hide the cost, and I try to save the money by myself," she said. "It's why this kind of thing has not spread among the general public. It's too expensive." Mariko used whatever extra money she could from her part-time jobs reading meters and clerking at the travel office, and also from selling cosmetics to friends out of her home. On Sundays she gave samisen lessons herself to two beginner students, but that brought in only fifty dollars a month.

Today Mariko was the student. Her class, a half-hour bicycle ride from the house, was in another Tokyo suburb, in the home of Mariko's aunt—the wife of her father's brother. The small wooden house in the traditional Japanese style had been built sixty years before, which made it ancient for Tokyo. "This house will collapse in an earthquake," Mariko's aunt told me. "I really worry about earthquakes." Mariko's aunt was a tiny woman, seventy-two years old, with such exquisitely smooth skin that I asked her what her secret was. She answered by telling me how hard she worked at giving samisen lessons, as if to say that all the activity kept her young. She gave lessons or took them herself six days a week and even made house calls for well-to-do wives of large factory owners. Once a week she taught until nine at night, which left her exhausted. "I feel like a frog," she said. On those days she was wound up tighter than a samisen string and needed a sleeping pill before bed. Mariko called her *Obasan*, Aunt, but in class she respectfully referred to her as *Sensei*, Teacher.

Today, Sensei had on an elegant black-and-gray-striped kimono. She sat with her legs tucked under her at the front of the main area of the house, a large tatami room with wooden beams and an old wooden ceiling. Next to her was a young man, a college student, said by the teacher to be quite talented. The two of them faced Mariko and three other middle-aged women students, who all sat with legs tucked under them, samisens ready. Sachiko and I watched from an adjoining wooden alcove that looked out on a well-cared-for garden of day lilies, azaleas, and hydrangea. A cool breeze blew into the warm room through the open windows as the teacher and college student began a plaintive, atonal singing that seemed to have no melody. A few moments later Mariko and the other women began accompanying the singing by plucking their samisens, which brought a haunting but oddly beautiful sound into the room.

Today, the class was practicing a famous lyrical passage from the Kabuki play *Kanjincho,* or *The Subscription Scroll.* (In Kabuki theater, passages of live song and samisen music from players onstage serve as a kind of Greek chorus for the actors.) As I listened to the dramatic music, I realized that even on an ordinary day in a modern city like Tokyo, the Japanese come in contact with their culture and their past.

The Subscription Scroll was based on the exploits of Yoshi-tsune, the samurai hero of the twelfth century Gempei War. Yoshitsune and his elder brother, Yoritomo, were on the same side at first but had a falling-out when Yoritomo became wild with jealousy over his brother's military victories. Yoritomo tried to assassinate Yoshitsune, which forced Yoshitsune to flee to the north. The music I was hearing in Mariko's class was the chorus for an episode in which Yoshitsune is trying to escape from his brother with a small band of retainers, all disguised as religious pilgrims. At a checkpoint on the way north, a guard almost recognizes Yoshi-tsune beneath his disguise as a porter. But then Yoshitsune's long-time aide, Benkei, dramatically saves the day by berating the "porter" for causing trouble and then striking him. The guard, who has long since realized who the religious pilgrims really are, is so moved that Yoshitsune's subordinate would strike his own master in order to save him that he lets the group go on its way. Benkei then weeps for the horrible disrespect that he was driven to commit against his master, and the music weeps with him. Or, in the words of the song sung by the student and teacher at Mariko's lesson: "Benkei has never cried in his life, but now he finally has. These are once-in-a-lifetime tears."

I looked over at Mariko. She plucked at her samisen and stared down, intent and serious, at some invisible spot on the floor. She later told me she could hardly make out the archaic Japanese of the lyrics, but she loved the passionate music. "I don't understand the words very well," she said, "but it's very rhythmical, emotional music. It's very easy for everyone to understand." She was right. Even I could recognize its force as it intensified toward the end. Suddenly I was completely happy and utterly surprised to be drawn in by such unfamiliar music in this old Japanese house with the lovely garden and the sensuous breeze. Mariko, I reflected, had led me in, quietly guiding me through a country that was becoming more comfortable and yet more foreign every day.

The music ended, and so did my reverie. Sensei briskly dispensed advice to her students, then announced it was time for lunch. *Bento*—elegant little lunches of rice, pickles, and fish in cardboard boxes ordered from a local shop—were brought out of the kitchen, and everyone ate, quite delicately and properly, I noticed, since they were at the respected Sensei's house.

Mariko finally relaxed when we went over to the nearby home of a fellow student after class, where we had some cool and deliciously nutty barley tea, a fixture of the Japanese summer. She pulled out a cigarette and gossiped and smoked until it was time to leave for the market to get chicken and other provisions for dinner. We talked a little about the Sanja Matsuri. Mariko, I noticed, was still annoyed by her husband's sulk. "Japanese men are big babies," she observed.

4

THE FESTIVAL OF THE DEAD

Mariko at the Ichomachi shrine

JUNE AND JULY

Sometime in the early morning hours of Thursday, June 13, Mariko's husband awoke in the hot, muggy night to find himself on a bank of the Arakawa, a river on the far northern border of Tokyo. He had no idea how he had gotten there and in the first moments of awakening had no idea where he was. That, in any case, is what he told his wife. Luckily a nearby road sign allowed him to determine his whereabouts, but he had trouble remembering what had occurred earlier that evening. As he told Mariko afterward, all he could recall was that he had gone out for drinks after work and then had taken a train to the end of a line. But where were his glasses? He must have left them in the train, or the bar. He got up, found a taxi—whose driver was presumably delighted to have the fare of another inebriated salariman—and sixty-five dollars later arrived home. Fortunately, he was no longer drunk, but unfortunately, it was now four in the morning. Mariko was in no mood to play the role of the docile Japanese wife.

"Where were you?" she demanded. Even by the standards of a Japanese husband, four in the morning was a little late. Mariko had stayed up worrying until two and then had fallen into an uneasy sleep. Chiaki and Shunsuke were worried too. Mariko knew her husband had had a girlfriend some years back—a bar waitress of some sort—as was typical of his generation of men in Japan, but she was certain that the affair was over. Now, as he told her the story of the river, she decided it was so preposterous that she had no choice but to believe him. Her husband, of course, had not called to tell her he was going out after work. He had something of a policy on the subject: If he had a scheduled event after work, or if he and a friend made plans in the morning to drink that evening, he called Mariko—sometimes. But it was a matter of male prerogative for him never to call if something came up suddenly at the end of the day—and "something" included deciding with a friend on the spur of the moment to head for the bars. He worked hard, he was under pressure at the office, and what was the point of a little spontaneity, such as it was in this country, if you had to get permission from your wife the way a twelve-year-old did from his mother? Takeshi viewed such a call as the ultimate sign of the henpecked husband. "If you have to tell your wife every detail," he told me later, "then you should go home instead of coming out with us."

Now that he was home in the predawn hours, Takeshi undressed, lay down on the futon next to Mariko, then thrashed around in his sleep. Mariko's samisen was nearby, and she was so afraid he might kick it that she got up and moved it from the room. The next morning she told him she had been worried he might ruin it.

"You're being overly dramatic," he said.

Mariko was furious. "I won't worry about you anymore," she spit out. "If something happens to you, the police can tell me."

She was in fact quite worried about him. True, arriving home drunk was seen as an occasional occupational hazard, if not a point of pride, for a male. By this standard, Takeshi was no better or worse than any other man she knew. Mariko, after all, had told me the first day I met her that she had a very good husband who arrived home drunk only twice a year. But for the past two weeks, this first half of June, he had been out drinking heavily two nights a week. Although he hadn't said anything to her, she suspected the cause was trouble at work. She knew vaguely that a big project he had been depending on—a contract for the electrical work in part of the new Kawasaki City Hall complex in an industrial suburb of Tokyo—was delayed. The delay did not mean any loss of income for him, but it was a blow to his company, and now he had too much time on his hands. Experience had taught her that he drank less when he was busy, more when he was idle. His unhappiness in a job that was not providing him with enough to do was becoming more and more of a problem, for him and for her. In a nation of supposed worker bees, Takeshi was a human face in the monolith of Japan Inc. He may have looked like an automaton as he left his house each morning, dutifully driving a company car an hour south to Kawasaki, but inside, I came to realize, he felt bored and trapped by his work.

To try to understand more, Sachiko and I had gone to see Takeshi a few weeks earlier, at a construction site in Yokohama where his company was installing the electrical wiring for one of the apartment buildings the Japanese call mansions. He seemed to be in a terrible funk. He had been with Nippon Electric for twenty years, his entire working life, and had risen to become one of the five assistant managers among the twenty-eight people in his electric-equipment division. Nippon Electric was one of the small construction-related companies that sprang up in the big building boom of postwar Tokyo and prospered, especially in the mansion business, during the big growth years starting in the 1950s. But now that the good times had peaked—land was increasingly scarce, prices were high, and people were less able to afford expensive new apartments in an economy that was slowing down—Nippon Electric's business was off.

Years before, Takeshi had had hopes for bigger promotions, but recently he had come to see his prospects as bleak. "I'm a baby boomer, so it's very competitive," he told us that day. "It's very hard to be promoted." It was another hot, sunny day, and we were sitting in his temporary on-site office surrounded by bulldozers and mountains of mud. On the desk in front of us were drawings of the project; each three-bedroom unit would rent for more than six thousand dollars a month. Takeshi wore a khaki work uniform and moodily smoked cigarette after cigarette. It occurred to me then that while Mariko was determined and focused, he seemed to drift through life, letting things happen, reacting but not acting. He told us that he had entered the electricity division of his technical college twenty years ago merely because his friends were there, and that he hadn't studied enough.

His work, he said, was what the Japanese call a three-*k* job, for *kitanai* (dirty), *kiken* (dangerous), and *kitsui* (hard). Although Takeshi was a supervisor and never did any of the physical work himself, he did wear a hard hat. In an increasingly affluent society, young Japanese were no longer interested in taking the three-*k* jobs, and it was even more difficult to find subcontractors, the men who did the unpleasant work of actually installing the wiring at muddy or cold construction sites. In recent years Takeshi's firm had had to turn projects down because it was understaffed, a growing problem among his competitors as well. Now companies in small industries throughout Japan, including those who supplied parts to Japan's big car manufacturers, complained that it was so hard to find employees that they had been forced to turn to the small community of young illegal immigrants from Asia. Thais, Pakistanis, Bangladeshis, Iranians, Filipinos, Taiwanese, and Brazilians of Japanese descent were working at many of these jobs, and it was not uncommon for groups of them to be holed up at night in rooms in the bleak outer neighborhoods of Tokyo, Yokohama, and Nagoya, harassed by the police and fearful that they would be discovered and arrested for having overstayed their tourist visas. But despite the need of small and large businesses to hire these immigrants, the Japanese Parliament had passed an immigration law that severely limited the number of unskilled foreigners entering the country. Japan was afraid that American-style social problems might otherwise result. Many companies hired illegally as a last resort, but Takeshi insisted that his company would not, and that in any case it was too expensive and difficult to teach non–Japanese speakers the necessary skills.

I asked him if he liked his job. "I don't know any other work," he said and shrugged. I asked if there was any work that looked better to him. "Sword making," he said, laughing.

Takeshi's malaise continued through June. Two nights after waking up on the riverbank, he arrived home late again, at two in the morning. This time Mariko said he was still drunk when he came through the door, but she bit her tongue. "I didn't yell because he was so drunk he wouldn't have listened," she said. The next morning, a Sunday, was Father's Day, another relatively recent American import, and also the day Takeshi was supposed to turn up for a class observation with Mariko at Ken-chan's elementary school. But he was so hung over that he slept until noon. Mariko, disgusted, left for the school alone, then went to teach her samisen class. She had her four students from one to five, and arrived home, exhausted, at five-thirty. It may have been Father's Day, but the thought of fixing dinner yet again for her hung-over husband was not appealing. Although she knew that he felt guilty under his bluster and indifference, she decided to try to turn the situation to her advantage.

"Today is Father's Day," she told Takeshi in front of the children. But then she added with biting sarcasm: "Although it seems like every day is Father's Day in this family." Knowing the kids were on her side, she decided to play her hand. Maybe Takeshi could do the cooking tonight? Yes, yes, said the kids. Takeshi, cornered and remorseful, agreed to make vegetables and beef, which he and the kids then mixed in with some take-out fried rice. Mariko napped. "Usually he's very unhappy to see me sleeping," she told me afterward. "He usually says, 'You're very lazy.' But during that day he didn't say anything. He knew what he had done."

Later, when Sachiko and I met Takeshi again at work, he indicated that he was indeed aware that his behavior was unacceptable. "She nags when I arrive home drunk," he said of Mariko, adding that he thought she was justified in doing so. But then he sounded the familiar theme that it was the pleasure and the right of the Japanese male to drink, even though he sometimes felt sheepish about the excess. "It can't be helped," he said. "We get drunk. And we are not allowed to get drunk at home. At first we think drinking with a colleague is just part of our jobs. But as we drink more, we feel great. Of course when you're drinking on the premises, you're okay. But when you start walking, or taking a taxi, you can't control yourself."

After Father's Day, Takeshi was on better behavior. At home after work, he had only his usual four to five whiskeys with water on the rocks. Things in the family returned to normal, at least for a while.

Takeshi's binges may have infuriated Mariko, but his drinking was not unusual in Japan. Nor was alcohol abuse considered an especially serious problem in Japanese society. Even Mariko, who usually calmed down a few days after one of his drunks, could rationalize his behavior as standard conduct for a Japanese salariman. Takeshi, like many Japanese men of his class and generation, relaxed every night he was home by drinking before and during dinner. "It's not a lot of alcohol," Mariko insisted of his four or five whiskeys, "because he has it with water on the rocks. It seems to be only one or two shots a glass." She thought he was probably "alcohol dependent," but in her opinion so were most men in Japan. Mariko, though, was not deluding herself. She knew from her experience with her brother, who had died in 1985, how lethal alcoholism could be, and she watched carefully for signs that her husband's drinking might be growing worse. Two years earlier, she had answered a questionnaire about problem drinkers in the *Mainichi*, the newspaper delivered each day, and was not entirely shocked to learn that by the standards of the questionnaire her husband had progressed from being "alcohol dependent" to being a full-blown alcoholic. After the Arakawa River incident, she happened to see an article about a hospital for alcoholics south of Tokyo, and at that point she told herself that if her husband stopped getting up for work in the mornings, she would force him to get treatment. As it was, he already had such bad hangovers two or three times a year that he vomited before going to the office. But at least he still got there.

More than anything else, Takeshi was a product of his culture. Public intoxication, particularly among the business class, is far more accepted in Japan than it is in the United States. Anyone who takes the late subways home in Tokyo sees the swaying, red-faced, glassy-eyed men, as well as more and more young women, desperately clutching the train straps in order to keep standing. Eventually any regular late-night rider will be greeted by the sight of a respectably dressed salariman vomiting in a subway car or station, maybe even in someone's lap. The other subway riders move aside, soundlessly, pretending that nothing happened. Drinking is seen as necessary for success in Japan's business culture, and essential for good human relations. In Japan's highly stratified companies, relaxing over a drink is often the only way men feel they can really relate to each other. "If you don't drink, people won't talk to you honestly," complained Kenji Shigemori, an official at the Ministry of Health and Welfare concerned with alcohol problems. Mitsuko Shimomura, who was the first woman in Japan to edit a major newsmagazine, also once said that she found it difficult at first to establish working relationships with her male reporters since she was hesitant, as a woman, to ask them out for drinks after work— the traditional method of bonding between Japanese employers and employees. It is not unusual to hear businessmen and officials at government ministries discuss their wild binges of the night before with a certain amount of pride, and it amused me that a good friend of the former governor of the Bank of Japan—the Japanese equivalent of the Federal Reserve Bank—described him with pride to the *Nihon Keizai* newspaper as a "heavy drinker." An official who cannot hold his liquor, however, is frowned upon. One of Japan's best-known political leaders was disparaged among many Japanese I knew as someone who got so drunk he frequently embarrassed himself, even though there was never a word of his habits in the papers.

And yet for the three years I was in Japan, I was frequently informed—by some alcoholism experts, some government officials, and Mariko herself—that alcohol abuse in the country was not serious. People maintained that it was the United States that had the real problem. "We have only one fifth of the numbers of people who suffer from alcoholism that you do in the United States," Kohjiro Sugino, the head of the All-Japan Sobriety Association, Japan's largest anti-drinking organization, told me proudly, and then added, as if he were letting me in on a big secret, "What we've heard is that this lowers the productivity of the United States." He went on to say that he had recently read a Japanese translation of an American book explaining that people shouldn't buy U.S. cars made on Monday or Friday because on Monday people have hangovers and on Friday they're too distracted by the prospect of beginning a weekend of drinking. I heard many Japanese cite this alleged phenomenon as a common problem in the United States.

In fact, statistics cited in recent international surveys have shown that the United States and Japan are moving closer together in per capita consumption of alcohol. Although Americans still drink more per capita, consumption is going down, while in Japan it is increasing. Health officials in both countries say they expect that if current trends continue, Japan's consumption will surpass that of the United States. For example, a survey by the Brewer's Association of Canada reported that the Japanese in 1990 consumed 1.72 gallons of pure alcohol per capita, compared with 1.89 gallons for Americans. Ten years earlier, Japan consumed 1.52 gallons per capita, while U.S. consumption was 2.15 gallons per capita.

Comparing the rates of alcoholism in both countries is more difficult. Survey methods differ widely, as does the concept of who is an alcoholic. In trying to figure out which nation had the dubious distinction of drinking more, I discovered that the profound difference in attitudes toward drinking in the United States and Japan was a dramatic example of the different ways in which each society perceives and handles its social problems. Over the years in the United States, for example, the definition of "alcoholism" has broadened to include not just physical dependence but such chronic problems as a preoccupation with alcohol, or an inability to cut down. Using this new definition, the National Center for Health Statistics conducted a nationwide survey in 1988 and estimated that some fifteen million adults in the United States, or about 8.6 percent of the population eighteen and older, suffered from alcohol abuse or alcohol dependence. At this writing, the definition of "alcoholism" is once again being made more inclusive, so the next set of statistics will probably show more alcoholics in the United

States than ever before. The high level of alcoholism in the United States, in other words, seems to be partly a matter of definition.

Japan, on the other hand, minimizes its social problems, as it has never easily admitted unpleasant, embarrassing truths about itself. Alcoholism surveys in the past decade are a case in point. Official statistics show that alcoholics, referred to as "severe problem drinkers," represent only 2.5 to 3.6 percent of the Japanese population as a whole—including children and babies. One reason American rates are higher is that they are percentages of the adult population only. The Japanese statistics are also less useful because many are based on responses to questionnaires like that devised by Kurihama Hospital, the leading facility for alcohol treatment and research in Japan, which was intended to identify only those drinkers who were in serious trouble.

The simple fact is that many Japanese men my husband and I knew well thought very little of getting drunk occasionally; for them, heavy drinking was a source of amusement, much as it was in the United States until a few decades ago. Finding statistics concerning this phenomenon is nearly impossible. However, studies show that alcohol-related liver disease in Japan is increasing. Furthermore, 50 percent of the Japanese population suffer from what is called a "flushing response," an unpleasant physical reaction to small amounts of alcohol. (Doctors say the syndrome, marked by facial flushing, heart palpitations, headaches, and nausea, is caused by an enzyme deficiency common among Asians but not among Caucasians.) Since the "flushers" drink less than nonflushers, and a large proportion of Japanese women are teetotalers, health officials suggest that certain segments of the Japanese population—chiefly middle-aged men—must drink a great deal to bring the per capita consumption rate so close to that of the United States.

The best evidence I could find of that obvious fact was a joint United States–Japan study sponsored by the National Institute on Alcohol Abuse and Alcoholism in Rockville, Maryland, and the

National Institute on Alcoholism at Kurihama Hospital in Japan. The project studied the drinking practices of four groups during 1984 and 1985: Japanese living in four areas of Japan, Japanese Americans in Hawaii, Japanese Americans in Silicon Valley, and Caucasians in Silicon Valley. The study found that the middle-aged Japanese men living in Japan drank more than twice as much as the middle-aged Caucasian men in California. Among the Japanese men aged fifty to fifty-nine—the peak of a man's business life, when drinking is most frequent and intense—56 percent were found to have "heavy drinking problems," compared with 11 percent of the Caucasian men in the same age group. A man was judged to have a heavy drinking problem if he answered yes to such questions as "Have you stayed intoxicated for several days at a time?" or "Have you awakened the next day not being able to remember some of the things you had done while drinking?" The survey sample groups, however, were small—518 Japanese men and 171 Caucasian men.

Interestingly, Japan does not have the problem of drinking and driving that the United States does—in part because penalties for drunken driving are especially severe in Japan, and because men, inebriated or not, usually take the subways home. (If they are senior enough, they are chauffeured home by company drivers.) To what degree alcohol abuse affects Japanese productivity is also impossible to judge, particularly since official employee absentee rates are among the lowest in the world. Like Mariko's husband, most men with hangovers drag themselves to work and let their colleagues cover for them in a system where the work of the group is more important than the performance of the individual. The bigger issue, of course, is that alcohol seems increasingly to be a release valve in one of the world's most pressurized and rigid societies—another price that the Japanese pay for their extraordinary success. Mariko knew this instinctively. When she cooled down after one of her husband's binges, she seemed understanding about his plight. "With other people, not the family, he cannot be free to speak his mind," she said sympathetically. "But then once he starts having alcohol with outsiders, he really wants to get drunk."

Two weeks after the riverbank incident, on June 30, a suffocating, miserable Sunday, Mariko, Takeshi, and Ken-chan decided to go on a family outing with thousands of others on the mobbed streets of Harajuku, a fashionable and popular shopping district. It was Ken-chan's idea. He wanted a toy, specifically a plastic model of his favorite cartoon character on television, and Mariko had agreed. Takeshi, still feeling guilty over his binges, was happy to have the chance to make up for his recent behavior. The two older children decided to stay home, considering themselves too sophisticated for such a trip.

Ken-chan and his parents left home around ten in the morning, taking a bus and then a train, which was packed, as on most Sundays, with families on outings together. Many fathers had not seen their children awake all week, but Sunday, father's day off, was the day for what Japanese men called with no irony "family service." Mariko hated the phrase because it implied that fathers had family responsibilities only on Sundays, and also that time with the family was an obligation, just like another aspect of a man's business life, such as golf games with business associates. (In fact, golf was often played on Sundays, which meant that sometimes a man would not see his children even one day a week.)

The train soon reached Harajuku, a trendy shopping area filled with boutiques, record shops, theaters, and teenagers, who poured in on weekends from all over metropolitan Tokyo. Mariko, Takeshi, and Ken-chan made their way through the crowds down Omote-sando, a graceful tree-lined boulevard the Japanese called their Champs Élysées, which was bordered by shops so expensive that Mariko would never have dreamed of walking into any of them.

There were $2,000 dresses in the window of the glass-and-steel Hanae Mori building, the headquarters of Japan's premier couturiere of conservative fashion, and $250 sweaters at Paul Stuart Japan, and sidewalk cafés, and paper fans, dolls, and other trinkets at the fake red pagoda of the touristy Oriental Bazaar. Their destination was Kiddyland, a child's fantasy and a parent's nightmare, with five overpriced floors crammed with stuffed animals, games, computers, and hundreds of kids on similar family outings. Ken-chan got his toy, and then the three went on to lunch at Shakey's Pizza, another of the popular American fast-food imports, like McDonald's and Kentucky Fried Chicken, that have proliferated in Japan. From there they took the subway over to Hibiya, in the heart of Tokyo near the grounds of the Imperial Palace, to see *Home Alone*, the big hit of the summer. As usual, there had been a six-month lag after the American opening before the film reached Tokyo. Like most first-run American movies, it would be one of the most popular pictures of the year in Japan—nearly as hard to get into as a hit Broadway show in New York.

Predictably, there were only standing-room tickets left. Mariko and the family gave up and decided to make do instead with some classic Japanese culture, the East Garden of the historic Imperial Palace, where the shogun housed his wife and concubines during the Tokugawa Era more than one hundred years ago. Today almost none of the buildings of the original Edo Castle remain, but the garden is still a peaceful respite from the city. The family arrived at the palace entrance called Otemon, then walked under the massive stone wall, built during the seventeenth century with slabs that were hauled on sledges through the streets of Tokyo by teams of one hundred men. The Imperial Palace grounds take up 284 acres in the middle of downtown Tokyo, a city with fewer parks per capita than almost any other in the world, but most of the lush green space is completely closed to the public on all but two days of the year—January 2 and the emperor's birthday. The East Garden is adjacent to the main grounds and remains the only part open to the public on a regular, if limited, basis. It is a pleasant enough place, with ponds, azaleas, iris, and pine forests, but it has none of the breathtaking beauty of the famous gardens in Kyoto that Mariko saw as a high school student. The palace, which cannot be seen from the East Garden, is a traditional Japanese wooden structure of seven buildings with graceful semi-gabled roofs, all connected by galleries and corridors; it is used mostly for banquets and other state occasions. About the only building on the palace grounds that the Japanese can see from outside the walls is, in fact, not part of the palace at all; it is the imposing but unused watchtower called Fushimi Yagura, one of the few surviving structures of the original Edo Castle.

Mariko found the East Garden quiet and natural, and she was happy to be there. Like most Japanese, she had respect for the emperor and followed the gossip about the imperial family—the crown prince's problems finding a wife were not going away—as avidly as anyone. But it was not a big part of her life. She lived only a half hour from the Imperial Palace, but this was the first time she had ever been there.

Dusk, July 13. As the shouts of children playing in the street joined with the ceaseless noise of the summer cicadas, Mariko came out of her house, stooped by the front gate, and struck a match to light a small bundle of dried reeds she had bought that day from the neighborhood florist. The little fire crackled and burned, and Mariko stared into it, feeling for a moment unusually peaceful. The flames lasted barely five minutes, but Mariko knew the small ritual was enough to help guide the soul of her dead brother back home from the spirit world for a short visit. It was the first night of Bon, the Buddhist Festival of the Dead, the time when the souls of the departed come home to enjoy the warm summer nights and the gardens lush from the rains and heat. Bon is celebrated in most parts of Japan in mid-August, but the dead come back early to Tokyo, in July. Mariko had started the fire while there was still light in the sky. She should have waited until dark, but she wanted her brother's soul home as early as possible; her feelings were still a little tender from the memorial service two and a half months before. When the flames had died, Mariko went back inside, to the family *butsudan*, or Buddhist altar, in her parents' room. The *butsudan*, a small wooden shelf in a corner, held religious objects and containers for burning incense; up above was a picture of her brother, who looked remarkably like Mariko. She placed on the altar the traditional seasonal offerings for Bon—things that the soul of her brother might like: eggplant, green grapes, cucumbers, tomatoes, sake.

Sake? For her brother? "Even if he died of too much sake," she told me quite seriously, "on this special occasion he should enjoy it."

Mariko, like most Japanese, did not consider herself particularly religious. Although she believed that souls live on, she said she did not believe in God, and like most people in the country she casually mixed Buddhism and the native religion, Shinto, depending on the occasion. She had been blessed as an infant at a Shinto shrine and married by Shinto rites, but her funeral would include the Buddhist ritual of *shoko*, in which mourners hold a pinch of incense ash to their foreheads, then offer silent prayers. Every New Year's Eve Mariko took a five-minute walk to the neighborhood's Buddhist temple, where she rang the big bell to usher in the new year auspiciously (the priests always struck the bell 108 times, to drive out the 108 evil desires of man). Then, in the first few days after January 1, she walked five minutes in the other direction to the Ichomachi shrine, which was Shinto, where she tossed a coin into the cash box at the front of the shrine, sounded the gong, bowed deeply, clapped her hands to wake up the god, bowed again, and then backed away so as not to turn her back on him.

Mariko's prayers—she simply and briefly repeated her requests in her head, without specific meditations or scriptures—would help ensure good health and fortune for her family for the rest of the year. All of her children had been blessed by Shinto priests, and when high school entrance exams loomed for Shunsuke, Mariko had gone to the famous Yushima Tenjin shrine near the old Tokyo neighborhood of Ueno and prayed to the god—a great Heian-period thinker who after his death become the deity of scholarship—for Shunsuke's success. For Chiaki's exams, Mariko had gone to a shrine at the top of Mount Takao, a day trip from Tokyo that happened to include a lovely and invigorating climb up steep pathways and forested hillsides. How could any of it hurt?

"Whenever I want to make a wish, I go to a shrine," Mariko told me, slightly embarrassed. She admitted she felt uncomfortable asking for favors, even from a god, because she wasn't one of the big financial supporters of the shrine. "In the routine of daily life, I don't do anything for the shrine," she said. "I don't contribute money, and I don't go regularly."

I asked to whom she prayed at the shrine if she did not believe in God. "I go there, but I don't have a strong consciousness that God is there," she said. "Maybe unconsciously. I go because I want to ensure that the whole family will be in good health."

We were as usual at Mariko's house, and at this point Sachiko broke in. "It's a very convenient god—do you understand?"

Mariko tried to explain. "Sometimes I can only believe in myself," she said. "But when I want to assure myself that I can get along with other members of my family, and that we will be happy, then I want to pledge to the god that I will be able to get along with the whole family. Or I want to protect the whole family. I consider a shrine a place to make a promise. Maybe I believe somewhere in my heart in the existence of a god. But I don't depend on him." But then she said that every January 7, after the New Year's celebrations, she took the pine branches that had decorated her home to the

Ichomachi shrine, where the priests threw them on a huge outdoor bonfire for a ritual burning. "I'm afraid if I don't do that, maybe I'll be punished," she said. "So maybe I might believe in God."

Mariko's religious views were wholly typical and not as confused as they seemed. Some 70 to 80 percent of the Japanese regularly tell pollsters they do not consider themselves believers in any religion. Like Mariko, they have made no deliberate choice about faith but have simply been born into and accepted the traditions of the indigenous folk beliefs of Japan, a loose mix that borrows gods and objects of worship from Shinto, Buddhism, Confucianism, and Taoism, the Chinese religion and philosophy based on the teachings of the "tao" or "universal way" of the great scholar Lao-tzu. Mariko's beliefs, such as they were, were unfocused precisely because they were so much a part of who she was. Like most Japanese, she held only vague notions of an undefined spirit world beyond her own. Life begins, according to the view of most Japanese, with the arrival of a soul, which develops, matures, and at death leaves the body; if properly honored by the surviving family members, it becomes an ancestral spirit to be worshiped for either thirty-three or forty-nine years, depending on local customs, and then finally is promoted to the status of a *kami*, or god, who lives, for example, in the mountains in the winter and in the rice fields in the spring. These are among the surviving practices of one of the world's most durable folk religions. Like most Japanese, Mariko took pleasure in the seasonal religious festivals, at one time tied to the harvest and fertility, that connected her to her community and all of Japan. But she never felt the need to seek any deeper meaning beyond them. The rituals were a comfort in themselves, aimed at achieving a certain peace of mind and tangible benefits in the immediate world—prosperity, recovery from disease, protection from bad fortune. There was also a strong element of fear—Mariko would never plan the wedding of one of her children to fall on one of the unlucky days known as *butsumetsu* in the Buddhist calendar. This, too, was typical. Even Japan Air Lines always schedules the inaugural flight of a new route on a *tai-an,* or good-luck day. The most international of Japanese companies regularly call Shinto priests to attend the dedications of new buildings; many also send their company cars and drivers to shrines to be blessed for safety. And in downtown Tokyo, the multibillion-dollar trading conglomerate Mitsui & Co. does not take lightly its location next to a small stone monument to Masakado, the fearsome warrior god. In the early 1970s Mitsui considered buying the hugely valuable real estate on which the memorial was built but decided not to offend Masakado by paving over the site. Over the years, there was talk in Tokyo that every desk at Mitsui & Co. was positioned so that none of the company's eight thousand employees would sit with his or her back to the god. When I visited the company, I saw the talk was unfounded—the desks faced any number of ways—but a company spokesman did tell me that employees had been known to inch their desks toward the proper orientation. In 1988, when a series of illnesses and accidents plagued one department within the building, Mitsui called in a priest to rid the floor of evil spirits. He brought over the traditional offerings of sake, salt, and rice, then blessed the entire department. It seems to have worked. Although Mariko could not easily articulate her religion, I came away with respect for it, not least because it was so seamlessly woven into her existence, whereas many Americans keep organized religion separate from other parts of their lives.

Not everyone in Mariko's family embraced religion in her unorganized way. Her mother and younger brother had both joined Rissho Kose Kai, one of the "new" institutionalized religions that play an important part in the spiritual and political life of modern Japan. Rissho Kose Kai, which now claims 16.7 million members, and Soka Gakkai, which claims more than 10 million, are the biggest of the religious groupings that were founded before the war but proliferated after it, chiefly among the devastated masses in the cities. Both Rissho Kose Kai and Soka Gakkai are lay organizations descended from Nichiren Buddhism, a sect founded in the thirteenth century by one of the great historical figures of Japan, the magnetic and strong-willed priest Nichiren. Nichiren preached that all truth was contained in the Lotus Sutra, the last sermon of the Buddha on Vulture Peak before he achieved the worldly detachment and inner peace known as nirvana, or enlightenment. Although historians say Nichiren arrived at his conclusions after a strenuous philosophical journey, the basic teaching of his religion comes down to this: Followers may achieve enlightenment simply by repeating the chant "Nam myo horenge kyo," or "Praise be to the wonderful Lotus Sutra."

In the 1950s Japan's leaders viewed Soka Gakkai and Rissho Kose Kai as outlets for the underprivileged and welcome alternatives to the Communist Party, but now both sects have become rich, conservative, and politically powerful voices of the establishment. Soka Gakkai controls one of the biggest of Japan's minor political parties, the Komeito, or Clean Government Party—part of the coalition under Prime Minister Hosokawa in 1993 and 1994—and also runs elementary and high schools, a university, a publishing house, and golf courses. Rissho Kose Kai, which has strong links to the long-ruling Liberal Democratic Party, owns an enormous pink main temple, a hospital, and the country's largest concert hall. Today the zealous proselytizing of both groups continues to attract the underdogs and ailing aged of Japan, who, in an intensely group-oriented society, feel a profound need to belong. Mariko's bedridden mother joined Rissho Kose Kai after members of the organization repeatedly visited her, promising a better life; Mariko's younger brother had joined after he left his last job because of his drinking. He often poured out his troubles with alcoholism at group meetings, and eventually became a kind of youth group leader. "But he was never saved from alcohol," Mariko said. "He always told me he didn't know why he joined the group. He used to say, 'I wish I believed the faith of this new religion—but I can't.' "

During the year I spent with Mariko, organized religion entered her life in another way; this developed from the simple fact that the Ichomachi shrine, a few blocks from her house, was one of the loveliest and most contemplative spaces in the area. Like many other shrines in Japan, it was shaded by gingko trees, and Mariko and others in the neighborhood had happy childhood memories of playing under their shade in the summer and sledding past them down the hills in the winter. There had been shock earlier that spring—on May 24, to be exact—when a crew of workers came into the wooded grounds of the shrine and cut down thirty trees, apparently in order to build a parking lot to be run for the benefit of the shrine itself. Although Mariko was not yet involved, the event would affect her life for the following year.

As the summer progressed, a small group of neighborhood activists sprang into action. Shocked and outraged by the once-lovely but now partly denuded hillsides, the group organized a signature campaign to protest the action and demand that thirty new trees be planted. One of the group leaders was also a member of an antinuclear group, and in June she took the tree petitions with her to a demonstration in Okinawa. Everyone signed. The Ichomachi activists had soon collected an incredible eight thousand signatures protesting the tree cutting, about half from the neighborhood and the surrounding ward, the others from all over Japan. At the end of June the activists presented the petitions to the ward council, which reacted as it often did in a political crisis: The situation was put under review. Plans for the parking lot were temporarily stalled, and the trees remained as they fell, on the ground—symbols to me of what would soon be a messy but revealing convergence of religion, politics, and the high costs of protesting the status quo in Japan.

5

THE PLEASURES OF SUMMER

The Tanakas on vacation in Hokkaido

AUGUST

High summer in all of its fetid misery and richness descended on Tokyo, bringing heavy gray skies, enormous white peaches, and evening fireworks along the overgrown banks of the Ichomachi River. The torpid brown flow was on the southern border of the ward, and just months earlier it had been swollen and rushing from the heavy spring rains. Now the river meandered off lazily in the heat toward Tokyo Bay, as lethargic as the sweating salarimen in the hundred-degree subways. Most people complained about summer in Tokyo, but Mariko had grown to enjoy the sultriness and the quiet. School was out, and one muggy Saturday she took Ken-chan on what had become an annual summer outing, to Toshimaen, a water park in the far northern reaches of Tokyo. One of Mariko's neighborhood friends and the friend's son went too, along with me, my husband, Steve, and our daughter, Madeleine. I even coaxed Sachiko and her son into coming—much to Sachiko's dismay, since she viewed such a trip as another summons to go far beyond the call of duty. Sachiko had none of my anthropological interest in the Japanese middle class at play, and Toshimaen was high on the list of places she avoided at all costs.

She did have a point. The place was a shabby, overcrowded, old-fashioned amusement park attached to a playground of seven swimming pools, most of them overflowing with humanity. There was a wave pool with imitation surf, a diving pool, a waterfall pool, and numerous giant slides. My favorite by far was the mammoth doughnut-shaped pool with a continuous current that carried bathers around a ring the size of a circular running track. Hundreds of bobbing heads were zipping along, like rush-hour commuters stuck permanently on the Yamanote Line, the subway that circled the city. Even at play, the Japanese seemed to be on a treadmill going nowhere fast. But it did look like fun.

We changed in the women's dressing room, a moist, cavernous space the size of an airplane hangar, where Mariko, like most of the Japanese women around us, stood in front of her metal locker and wiggled discreetly into her bathing suit while wrapped in a towel—a champion at the technique Japanese women use to avoid exposing private parts or unnecessary flesh. Outside in the sticky air we spread out on an inviting spot of concrete. Ken-chan immediately had to have a hamburger; Sachiko's son headed for the diving pool. Steve and I took Madeleine into the waterfall pool, then headed over to check out the giant slides. Mariko and Sachiko sat and talked. Neither had any intention of actually getting into the water, and by then the sky had grown overcast and the air clammy. The crowds thinned out. By late afternoon it was almost too cool to swim, but Ken-chan and Sachiko's son wanted to stay, so Mariko took them over to the adjoining amusement park. There she met up with her friend and his son. As the three boys ran off toward the roller coaster and the cotton candy, Steve, Madeleine, Sachiko, and I headed home, leaving Mariko sitting with her friend near a bandstand where a screeching rock band was making it impossible to think. But Mariko seemed perfectly happy. She smoked a cigarette, sipped a beer, talked to her friend, and watched the summer dusk fall as the world walked by.

I now see that the summer was an interlude, a natural breather, between the intensity of our first interviews and the revelations that were to come later. In Mariko's house the cozy leg-warmer under the table had long since been put away. On the still afternoons we sat in the insufferable heat drinking endless glasses of barley tea in a futile attempt to stay cool, while a fan blew the stifling air from one corner to another. Kiri-chan, the cat, sensibly parked herself right in front of it and never moved. The house had that smell of summer mildew common to all traditional Japanese wooden houses, and everything in it seemed damp. Without air-conditioning, I had a hard time concentrating, and so did Mariko and Sachiko. After the drama of the spring interviews—Mariko's brother's death, her husband's drinking, her parents' story of World War II—none of us could summon the energy to move forward.

I learned more when we just relaxed and meandered from topic to topic. One Wednesday after Mariko's samisen lesson at Sensei's house, she and her classmates bowed and told their honored teacher thank you very much, then skulked off like guilty schoolchildren for a vaguely sleazy girl's-afternoon-out of karaoke, or singing to recorded background music. Karaoke is usually performed by inebriated salarimen who like to belt out Frank Sinatra's "I Did It My Way" (still one of the all-time hits among karaoke tunes) in nightclubs and bars. But housewives, who rarely go out in the evenings, had no opportunity for karaoke until a few years ago, when the idea of the "karaoke box" was born. The "box" is a tiny room with an elaborate sound, light, and video system, usually one of several in a storefront sitting alongside the rice shops and vegetable markets in any suburban shopping district. It is open during the day, is less expensive and disreputable than going to a karaoke bar, and can be rented by the hour.

So there we were—Mariko, her four friends, the nine-year-old son of one of the friends, Sachiko, and me—in our very own box, a black room about six feet by six, all of us wedged onto a horseshoe-shaped red sofa around a little table crowded with potato chips, muffins, beer, and cigarettes. Not surprisingly, the place smelled of stale smoke. Colored lights beamed from the ceiling, the disco sound throbbed, and icy gusts blasted from the air conditioner. It felt as if we were sitting inside some kind of space-age refrigerator. The five other karaoke boxes in the shop were identical, and all had see-through glass doors—the result of a new regulation that had been imposed in order to stop teenagers from using the boxes for sex.

Mariko, Kirin beer in hand, selected "Blue Stardust," a Japanese golden oldie by Yuzo Kayama, an enduring pop singer who had first become famous a quarter century ago. "Ojin," she said, laughing, using the Japanese slang for a boring middle-aged man. A dreamy nighttime scene of Shinjuku skyscrapers popped up on the TV screen; as the music started, the words to the song appeared at the bottom. Mariko held on to her microphone and in a deep, low voice, enhanced by the sumptuous sound system, let loose in Japanese with:

> "I see the stars in the sky,
> One star looks like you,
> And the star seems very sad . . ."

Her voice was good, and in this womb with friends and beer she was uninhibited. "You can free youself by singing in a very loud voice," she told me afterward. "You don't have to put on any pretenses. It's an escape from stress."

We moved on, through the selections. One friend sang "Yesterday" by the Beatles, in English, as the screen showed scenes of lovers kissing under a waterfall and along the East River in New York. "Moon River" followed, with incongruous shots of a Ferris wheel and a merry-go-round. The women decided it was my turn next and selected "Only You" by the Platters for me. Mariko stepped in to help, competently singing the English words as they appeared on the screen.

We moved on to "Calendar Girl" by Neil Sedaka, then an *enka* song. *Enka* is the dark, brooding popular music, usually about failed and tragic love, preferred by Japan's middle-aged. Mariko liked it; Sachiko hated it. Everyone sang out in a suitably doleful tone:

> "You're always watching the waves coming in
> And watching for the man to come back . . .
> And he's married . . ."

On the television screen there appeared a shot of a woman lying dead alongside some cherry blossoms. Even for *enka*, this was a bit much. Everyone laughed—probably not the reaction the video's makers had in mind—and then kept on singing.

By far the best selection of the day was a real crowd-pleaser: "Love Comes Suddenly," the theme song from *Tokyo Love Story*, the big television soap opera from the winter before. Everyone joined in lustily in the smoke-filled darkness:

> "So many men pass by,
> Even women love crazily,
> Love affairs come suddenly and go suddenly . . ."

The song is something I will always associate with that summer. *Tokyo Love Story* had been on the air from January to March— Japanese television shows frequently run only three months, like protracted miniseries—yet in July the song was still one of the most popular in Japan. You could hear it everywhere, in taxis and on the radio, in health clubs and bars. Every Monday night when *Tokyo Love Story* was on the air, high school girls all over Japan positioned themselves in front of their television sets from nine to ten and watched, transfixed. Chiaki once told me that if she didn't see *Tokyo Love Story* she had nothing to talk about at school the next day. It was one of the top-rated shows in the history of Fuji-TV, Japan's most popular television network, known for its high-quality junk.

Tokyo Love Story revolved around the lives of five twenty-something friends starting out on their own in Tokyo after college. They all became romantically entangled as the weeks progressed, but the character who carried the show was Rika, a pretty, preppy-ish office lady, or O.L., invariably dressed in expensive blue blazers, penny loafers, headbands, argyle sweaters, and lots of red, white, and blue stripes. She had bangs, a fresh face, and a very modern attitude; in the series' most memorable moment, much discussed in Japan, she took the initiative and simply said, "Let's have sex," during a romantic moment with one of her male costars. The producers had aimed the show at Japan's young generation, but Mariko found herself hooked after the fourth episode. "I never heard about it from anybody my own age," she admitted. But she said it reminded her of her own single days in Tokyo, those six years between her high school graduation and her wedding when she worked at the Japan Travel Bureau and was relatively free. "I can still remember that feeling that those young men and women in the show had," she said. "I can still feel that kind of excitement about love."

At the time, the show was the most famous of what the Japanese call "trendy dramas," a new genre that underscored the growing power of television as a marketing force and a definer of modern culture in the lives of the Japanese. This was one way in which Japan really was like the United States; the characters in

Tokyo Love Story became nationwide personalities and were talked about as if they were real. Mariko and Chiaki eventually took to watching the show together. Chiaki would prop herself up on cushions on the floor, her legs under the warm *kotatsu;* Mariko would sit nearby and point out that the independent and direct Rika was not the kind of woman that Japanese men like to marry. "A man would have to be very strong to handle her," she said. It was an observation, not a criticism, since Mariko considered herself of the same sort. "I am not a Japanese man's type of woman," she once told me when we were talking about the show. "I do what I want. I have initiative. I go according to my own schedule. Most Japanese women do what their husbands say."

Tokyo Love Story was created for television by Tooru Ota, a thirty-two-year-old former police reporter for Fuji's main news show and a 1981 graduate of the elite Waseda University. Ota, who functioned as a kind of wunderkind director-producer, had gathered dialogue and ideas for the show by reading the women's magazines and taking two or three O.L.s at a time to dinner. "I would draw stories out of them, and just listen," he told me. "It was a job, although other people thought I was fooling around." When I went to see Ota one afternoon at the Fuji TV studios, he happily admitted that the trendy drama was in fact a gussied-up version of the stodgy television melodramas of five years before— when the locations, music, interior design, and fashions were, in his words, very *dasai,* or "country." "I wanted to change the wrapping—although not the gift itself," he said. The first trendy drama appeared in 1988, dazzling its audience with characters who wore clothes by Comme des Garçons, worked as fashion stylists, and lived in high-tech apartments in chic areas of central Tokyo. "The dramas captured the heart of the typical O.L., who makes photocopies and tea for men all day long," Ota said. The lifestyles in the show were of course utterly out of reach of the typical O.L., who lived at home with her parents. "It was completely unrealistic,"

Ota admitted. The fashion parade continued in subsequent shows until, in Ota's words, "the audience got sick of it." For *Tokyo Love Story*, things were scaled back, but not completely. "If I get too close and show reality," Ota said, "the audience won't watch."

I was always struck by the opening of the show, which managed to make Tokyo, one of the more prosaic spots in the world, look like a city of poetry and love. As the theme song that Mariko and her friends had sung in the karaoke box throbbed, dreamy shots of fountains, skyscrapers, and lovers kissing appeared on the screen. Tokyo was nothing less than a glamorous, fast-paced capital. People rushed through the streets, ran off subways, dashed to public pay phones to rendezvous for dates. I was suddenly excited to be living in such a marvelous place. The characters met for drinks in wood-paneled bars, dined at elegant French or Chinese restaurants, and once went away for a naughty winter weekend at a secluded hot spring in the Japan Alps.

And yet the basic appeal of *Tokyo Love Story* was in the sophisticated Rika, who showed she had enough heart to fall in love with Kanji, the country boy from the provinces who worked in her office. Although Rika lost Kanji in the end to a more traditional Japanese woman, she could tell him in the last scene of the series, when they ran into each other on the street three years later, "I still think of the time I loved you as very important. When I'm depressed, I think of it, and it makes me very happy." Rika wasn't manipulative, and she wasn't looking for just an *asshie-kun*—a slang expression, derived from the word for "leg," used for a boyfriend who has a car and is besotted enough to chauffeur a woman wherever she wants to go. "Before, a lot of girls looked for an *asshie-kun* to play love as a game," Ota said. "But Rika had a different attitude. She loved Kanji from beginning to end."

The actress who played Rika, Honami Suzuki, was less impressed with her character than were her fans. "There are no Rikas in this world," she told me when I caught up with her at a studio in

Roppongi, where she was posing for photographs for a women's magazine. "Rika is a creation—like Mickey Mouse. The reason people say that Rika is a new Japanese girl is because she says very definitely yes or no. But Japanese don't like to do that, and young girls aren't able to have that kind of attitude yet. . . . Generally, women get married. Rika should get married someday, and get old."

The television was always on in the evenings in Mariko's house, bringing not only *Tokyo Love Story* but also a regular diet of cartoons, sports, news, game shows, quiz shows, cooking shows, and such travel shows as *Dreamy Trip*, a completely banal but to me strangely irresistible series. Each episode of *Dreamy Trip* sent a different Japanese movie or television star to a place known for its beauty and culture around the nation and usually included an overnight stay at a hot-spring resort, with the inevitable shots of the travelers earnestly sampling the local fish, mushrooms, or tofu. Everything was always the same—the *ahhh*s in the steaming waters of the hot spring, the appreciative *mmmmmm*s after the food-tasting, the pleasing stroll through the spot's main attraction. The Japanese do not like surprises when they travel, and *Dreamy Trip* always peddled more reassurance than adventure.

One night that summer Chiaki and Ken-chan were sprawled in front of the television set watching a popular cartoon show when I came over for dinner. I said hello to the kids, then went into the kitchen to see how Mariko was doing. Since February I had eaten her snacks and smelled intriguing salty-sweet aromas throughout the house, and now I was curious to see how Mariko prepared meals for a family of seven in a kitchen that was perhaps ten feet by four feet and looked as if it had been jerry-built over the years. It was crammed with a small Toshiba refrigerator, a set of two gas burners, and a large cabinet for dishes. Since there was no counter space,

Mariko used a wooden cutting board over the tiny sink. Connected to the kitchen by a door was an old wooden bathhouse. It had been a separate structure in the old days, when the water had to be heated by a wood-burning fire. The bath was now heated by gas, but there was still only cold running water elsewhere in the house, which was not unusual in Japan. Mariko made do in the kitchen with her "boiling water machine," an appliance that brought scalding water to the sink through a separate pipe and faucet.

For dinner Mariko was going to serve raw tuna with rice in bowls, topped with shredded dried seaweed and *shiso* leaves, a sharp, pungent herb used throughout Japanese cooking. There would also be miso soup—miso is fermented soybean paste—and a dish of simmered sliced carrots, radishes, and fried fish cakes. There would be broccoli in a mustard-soy sauce and boiled fresh soybeans in their pods, a favorite snack with beer in the summertime. As always there would be rice and Japanese pickled cucumbers. This was to be an ordinary dinner, but Sachiko had brought pork cutlets for the occasion. Mariko was planning to make them into *tonkatsu*, a breaded, deep-fried specialty, one of the most popular meat dishes in Japan.

I watched and took notes as Mariko moved fast. First she chopped the small pinkish roots from the leafy green *myoga* plant, native to the mountains, that grew in the patch of dirt in her backyard; they would add a sharp zest to the miso soup. Her technique with the knife was as rapid and precise as that of a professional chef, and when I asked, she told me she had learned years ago in a high school cooking class. A pot of the soybeans boiling in water with a teaspoon of salt rested on one burner, and on the other was chopped eggplant boiling in water for the miso soup. To the eggplant and water Mariko added the miso, a thick, salty, protein-rich, low-fat paste that looks like peanut butter. Mariko stirred the mixture with two large chopsticks, then added the chopped *myoga* roots and some *dashi*, an all-purpose broth that gives Japanese cuisine much of its distinctive flavor. But it was instant *dashi,* not homemade. Mariko apologized, knowing that a generation earlier, any self-respecting Japanese housewife was expected to make her own *dashi* by painstakingly shaving flakes from a dried fillet of bonito fish, then simmering them with dried sea kelp. The fresher the bonito flakes the better, and every Japanese housewife knows that the best dried kelp is harvested from the subarctic waters off the northern island of Hokkaido. Ever the traditionalist, Mariko often did make her own *dashi,* saving the instant *dashi* granules for those days when she had no time.

Mariko stirred the miso soup and set it aside, turning her attention to the simmered carrots, radishes, and fried fish cakes. She put them in a pot and added sugar, soy sauce, *dashi,* and salt. By now the broccoli was parboiled to a crisp-tender bright green. She made a marinade of soy sauce and Japanese mustard—hotter and darker than the American version—then drained the broccoli and tossed it around in the dressing. Until recently, broccoli was not used in traditional Japanese cooking, but Japanese appetites are becoming increasingly Westernized. Schoolchildren now eat spaghetti and macaroni and cheese as much as they do sushi and rice cakes. The favorite food of sixth graders surveyed in 1989, for example, was hamburgers.

Turning to the pork *tonkatsu,* Mariko heated up a mixture of fresh and used cooking oil in a deep pot. "That's what makes the *tonkatsu* brown," she said. She beat two eggs with water in a bowl, adding flour to make a lumpy batter. Using her hands, she dipped each pork cutlet in the batter and then rolled it in some bread crumbs taken from the freezer. I watched as the cutlets sizzled noisily in the oil.

"Frying is the most difficult part of cooking," she said. "The oil has to be really hot for meat, but not so hot for vegetables. I didn't know how to fry when I was first married." She expertly chopped a head of cabbage to accompany the *tonkatsu.* Chiaki, meanwhile, was out in the living room waving a Japanese fan over the rice to cool it off; Mariko had put it in a big wooden tub and dressed it with a mix of vinegar and sugar. Mariko then put the cooled, slightly sweet rice in red lacquer bowls and on top arranged pieces of raw tuna. Normally the fish was prohibitively expensive, but in this case it was a great bargain because Mariko had known to buy it late that day at a basement market in Shibuya that, like many stores, marked down the raw fish that would not be fresh enough to sell the next morning. Mariko had paid only eight dollars for enough tuna to feed her whole family; a few hours earlier, it would have cost three times as much.

Like most Japanese housewives, Mariko shopped every day, a custom that endured from the time when families had only tiny refrigerators or none at all. Mariko's modern refrigerator could easily hold half a week's worth of food, but never would it have occurred to her to plan ahead for several dinners and shop for them all at once. Partly this was because she could buy only what would fit in her bicycle basket. Although I suppose she could have made some arrangement with her husband to use the company car, shopping once or twice a week like an American was simply not a part of her mentality. Like most housewives, she believed it was one of her responsibilities as a mother and wife to buy the freshest food available; although she used convenience foods like instant *dashi* and cubes for curry rice, she never bought frozen vegetables or dinners, which in any case were not available in any great variety. Then, too, if she went every day she could plan meals around whatever was on special—for instance, a large package of chicken legs, more than enough to feed her whole family, that was on sale for four dollars when I went with her to the neighborhood market one day that summer. The market, part of the large Marufuji chain, looked like any medium-sized modern grocery store in the United States, except that it was far cleaner and had faster checkout clerks, virtually perfect, blemish-free, often individually wrapped fruits and vegetables—and food prices that were two and a half to three times higher than those in the States.

Japan's exorbitant food prices are of course well known around the world, but Mariko avoided the extremes. She never bought any of the infamous hundred-dollar Japanese melons, for example. Few Japanese do, since they are meant only as expensive gifts and not for ordinary consumption. (They taste fine, but definitely not like a hundred-dollar piece of fruit. The high price is for the utterly symmetrical shape and flawless skin texture, and for the meticulous labor that goes into growing them that way.) Mariko, like most housewives, simply bought whatever everyday fruit was in season, always prominently displayed by Marufuji at decent prices. In the winter there were enormous, sugary hothouse strawberries and juicy, sweet *mikan,* the native mandarin oranges. In the summer came succulent peaches and watermelons, and in the fall were persimmons and the delicious Japanese "pear-apples" called *nashi.*

There were a few imported American foods at Marufuji, chiefly beef and citrus, which Japan had finally allowed into its domestic markets after years of intense pressure from the United States. But even though the prices were cheaper than those for domestic beef and citrus, Mariko rarely bought them. Her resistance was typical, and one reason why exporters of American products find the Japanese market so hard to crack. Mariko, for example, did not like the bright red appearance of lean American beef. "It looks bad and seems very hard to chew," she said. I was grateful she did not try to tell me that Japanese intestines are longer than those of other nationalities and that therefore American beef is not suitable for digestion—a view of Japanese "uniqueness" put forth by no less an authority than the former chairman of Zenchu, the association of Japan's agricultural cooperatives, in 1982. Mariko simply preferred the juicier taste of Japanese beef, the kind marbled with so many layers of white fat that American visitors look on it as a kind of lethal and illicit drug.

Mariko also stayed away from most U.S.-grown oranges, and understandably so, given the ill-tempered campaign waged in Japan about the perils of eating American citrus fruit. The campaign continued well after Japan yielded to American pressure to remove its barriers to citrus imports. One video I saw, "But Are You Still Going to Eat?," reminded me of a World War II propaganda film; it was filled with shots of hospital beds holding Japanese children with tubes up their noses as a narrator warned that both food imports and the number of sick children were increasing in Japan. The video was made by a private production company that, despite its denials, was obviously linked to the politically powerful farmers' union. It was chiefly sold as a cassette to food cooperatives and schoolteachers.

"But Are You Still Going to Eat?" was never broadcast on national television, and Mariko never saw it. But parts of another food video released in 1990 were shown many times on Japan's major networks, and its message soon made its way into stories about food imports in Japan's biggest newspapers. The video claimed that the major ingredient in the chemical defoliant Agent Orange was regularly applied to the skins of American lemons sold in Japan. The same ingredient is in fact approved by the Japanese government for use as a herbicide by Japanese farmers, and the Ministry of Health and Welfare has said that American lemons pose no risk to Japanese consumers. Nevertheless, the video had a significant impact. Around the time of its release in 1990 there was a sharp drop in sales of Sunkist lemons in Japan.

Mariko admitted that there were probably even more chemicals in Japanese produce—American agricultural officials in Tokyo say Japanese farmers use seven times more pesticides than farmers in the United States—but she nonetheless avoided the American fruit. "I feel more relaxed about Japanese food because it's grown in Japan," she said.

Mariko spent only about two hundred and fifty dollars a week on groceries for the whole family, which would be a large sum in the

United States but in Japan was an impressive example of her ability to cope with the highest food prices in the world. She was a great bargain hunter, and on the day I went with her to Marufuji she spent less than twenty-five dollars for a shopping cart that included not only chicken legs but chicken breasts, broccoli, eggs, cucumbers, a giant white radish, pickled plums, fried tofu, fish cakes, and mushrooms—plus a syrup that she would freeze to make popsicles for her kids. At one time she wrote down everything she spent in a week, but she had long ago given that up. "If I could do it so there would be some money left over, I would," she said. "But it doesn't help." Her frugality ran counter to the myth that the Japanese are not price-conscious, and her behavior, I suspect, was typical.

It was now seven-thirty and dinner was on the table. Mariko had been cooking for almost an hour and a half. We sat down and spent the next hour happily eating and drinking in front of the television set. The food was delicious. Mariko's husband had not turned up, and as usual she had no idea when, or if, he would be home.

The Tanakas went on vacation the last few days of July and the first few of August, taking a full and unprecedented week in Hokkaido, the northernmost of Japan's main islands, a mountainous, windswept outpost of dairy farms, alpine flowers, and a few unspoiled national parks. Mariko, the former agent at the Japan Travel Bureau, had planned the entire trip, literally down to the last bus stop. When she got back she showed me her pre-trip notes: July 31, 9:07 A.M.: Train from Noboribetsu, a crowded and gaudy hot-spring resort famous for its forty different mineral pools, arriving at 10:13 A.M. in the town of Tomakomai. Then a bus at 10:45 A.M. from Tomakomai, arriving 11:29 A.M. at Shikotsu-ko, a large volcanic lake in southern Hokkaido ringed by mountains and forests. Lunch at the lake, then another bus at 14:55, arriving in Sapporo at

16:13. Hotel reservations, relevant phone numbers, and prices, even for the bus trips, were all recorded in advance.

"Maybe it's because I worked for JTB," Mariko said, shrugging, when I expressed incredulity at the detail. "And also, it was fun for me." I was beginning to get further insight into the most punctuality-obsessed country on earth. In Japan, the trains not only run on time, you can set your watch by them. Arriving ten minutes late at a party almost guaranteed you would be the last to get there. It sometimes seemed I spent most of my time in Japan frantically rushing to get to interviews at just the right moment and then always having to apologize for being three minutes late. Once a Japanese friend invited me to her home for dinner—at 6:10 P.M. At first Mariko had tolerated it when Sachiko and I arrived at her house twenty or thirty minutes late, but eventually even she got mad and complained to Sachiko. After that we were almost always on time. When I asked Mariko about her vacation, she told me how they had deviated from her master itinerary, as if doing so had been an act of mischief and adventure.

As Mariko recounted it later, the Tanakas arrived in Hokkaido by overnight train from Tokyo. Chiaki and Ken-chan were along, but the sixteen-year-old Shunsuke had decided to stay home, go to his high school football practice, and enjoy a rare week alone without his parents and siblings. Mariko, knowing he felt much too old for a family vacation, didn't press him.

Highlights of the vacation included the stay at the Noboribetsu hot spring, where Chiaki and Mariko went through the special "slimming course" of mineral pools, steam bath, and sauna three times. "It didn't work," Mariko said. "I ate too much." In Sapporo, the modern and characterless Hokkaido capital, they stayed in a modest hotel with a "family room" for four that cost $250 a night, a decent rate in Japan. Mariko and her husband went out one evening for drinks in Susukino, a famous after-hours district known also for its porn shows and "soaplands"—establishments where prostitutes provide hot, soapy baths prior to their usual services. (In Susukino, there were soaplands based on "themes" such as a hospital, Hawaii, and China. One place fulfilled a well-known male fantasy by having the women dress as schoolgirls.) With their kids, the Tanakas also saw a sea-animal show in nearby Otaru and Herring Mansion, a large house built on a fortune made in fish. By car they toured three crater lakes, then drove to the Nossapu Strait on the eastern coast and peered north toward the Kurile Islands, a disputed group of islands that the Japanese say are unlawfully occupied by Russia.

By far the best part of the vacation, at least for Chiaki, was a side trip to see a small piece of property, only a sixth of an acre, that the Tanakas owned in southwestern Hokkaido. Takeshi had bought it through a friend in 1974 for $3,500. The family had decided that Chiaki should have it when she grew up; there was at present no water or electricity on the land, but she could build there someday. Mariko showed me a picture of it, and I was struck by the beauty of the stands of white birches and lush ferns surrounded by cornfields and farms. It was unclear to me what Chiaki had in mind for the property, but the sight of it put her into good spirits for weeks. The entire vacation was in fact a reprieve in the usually contentious relationship between Mariko and her moody daughter, and the two found that they enjoyed each other's company. When the Tanakas returned to Tokyo by plane, everyone was in good humor.

The seven days had been the longest vacation of Mariko's life. In total, the week had cost the Tanakas $3,000—more expensive than a package deal to Hong Kong or Thailand. The Tanakas considered the cost reasonable and had paid for the trip with money they had received in rent from tenants who had lived for four months in their old house. Mariko's husband did not like playing landlord, but in this case some old friends had needed a place to stay, and he was happy to have an unexpected windfall.

Like most Japanese, Mariko and her family rarely spent more than a few nights away from home each year. Even though Japanese at most large companies get two weeks of paid vacation, many feel pressure in Japan's workaholic culture not to take any time off at all. No worker in Japan likes to admit that he or she is dispensable; more important, perhaps, is that pay is often geared to how much work a unit produces, so that people are afraid of being held responsible for lowering the output of their "team." Mariko's husband felt pressures like these at his office, even though many weeks went by when he was idle.

Although more and more Japanese were traveling overseas—mostly to South Korea, Australia, and the United States—Mariko told me she had no immediate interest in taking vacations outside the country. In fact, most Japanese have never been abroad. In any case, I think Mariko's years booking domestic travel arrangements for JTB had turned her into a *Dreamy Trip* kind of enthusiast. "I want to see all of Japan before I go overseas," she told me after the vacation. I asked why, and she pointed to a shriveled slab of dried salmon she had brought back from Hokkaido: "Even if I'm living here, I don't know this kind of food. It's amazing to me that there are so many things to see and eat in Japan." More international-minded Japanese might have called her provincial, but at least she didn't want to go in lockstep on Hawaiian shopping sprees with the self-contained Japanese tour groups, famous for staying only at Japanese hotels, eating only Japanese food, and sightseeing only from the confines of the Japanese tour bus. I also came to understand the diversity in Japan under its homogeneous surface. Beyond the identical-looking rice fields, parking lots, fast-food joints, neon signs, and uniformly designed hotels and train stations, the distinctions among Japan's regions could be discerned with a careful look. My own most pleasurable memories of Japan come from the vacations we took in the mountains of Hokkaido, on the beaches of Okinawa, or wandering through the Japanese porcelain-making towns of Kyushu. Even on the small island of Shikoku, where there are no particularly famous sights, it was relaxing to drive from city to city, sampling the local specialty, bonito broiled over a pine-needle fire, in Kochi, or taking the waters in the nineteenth-century wooden bathhouse near Matsuyama on the Inland Sea. I told Mariko all about that "dreamy trip" when I got back. The former travel agent was, of course, well aware of Shikoku's attractions, and was hoping to travel there herself.

The summer passed by. Takeshi got drunk again one hot night in August when he went with Mariko, Ken-chan, and two other couples and their children to Chinatown in Yokohama for dinner. The other men got drunk, too. "Only one of them could walk straight after dinner," Mariko recalled matter-of-factly. "But they didn't want help from the wives, because that would have been admitting they were drunk. So I held up my friend's husband, and my friend held up my husband." Back home at the train station, Takeshi complained bitterly to Mariko about having to leave the restaurant before he was finished drinking. "It depends on his mood whether he's a cheerful drunk or a nasty drunk," Mariko said. Once, during one of his nasty drunks, she said, he tried to break the TV. But that night all he did was race Ken-chan home, an event he could not remember the next day.

In late August, Mariko savored another fixture of late summer in Japan, the annual high school baseball championships televised from the Koshien Stadium near Osaka. The tournament was a national obsession, and she kept track of the early rounds by tuning in for a short time each day. But for the final game on August 21 she parked herself in front of the television set at one in the afternoon and did not move until it was over three hours later. The rest of the nation was similarly transfixed. Activity slowed at offices all over Tokyo, department store windows displayed inning-by-inning scores, and once, during our own vacation, we even saw hikers in the mountains pause in their ascent of the summit to press transistors to their ears. The Japanese have taken baseball, the quintessential American sport, and transformed it into a kind of Japanese martial art in which concentration, training, and dedication to the team are paramount.

Koshien, as the Japanese call it, is the nation's single biggest sporting event, a kind of World Series, Olympics, and Sumo championship in one. Professional baseball may draw bigger crowds throughout the year, but every August Japanese fall for the mix of youthful innocence, samurai spirit, and team fanaticism displayed on the field of Koshien and in its many legends of athletic zeal. As Robert Whiting recounted in *You Gotta Have Wa*, one Koshien star, a right-hander, pitched his final game with a broken left arm in a sling. Another pitched his team to victory despite a ruptured blister on his hand; when a teammate expressed worry about the blood dripping from the pitcher's fingers during a meeting on the mound, the pitcher begged him not to tell the team manager, for fear that he would be taken out of the game. Their dedication is excellent preparation for the major leagues, where players actually intensify their training during the suffocating summer season, believing there is no limit to what practice can do.

Most Japanese high school teams practice every day of the year, morning and afternoon, with only a brief break at New Year's. During summer and winter vacations they go to baseball camps, where training sessions can include marathon all-night workouts. Koshien is their great battleground, a reflection of the single-minded and intense spirit of Japanese youth and—as Japanese commentators invariably point out—of the nation itself. Mariko's husband watched Koshien too, although his tastes were more for the Yomiuri Giants and other gods of professional baseball. But for Mariko, the high school championships were an emotional release, like the karaoke box and the shrine-carrying festivals. Like many

Japanese, she always wept at the end of the final game. "To look at the players, I can feel their enthusiasm, seriousness, and purity," she told me. "I can feel how they feel, so I cry." That summer she wept when she and the rest of the nation could see that the star pitcher obviously was suffering from a terrible arm injury. Naturally, he was left in the game. "The life of a baseball player is so short," she said, referring to the star pitcher as if he were a tragic hero. "He's already damaged his elbow."

The Koshien that summer was marred only slightly by the interruptions of bulletins from Moscow, where Mikhail S. Gorbachev was ousted in a coup attempt and then restored to office. Mariko first heard the reports on the ten P.M. news that Gorbachev had "stepped down" for "reasons of health." She knew it was a lie, like everyone else—everyone, that is, except for Japan's pathologically cautious political leaders. While President George Bush denounced the military putsch, Prime Minister Toshiki Kaifu remained silent, obviously worried about offending someone. "I paid no attention to Kaifu-san," Mariko said, "but I thought Bush-san was great. He was very outspoken when he had to be. Kaifu-san didn't say anything."

We were talking a few weeks after the coup at Mariko's house, drinking tea, as usual, and snacking on boiled sweet potatoes and the first pears of the season. It was a slow, rainy, sleepy afternoon, a good day for napping. Mariko and I had had only passing conversations about politics, so now I asked why she thought Japanese leaders are so deferential and timid.

"It's not only Kaifu," she said, "but all Japanese. When we are asked to say something on a very important occasion, we can't say anything. Even me. This is a very private conversation, so I can say what I want. But not in public." Japan, she said, has always had "no-energy" prime ministers. "As a whole, we don't know anything about politics."

The conversation meandered on. Mariko frequently voted for the Socialists, and was no fan of the ruling Liberal Democratic

Party—many Japanese women weren't—because she saw it as a "rich, wealthy, not-the-people's party." I looked over at the copy of the day's *Mainichi* newspaper lying in a corner of the room, and there on the back display page, as if to prove her point, was a story about an official of a huge real estate company who had given a leading politician of the LDP a contribution of $2.4 million—just another disclosure in the long-running corruption-and-kickback scandals that had led in 1989 to the forced resignation of Prime Minister Noboru Takeshita and many in his cabinet. On page one was another story, about questionable bank loans that had gone to LDP candidates in Hokkaido. The stories were evidence not so much of crimes as of the cozy relationship and the trading in favors between business and government in Japan. Mariko glanced at the headlines but did not seem to get too excited. It was not until after I left Japan, in 1993, that the accumulation of scandals would help bring down the most powerful titans of the ruling party and usher in a reform prime minister on a wave of revulsion against corruption. But the reform government lasted only a year before it, too, fell victim to corruption scandals and its own internal divisions.

In the summer of 1991, Mariko was resigned to the existence of corruption and the unchanging nature of politics in Japan. Like most Japanese, she was vaguely uneasy about throwing out of office the party that, for all its faults, had transformed the nation into an economic superpower, even if its leaders had feathered their own nests in the process. "Living in Japan, we're used to it," she told me that day, referring to the scandals. "We get angry inside, but we don't know how to deal with it. People vote for the LDP to maintain the standard of living here. People think of low crime or high literacy and they give credit to the LDP. I don't want to believe that, so I vote for the Socialists. Unfortunately, the Socialist Party doesn't have so much energy. So I voted for a while for the Communist Party. But in honesty, if I think deeply about it, I'm happy with the LDP." I pointed out that she had just contradicted herself.

Her answer was that the LDP and a strong opposition party should probably take turns in power.

I asked her what she wished she could change in Japan, and it was clear that she felt that the country's prosperity was not being shared by the average person. "Look at this house," she said with exasperation. "We're told we're rich, but look at our standard of living."

The conversation began to peter out. Mariko mentioned that two days earlier her husband had come home drunk again, and very tired.

"He gets depressed when he's tired," Mariko said.

"Because of the fundamental loneliness that everyone has," Sachiko said.

"Yes," Mariko said emphatically. I was not sure whether she was referring to her husband, herself, or both. "I try to ignore it, and not think anything about it. I try to sleep."

At the end of that summer, Sachiko and I had another adventure together—an appointment with some leading mobsters in the old downtown area of Asakusa. I wanted to meet the local gang called the Takahashi-gumi (or Takahashi Syndicate), which had clambered all over the portable shrine carried by Mariko at the Sanja Matsuri festival that spring. They were a distinguished group, at least according to a glowing article about them in *True Story Age*, a sort of *yakuza* fan magazine, which reported breathlessly on their exploits during their eighty-year history. "The first boss was as big as a sumo wrestler and a man of extraordinary strength," the magazine said. "Even in his closing years he could lift two or three young men up in his arms and easily smash their heads." This was in the early part of the century, when the influence of the Takahashi-gumi paralleled the prosperity of Asakusa in its heyday, and a "well-informed local" described in glowing terms what was obviously a well-oiled protection racket. "The smallest construction work could not proceed without the Takahashi-gumi's acknowledgment, and the same was true when opening a restaurant or coffeehouse," he was quoted as saying. "All the cinemas and entertainment halls were in their grip."

The Takahashi-gumi now had 200 members, according to the magazine—down from the 2,000 to 3,000 of its golden age—but it remained important. In the boom years of the 1980s, the *yakuza* generally moved from the fringes of society into the mainstream—major real estate development, the stock market, national politics, and the international art market. By the 1990s, the police estimated, there were some 90,000 *yakuza* nationwide in 3,300 different groups affiliated with three major syndicates. Their total income was estimated by the police at $10 billion, but many people thought the estimate was low.

One does not, of course, simply ring up the local boss and ask for an interview. The *yakuza* may operate in a far more open manner than the mafia in the United States, but certain Japanese formalities must be observed. One needs a proper introduction. To get this, I requested an interview with the finest intermediary possible, respected and trusted by the *yakuza*: the Asakusa police.

"Would you like to interview some *yakuza* bosses?" Toshio Hara, the Asakusa police department's *yakuza* specialist, asked me at the close of our conversation.

"Yes," I said.

"I'll call them for you," he offered genially, "and tell them you'll be stopping by."

The *yakuza* have had close links with the police at least since the time following World War II, when they helped in keeping order, particularly in disposing of once-violent Communists. In return, the police looked the other way while the *yakuza* went about their business, but nonetheless kept tabs on mob activities. The police told me there were 1,100 *yakuza* members in Asakusa, in eight main groups, earning income from selling drugs, gambling, prostitution, protection rackets, and extortion schemes among local shopkeepers.

So there we were, on September 17, Sachiko and I, in the headquarters of the Takahashi-gumi, sitting alongside Koiichi Kikuchi, the head boss, on a dark brown leather sectional sofa, surrounded by eight of his sub-bosses and much Takahashi-gumi and other *yakuza* memorabilia. On one wall of the room in a nondescript corner office building were wooden plaques with the names of all the bosses of the other gangs in Tokyo, dutifully sent to Kikuchi when he became president of the Takahashi-gumi. There were also an ornate grandfather clock, a coffee table covered with a fussy lace cloth, and numerous scrapbooks and videotapes of past Sanja festivals. Kikuchi, a wiry man wound tight as a spring, was wearing a blue-gray suit, a light blue shirt monogrammed with *K. Kikuchi* in English on the cuffs, and an expensive silk tie. He proudly showed me his gold belt buckle and his diamond cufflinks. "We only wear the best brands," one of the sub-bosses informed me. The other men were similarly attired; one of the sub-bosses, who had met Sachiko and me at a nearby hotel and brought us to the headquarters, was in orange linen pants and an olive silk blouse and was carrying a green lizard purse. Several men had their hair in the tightly coiled short perm style much favored by the *yakuza*. All but one were missing a part of one of their little fingers, a well-known *yakuza* sacrifice carried out to show remorse for misbehavior.

Kikuchi soberly informed me that construction was the main business of the group. "The members are all entrepreneurs," he said. He went on to explain that the Takahashi-gumi did not extort money from shopkeepers and in fact did not like to receive such money. But could he help it if the shopkeepers handed over the money to the Takahashi-gumi of their own free will? In fact, the police say the *yakuza* rarely issue overt threats—all they have to do is show up. Therefore they are almost impossible to prosecute.

"The shopkeepers pay donations for protection from us against people who do really bad things," he explained. "These are people who are violent, who cannot be handled by the police. So we are like the unofficial police. Besides, the police are salaried workers. We are willing to sacrifice ourselves. We are more dedicated." With all the gentleness of Marlon Brando in *The Godfather* describing himself as a simple community problem solver, he gave me an example. "Say you marry a very terrible husband," he said. "He beats you, and you find out he has a second or third wife, and you go to the police, and they won't help you. So then people say, 'Go to Kikuchi.' " Usually all that Kikuchi had to do was send a hench- man to the husband's door, where a subtle display of a truncated little finger was like an offer that no one could refuse. "The true policy of the *yakuza*," Kikuchi said, "is to help weak people and fight against strong people. Since the Edo Era, the government has used the *yakuza* for things that the police can't handle."

It is true that the *yakuza* are well known in Japan as fixers and mediators in nasty domestic and neighborhood disputes. I know of someone who was in a motorcycle accident and was tempted to turn to the *yakuza* when he could not get any damage payment from the truck driver who hit him. Only half in jest, the writer Murray Sayle says that the *yakuza* in Japan simply perform the function that lawyers do in the United States. Japanese properly think of American society as overly litigious, but since there are only 13,000 lawyers in all of Japan (compared with more than 800,000 in the United States), the *yakuza*, by pressing other peo- ple's grievances through a system more efficient than the courts, are clearly filling some sort of vacuum.

But Kikuchi's romantic description of the *yakuza* as rough but righteous fighters against injustice has been overtaken by recent disclosures of how violent and dangerous the *yakuza* really are. In 1992, the film director Juzo Itami was attacked by three gangsters in front of his house a week after the opening of *Woman Mob*

Fighter, his movie about an anti-mob lawyer. They slashed his face, neck, and left hand, leaving him disfigured for life. "They cut very slowly; they took their time," Itami, the director of *Tampopo* and *A Taxing Woman,* told *The New York Times.* "They could have killed me if they wanted." Later that year, Shin Kanemaru, at that time Japan's most powerful politician, was forced to resign from his seat in Parliament and as vice-president of the ruling party after he admitted accepting $4 million from a mob-connected trucking company. It later was disclosed that the ruling party had turned to the *yakuza* for help in quieting the sound trucks that in 1987 were mocking the party's candidate for prime minister in the streets of Tokyo. Rightist groups and the mob are well known to be in bed with each other in Japan, but when the party's dealings eventually became public, even many cynical Japanese were shocked to find out that organized crime was functioning at the heart of Japan's political system.

Kikuchi of the Takahashi-gumi did not move in such select circles, but he was nonetheless a large fish in the small, scummy pond of Asakusa. When he took over the gang in 1988, he was the first boss to come from outside the founding family, a tribute to his doggedness. *True Story Age* described Kikuchi as a "pugnacious youth" who dreamed of becoming a *yakuza* while growing up in the boondocks north of Tokyo. "I wanted to become a *yakuza* from the very beginning," Kikuchi told me. He joined a less prestigious gang before hooking up with the great Takahashi-gumi at the age of seventeen. He endured the torturous initiation of being used, he said, "like a dog and a cat." He made rice, polished shoes, did laundry—and recalls being beaten at whim.

"But now you can't do that in the modern *yakuza*," he assured me, referring to the beatings. "If you do that, people will leave."

"We still beat," one of his sub-bosses interjected, prompting a murmur of agreement that compelled Kikuchi to clarify his statement.

"People are still beaten if they don't do things properly," he explained. "Or if they sleep late, or if they're not on time."

Kikuchi had spent seven years in jail and readily admitted to me he had killed a rival gang member—in self-defense, of course. Jail for the *yakuza* was accepted as a necessary sacrifice. "None of us like it," another sub-boss said. "But it's something we have to do."

Lunchtime. Kikuchi suggested we continue the conversation over sushi, and soon Sachiko and I were seated on a tatami mat at a neighborhood restaurant surrounded by ten muscular men in shiny suits with abbreviated little fingers. As we ate delectable raw tuna and sea urchin, I noticed that the proprietor seemed quite eager to please. Unfortunately, in the more relaxed setting, the mobsters now turned their attention to us.

Did we have children?

Yes, we said.

Then why weren't we home?

"I think women should be with their babies all day long," a sub-boss sitting next to me said.

"We don't like our women to leave the house," Kikuchi agreed.

"We are still living in a feudalistic society," another sub-boss informed me.

"If the husband can make money, the woman should stay home and take care of the family," Kikuchi said.

"That especially applies for our wives," one of the sub-bosses said. "It's very strict."

"I can buy my wife rings," Kikuchi said. "I can give her any-thing. I want her to stay all day at home."

Sachiko and I let this drop as Kikuchi moved on to a new subject.

"We can't go to the United States," he complained. "We are on an international blacklist. The Japanese police and the FBI have strong connections."

"It's unfair," said a sub-boss.

"And your mafia is so much worse," Kikuchi continued. "The big difference between the American mafia and the *yakuza* is that we try to help people, but the American mafia hurts people with drugs." In fact, authorities say, many *yakuza* gangs are heavily involved in drug trafficking in Japan, although Kikuchi insisted that the Takahashi-gumi was not one of them. "I don't like the groups who handle cocaine," Kikuchi said.

Lunch over, Kikuchi had a new idea: Would Sachiko and I like to come with him to a karaoke bar for a quick sing-along? We apologetically declined the chance to slip into a darkened corner of Asakusa in mid-afternoon, saying we had to get home to our neglected children. In any case, it was only three. One of the sub-bosses informed Kikuchi that the karaoke bar did not open until six.

"Use your power to open it," Kikuchi said gruffly.

It seemed a good time to go. As Sachiko and I got up to leave, Kikuchi insisted we be driven to the subway station by a car from the Takahashi-gumi fleet: a Mercedes SEL 600, which sells in Japan for around $200,000. Kikuchi proudly told us that the Takahashi-gumi owned some fifty Mercedeses—a switch from three years before, when the fleet had been mostly Cadillacs. "American cars are not popular here," Kikuchi informed me. "Also Cadillacs are fuel guzzlers." Detroit had lost again. We said good-bye, then spent a few silent minutes in the buttery leather seats of the Mercedes. At the subway station we made our getaway.

Afterward we told Mariko all about it. She was amused, especially since it was her participation in the shrine-carrying festival that had triggered this bizarre side trip in the first place. I had the sensation once again of letting Mariko point the way to deeper layers of the society. Mariko seemed happy to watch from the sidelines as I explored her Japan—until the day Sachiko and I told her we had plans to go to Asakusa to interview the head of the Sanja Matsuri and visit a storehouse to see one of the three major portable

shrines up close. "I want to come," Mariko said. Now she was reacting to my reactions to her. I was no longer a social observer but was
a participant in her life. I knew from the start that my presence
would change her life in subtle ways. But this detour seemed harmless, and I thought we would both learn from it.

The portable shrine was stunning—a gleaming, glittering
palanquin of brass and gold plate, built new in 1950 after the
original was destroyed in the firebombing of Tokyo during World
War II. Mariko, silent and respectful, intently inspected the
shrine's mythical golden birds and the rich purple braiding along
the sides; there had been no chance in the chaos of the festival to
study such exquisite workmanship. She made a full circle, taking
in every detail. "This is the one I carried," she said quietly.

On the way home, Mariko, Sachiko, and I stopped for a quick
bowl of noodles at an Asakusa restaurant, then headed for the subway station. It would take forty-five minutes on the train to get to
the other side of Tokyo, so Mariko wanted something to read. She
bought an issue of *Croissant,* a popular Japanese women's magazine,
because a line on the cover promoting a story inside had caught her
interest: "I Can't Be Someone Who Is Loved by Everybody." The
story promised to show women an "honest way of living." There
were also articles on remodeling rooms and cooking easy family
meals. When the train came, Mariko quickly found a seat, opened the
magazine, and remained absorbed during the whole trip home.

6

BACK TO SCHOOL

Kindergarten students exercising

SEPTEMBER

I don't know anything about the war—do you?" the teacher of Ken-chan's fourth-grade class said to her thirty-five students. "Maybe your grandfathers know about the war, or your grandmothers. Have you ever heard war stories from them?"

A half-dozen hands shot up.

"The American planes were in the sky, and my grandparents saw them," said a boy.

"My grandfather was shot and lost a toe," said a girl.

"My grandfather still remembers the sound of the tanks," another boy said.

The teacher, a brisk and direct nineteen-year veteran of two Tokyo elementary schools, was herself too young to remember firsthand the catastrophe of World War II in Japan. But Sensei—

which is what the students called her, for "Teacher"—nodded at her students appreciatively. "During the war, women had to raise their children by themselves, and feed them, even when there wasn't enough food," she said after the students had spoken. "So it was the hardest time for both men and women. Nobody in this class knows about war, although you might have seen the Persian Gulf War on TV."

It was September 20, 8:50 A.M., a gusty Friday under a slate-gray sky, the height of the typhoon season, my first day to observe one of the world's most successful education systems at work. I was in the back of the class with Sachiko, near a window looking out toward the school's far side, an expanse of concrete painted a dreary mustard-yellow and streaked black from years of typhoons. Although Mariko's neighborhood was itself not especially affluent, Ichomachi Elementary was a public school in one of the richest wards in Tokyo, with students who came from some of the city's most prosperous white-collar and middle-class families. The school, however, had scarcely changed since Mariko had gone there three decades before. A spartan sensibility, common to all Japanese schools, prevailed. The down-at-the-heels rooms were heated in winter by kerosene burners at the front of the class. The students sat at beat-up wooden desks, in three neat rows of twelve, and were expected to sweep and mop their own classroom floors. And yet the day I was there unfolded in a cheerful chaos. The students were well prepared, engaged, and even raucous, and during class discussions the teacher tolerated a noise level far beyond what would have been allowed at a comparable American school. There were no uniforms, just boys in shorts and girls in skirts and sweatshirts branded with a picture of the ubiquitous "Hello Kitty," the most popular cat in Japan. Student artwork and a pet goldfish brightened the otherwise functional room, which like the rest of the school smelled of the serious business of childhood: chalk, old gym clothes, poster paint, and sticky white paste. Outside, two weathered Chinese windmill palms shaded the gravel playground, which was edged on one side by a rowdy chicken coop. At one time there had been a pet rabbit, but he had been killed by a cat. All in all, Ichomachi Elementary seemed a lively, inviting place, a school I would happily have used for my own children; it had none of the feeling of oppressive rigidity and rote learning that is said to characterize the Japanese education system. It was a good introduction. Only later, at Shunsuke's elite private high school, would I see the more notorious downside.

The war discussion at Ichomachi that morning was prompted by "One Flower," a tragic short story of war and loss. The class was reading the story one painstaking line at a time, slowly digesting the difficult new Chinese characters, or *kanji*, that appeared in the text. I was struck by the sophistication of the vocabulary and also by the rigors of learning to write one of the most difficult languages in the world. The students in this class could read and write at best 400 *kanji*, and over the next five years they would need to master at least 1,545 more (out of some 40,000 *kanji* in all) just to be literate enough to read a newspaper. Plain memorization is still the way children learn *kanji*—no one has figured out any more novel or interesting way to teach children how to read—which is one reason why rote learning is so emphasized in Japan.

Even more striking than the demands of the language was the short story itself, a heartbreaking tale about a little girl named Yumiko whose father goes off to fight in World War II. I was surprised that fourth graders were reading about one of the bleakest periods in the history of Japan; students in the United States generally read *The Diary of Anne Frank*, for instance, when they are older. And Yumiko's story was not unique. Japanese literature and children's books are filled with miserable stories about the sacrifices that Japan had to make during World War II. One of the most famous is "The Pitiful Elephants," a horrific tale about Tokyo zookeepers who starve three beloved elephants to death as an act of mercy. The zookeepers are afraid that bombs from the American B-29s during World War II will break the animals' cages, causing the elephants to run wild through the city. On one of the last pages of the book, as the elephants lie dead at the zookeepers' feet, the zookeepers raise their fists toward the American planes in the sky and cry, "Stop the war! Stop all wars!" Not only is the story unbearably sad, but it treats the war as a disaster visited upon a peace-loving Japan. Mariko grew up on the story, as did her children; it is read aloud on Japanese radio every year to mark the anniversary of Japan's World War II surrender. Probably no other nation inculcates the horrors of battle into its schoolchildren to the extent Japan does—although without any discussion of Japan's responsibility for World War II. The result, in any case, is a citizenry that may be the most truly pacifist on earth. I often thought that General MacArthur would have been pleased with the pacifism, if not with the means toward that end.

The story of "One Flower" that Ken-chan's class was reading that morning begins with the phrase "Give me only one." The story then explains that these were the first words that the little girl Yumiko knew. The war was at its peak, there was not enough food, and Yumiko was always hungry, always wanting more. But she was taught to ask for "only one"—one more potato, one more rice cake —because that was all her impoverished parents could afford. "Everything is 'only one,' " Yumiko's father sighs. "She knows the pleasures of only one. Maybe she won't even have one happiness." On the day the father leaves for the war, his wife makes rice cakes. Yumiko, desperately hungry, eats all the rice cakes before they get to the train station, each time crying for "only one" more. As the train approaches, Yumiko's father tries to quiet his hungry child as he says good-bye, perhaps for the last time. "I give you only one," he says, presenting a solitary cosmos flower to Yumiko and boarding the train. Then he stares silently through the window at his daughter and her flower as the train pulls out of the station.

At this point Sensei asked the students to stop reading and answer questions based on the text. "I want you to imagine the father's feeling when he leaves the station looking at the cosmos flower," she said. "What is he thinking?"

"That he might not come back from the war, but even if the cosmos flower dies, maybe Yumiko will remember him whenever she sees other cosmos," a girl answered.

"He wants his daughter to be like a cosmos flower," another girl said.

"He is thinking, 'I will go to war, but don't forget me. This will be my last present for you,' " said a boy.

The teacher nodded. "So one cosmos flower means a lot," she said.

Moving quickly, she read the rest of the story to the class herself, picking up ten years later. Yumiko and her mother live alone, and the father has never returned. "Yumiko doesn't remember her father's face," the teacher read. "Also, she doesn't remember the flower. But her house is surrounded by cosmos. Inside you can hear the sounds of a sewing machine. Yumiko asks, 'Mother, which do you prefer—meat or fish?' The sewing machine stops for a while. But when the machine starts making noise again, Yumiko walks with her shopping basket to town, through a tunnel of cosmos."

The story was over. There was silence in the room, and Sachiko and I were wiping the tears from our eyes. Then we noticed that the story seemed to have no discernible effect on the emotions of the fourth graders. Were they too young? Had they been too absorbed in poring over their letters? Were they used to stories like this? After "The Pitiful Elephants," maybe this was nothing. Or maybe you just had to be a parent to appreciate the wrenching pain of the story's conclusion. Whatever the case, Sensei was not wasting a minute, and now she called individual students to the front blackboard to write *kanji* they had learned in the story. Soon a girl was chalking out the *kanji* for the word "designate," written with seventeen strokes. (Many *kanji* contain even more.) This one had a certain logic: the top part was made up of the symbol for "finger" while the bottom was the symbol for "settle." Sensei looked on approvingly. "Very good," she said.

Arithmetic was next. Problem: 215 people have to blow up 2,580 balloons. How many balloons for each?

"I saw a great balloon at the toy store," a boy offered from the back of the class.

Sensei ignored him, not breaking her pace. "You have to divide 215 into 2,580," she speedily explained. "This is the first time you've had three digits for the number that is used to divide." She asked for volunteers to do this calculation and similar ones at the blackboard, which caused an instant clamor. Hands waved in the air frantically. One by one the students went to the blackboard, but long division with three-digit divisors proved difficult. A girl in bicycle shorts with a pink plastic barrette holding up her ponytail struggled to divide 395 into 2,785. At the start of the lesson, a boy who had got only one problem right on the previous evening's homework had been asked to divide a two-digit number, 42, into 7,707. As he hesitated, Sensei gently encouraged him. "All you have to do is concentrate," she said. "You're doing fine."

The day moved on to gym—two laps around the track, exercises, and flips on the parallel bars, all under the guidance of Sensei, who, like the other teachers, had to change into gym clothes each day and double as the class athletic instructor. Then came lunch: rice cakes, fried Chinese noodles with pork, a bean-sprout salad with carrots and spinach, milk. The meal was brought from the school kitchen to the classroom, where the students had made little tables of four desks each. As Western classical music was piped in over the intercom, Sensei, with the same lunch at her desk, led everyone in a singsong chorus of *"Itadakimasu"*—literally, "Thank you, we are going to receive this treat"—the Japanese expression of gratitude for everyone and everything connected with making a meal possible, almost like a grace. The kids dug enthusiastically into their food with chopsticks, and I soon saw that lunch was not downtime. As everyone ate, Sensei led the students in a discussion of current events, asking them what they had seen on the television news the night before.

"A Northwest Airlines jet had a problem yesterday, but forty-seven people landed safely," one student said.

"I watched a boxing match last night," another offered.

Sensei nodded, mentioning a recent typhoon that had caused extensive property damage. The students finished eating, and after a chorus of "Gochisosama"—literally "It was a real feast," always said after meals—they began their daily sweeping and mopping of the floor. Normally Sensei helped them for twenty minutes, then let them finish in a tumult while she escaped for a calming cup of tea in the teachers' room. It was her only real break of the day, but she took no more than a quarter of an hour. Today, however, she did not get even that, since I had made an appointment to talk with her.

Away from the ruckus, I asked first about the purpose of the cleaning. "The classrooms and desks are used by the students, so they should be cleaned by them," she said, as if it were obvious. "At home, they hardly ever clean. This teaches them cooperation."

Sensei was a slender woman of about forty, well turned out in a bright orange blazer and a straight black skirt that hit just above her knee. Her long, straight hair was held in place by a headband, which gave her a collegiate look. Although she rarely smiled in class, she had a kind, confident air and when necessary could keep the class under tight control. She had a ten-year-old son, who was a fourth grader at a different school, and a husband who worked at home selling fertilizer for golf courses. After nearly two decades of teaching she made $50,000 a year, more than most of her American counterparts with comparable experience. (The average salary in the United States for public school teachers aged forty to forty-nine is $33,690.) She liked her job, which commanded great respect in Japanese society, and the hours were good. "Teachers hardly ever quit after they have children," she said.

She was happy at Ichomachi. "The mothers are very involved, and you don't really have to teach the students manners and etiquette," she said. In a later conversation, she told me that of thirty-five mothers in Ken-chan's class, fifteen worked outside their homes in full-time or part-time jobs. I was curious if she saw any differences between the students whose mothers had outside jobs and those whose mothers did not. "There's no difference," she replied briskly, but then I realized I was talking to someone who was a working mother herself. "On the contrary, the kids with stay-at-home mothers are less self-controlled and more dependent on others when there are problems."

After the classroom cleaning, it was time for "Morals," which on this day turned out to be an exercise in group problem-solving that deteriorated into total anarchy. It was hard to tell whether I was witnessing a breeding ground for the famous Japanese consensus-building style of decision making or simply the inevitable mayhem when thirty-five ten-year-olds try to work together as a group. Later, when I asked the teacher about the purpose of the exercise, she told me that the Education Ministry set guidelines requiring that elementary school students learn how to work together in a cooperative spirit. I'm not sure what I saw could be called cooperation. But it was entertaining.

The teacher began by telling the students that they had to organize themselves into four teams for a future game of dodgeball. She then stood off to the side. Ken-chan and three others, apparently acting on their own, went to the front of the room to select players. No one objected. At this point I assumed they would take turns picking team members, which I figured would take about five minutes. I wondered what the class would do for the rest of the time.

I need not have worried.

"It's not going to be fair if all the strong kids end up on the same team," a boy immediately objected.

"But how do we know who's strong?" another boy said.

"Well, please tell us if you're strong," Ken-chan said.

Nobody liked this idea, and a long discussion began about the best method of determining who were the strongest. Shouting and chaos ensued. Finally, the class members reached agreement to vote on two propositions: one, that the strongest be determined by an all-class vote; and two, that the strongest be determined on the basis of the recommendations of individual students. The first proposition won, meaning that four strong boys and four strong girls, a pair for each team, would be designated by democratic means. Over much shouting, nominations were taken from the floor. Ken-chan began writing down their last names—Kono, Kobayashi, Nakano, Honda, Suzuki. It was decided that everyone could vote twice, for two girls and two boys. The shouting continued.

"Quiet please!" Ken-chan bellowed, to no effect.

At long last, the voting began, and the strongest four boys and four girls were selected. Each team now had two members; the process had taken more than half an hour. But now what? How to choose the rest?

"Now we have to find the people who are very good at dodging the ball," a girl said.

"We have to do this again?" complained a boy in the back. "It's a lot of trouble to find out who is good at dodging the ball."

"This is taking too much time," another girl agreed.

The class responded to these voices of sanity with more shouting. Finally—incredibly—they decided to have yet another vote, this one on whether they should go to the trouble of determining the good dodgers or should just choose the remaining team members "at random."

"How do you choose at random?" a boy asked.

The shouting grew louder. Anarchy reigned.

Finally Sensei, who I thought had showed astonishing restraint, stepped in. "This 'at random' idea is too vague," she said crisply. She suggested a lottery. The class put it to a vote, and mercifully, five minutes before the final bell, the lottery idea was approved and the rest of each team was selected.

"Now I don't want to hear any complaints about whether the teams are fair or not," the teacher said sternly. "You've all been selected by vote or lottery. The game will be two Thursdays from now. Part of your homework is to think up names for your teams."

"How about the Piranhas?" somebody suggested.

Americans weary of hearing about the failings of the education system in the United States might at first look at the results of Japanese schools with awe and envy. Japan's rate of illiteracy is less than 1 percent, among the lowest in the world. In the United States, the Department of Education estimates, 21 percent of the adult population have only rudimentary reading and writing skills—enough to pick out key facts in a short newspaper article, but not enough to write a letter about an error in a credit card bill. In Japan, 97 percent of students complete their high school education; in the United States, 88 percent do. On international math and science tests, Japanese students score higher than students from any other country. And while the excellence and accessibility of American university education are unrivaled in the world, and the United States is far more successful than Japan in turning out a highly creative elite— the Japanese are painfully aware that they have produced only a handful of Nobel laureates—the Japanese are masters of educating an entire country to a standard that the United States has not begun to approach.

Japan, of course, is one of the world's most homogeneous societies because it has not absorbed any large communities of immigrants with other cultures or languages. Most schoolchildren in Japan come from more or less the same background: stable, two-parent, middle-class homes. Only five percent of Japanese children grow up in single-parent families. In Ken-chan's fourth-grade class, only four of the thirty-five students were from what the teacher called "broken homes," and three of those were "broken" because of the death of the father, not divorce. Japan also has no severe pockets of poverty, few drugs, and no enormous chasm between urban and suburban school districts. The Japanese school year is longer than the American by sixty days, which means that from first through twelfth grades Japanese students actually receive two more years of schooling than Americans.

Japanese education is as homogeneous in its approach as the students it serves. The Japanese often point out that the chances are good that a sixth grader in Hokkaido will be studying the exact same writing or history lesson as his counterpart in Okinawa fourteen hundred miles away on the very same day. National standards and curricula are set at the Education Ministry in Tokyo, and all public schools receive more or less the same funding and services. Class size is large, usually above thirty, but most students can keep pace, meaning that little money is thought to be needed for remedial programs and that more can be spent on art and music—often considered "extras" in the United States, but considered basics in Japan. (By sixth grade, all Japanese students are expected to know how to read music and play two instruments.) In addition, there are no emotional debates about the language of instruction, since all students not only speak Japanese but have been taught to read and write the phonetic hiragana alphabet by their mothers before they enter school. Indeed, mothers are crucial to Japanese education. Like Mariko, the majority are still deeply involved in their children's schools, particularly at the elementary level. Mariko served as a committee chair of the PTA, helped organize school outings and events, and with the other mothers arranged annual parties for the former teachers of her children. Seeing to her children's education was a serious job, much valued in Japan; after all, their success would be her success.

Given these advantages, Japan finds it can invest less money in education than America does. In the school year 1990–91, the United States spent 6.9 percent of its gross domestic product on education; the Japanese spent 4.9 percent. In the same year, the Japanese government spent $3,429 for every student enrolled in secondary school; the United States spent $6,296.

And yet the success of the Japanese education system has come at a price. Certainly no Americans I know would want their children educated in the restrictive and mind-numbing atmosphere that I observed in Japanese secondary schools, where all intellectual energy is focused on passing entrance exams into high school or college. At their best, American high schools strive to open up the broadest possible world to young men and women, forcing them to think, question, and judge. But even the best Japanese high school education is still an exercise in memorization, standardization, and correctness. "High school does not represent an opening up of choice, but a narrowing down of focus," writes Thomas Rohlen, the author of *Japan's High Schools*, the best book in English on Japan's education system. "The overwhelming reality is not one of growing independence, but of certain inescapable givens about the relation of studying to future social status. . . . It is a tight regime that does not encourage personal dreams, experimentation, individual variety, or idealism."

That seemed to be the case at Azabu High School in Tokyo, the elite private boys' school that is the alma mater of Japanese cabinet ministers and company presidents. On the day that I visited the school to see how Japan was educating its next generation of leaders, I ran into Yutaka Kobayashi, who had been an exchange student during his junior year, from July 1990 to June 1991, at West Boylston High School in Worcester, Massachusetts. Kobayashi, a tall, athletic, confident student who dreamed of becoming a heart surgeon, heard that I was in the headmaster's office and sought me out, offering to be interviewed about the differences he had experienced between the Japanese and American education systems. I guessed that he felt out of place at Azabu after a year abroad, and I was right—he told me he was repeating his junior year because there was "no way" he could pass his college entrance exams without it. His old friends, meanwhile, had moved on, and were spending night and day stuffing massive amounts of information into their brains. "We study only to pass the examinations to get into college," he told me ruefully.

Kobayashi looked back on his year in the United States as "my treasure"—even though the calculus class he took repeated what he had learned in Japan the year before, and his physics class covered material he had studied two or three years before. He was also taken aback by the geographic ignorance of some of the American students, who asked him if Japan was in China. All in all, though, his year at West Boylston was like feasting at a banquet. At Azabu, as at other Japanese high schools, he was allowed to participate in only one extracurricular activity, but in Massachusetts he played tight end for the varsity football team, was chosen most valuable player in track and field, sang in a local church choir, skied, went to the mall with an American girlfriend, and for the first time in his life expressed his opinion in class.

"A Japanese class is not a class but a lecture," he told me. "The core is the teacher. We take notes and listen to his explanation. That's all. But in the United States, we discussed a lot. Americans can express their own opinions. They can think. They can express their originality. And we can't."

I found many other Japanese with similar complaints. Among intellectuals especially there is an increasing sensitivity to foreign criticism that Japanese schools are churning out nonthinking robots to supply the nation's economic machine, and a genuine debate about why Japan fails to turn out creative, independent thinkers.

"Japanese education works against the cultivation of intellectual ability," Shuiichi Kato, an author and a well-known critic of Japanese schooling, told me. "It does provide a supply of qualified labor to Japanese industry, but it is not quite good enough for producing really outstanding people in any field."

And yet while the government, the media, teachers, and parents cry publicly for reform, particularly in the "examination hell" that overshadows junior high and high school, in private few parents have the courage or incentive to opt out of the system. Like the liberal American parents who support public education in principle but send their own child to a private school, no Japanese parent wants to sacrifice something as important as a child's future to an abstract ideal, in this case the goal of developing free spirits. As Rohlen writes: "Time and again one reads how examinations are ruining the schools, the young, and Japanese society; how cramming produces warped personalities, crushes enthusiasm, and nips creativity in the bud . . . Japan's examination hell has been around for a long time. Hardly a soul in the entire country will say anything publicly in its favor, yet private behavior feeds the competition."

Mariko was a good example of a mother torn by the debate. As I had first heard during her heated exchange with Sachiko, she did not approve of the growing number of cram schools that exist solely to prepare students for entrance examinations for private schools. She refused to send her children to them during their elementary years, even though so many of Ken-chan's fourth-grade classmates were enrolled that he pestered her to let him go. But by junior high she relented, knowing that her children needed the cram schools to get into a decent private high school and ultimately succeed in Japanese society.

Although Japanese educators say the race toward private school is a reflection of the affluence experienced by Japan in the past two decades, education has been highly valued in Japan throughout its history. Confucianism and Buddhism have always promoted learning. In the seventeenth century the Tokugawa Shogunate ensured that education would be the preserve of the top quarter of society —particularly the samurai, whose sons were inculcated with the idea that loyalty and obedience are superior to independence of thought. Universal, compulsory education was not established until 1872, after the Meiji Restoration, when it became part of the general Japanese mania to catch up with the West. Even McGuffey's Readers were translated into Japanese in this period.

Encouraged by the United States, the fledgling Meiji government sent five young women off to study in America for ten years. One was a six-year-old girl named Ume Tsuda, whose father, a great admirer of the West, saw the trip as an extraordinary opportunity for his youngest daughter. In the words of Yoshiko Furuki, the author of the Tsuda biography *The White Plum*, the student exchange and the new system of Japanese education were "status symbols for a country that desperately wanted to be recognized as modern." After Ume Tsuda returned, she established Tsuda College, Japan's first institution of higher learning for women.

By World War II, Japanese education was nationalistic, authoritarian, and devoted to inspiring the nation for combat. After Japan's defeat, Occupation leaders set about trying to transform the defeated country's educational system into a tool of democracy, believing, perhaps naïvely, that reform would produce citizens who were more independent and free-thinking. A mission of American educators concluded after a month of study in Japan that what the country needed was school boards and PTAs, more teacher initiative, and the American system of six years of primary school, six years of secondary school, and four years of college. They also suggested that the Roman alphabet replace Chinese characters in the written language—an absurdly farfetched idea, though exasperated foreigners struggling to learn Japanese often wish it had been carried out.

The American model basically failed. It was unsuited to the Japanese, who preferred a highly structured national curriculum to teacher or community initiative. The American Occupation shut down officially in 1952, and in the years of phenomenal growth and optimism that followed, most Japanese families became ambitious for college educations for their children. Grueling entrance exams for private junior highs, high schools, and colleges, and even for some public ones, were seen as the way to weed out and progressively narrow down the oversupply of applicants. One subtle underlying trend has been that the system has eroded Japan's famously egalitarian society, since students whose parents can afford the expense of cram schools and private schools are at a great advantage. Rohlen cites statistics, for instance, showing that an increasing proportion of national university students come from households with incomes in the top 10 percent.

Mariko's family was a classic example of a postwar household striving to make sure its youngest generation got a share of society's new riches. The good news was that the Tanaka family's new generation had already surpassed the accomplishments of the old. Mariko had never gone to a university, and her husband had been educated at a technical college, but Shunsuke had passed the exams for one of the four private high schools attached to Waseda University, one of the most prestigious schools in the nation. Unless Shunsuke completely neglected his studies—and he was walking a perilous line, as I was soon to learn—he would be able to enter Waseda with relative ease, assuring himself of the ticket into Japan's business or bureaucratic elite that his father could never have imagined for himself.

It certainly seemed that this was an example of the Japanese meritocracy in action, but I was soon to see that there were hierarchies within hierarchies, and that Shunsuke's entry had been through a kind of side door. For starters, Shunsuke was a student at Waseda Commercial High School, which, in the stratified hierarchy of high schools, known backward and forward by every parent in Tokyo, was somewhere near the top, but far from elite. Whenever I mentioned to another Japanese that the son in the family I was studying went to Waseda Commercial High School, the reaction was invariably, "That's good, but it's not the best." Men usually said, "Oh, that's the baseball school"—referring to the school's superb baseball team and the famous but less than academically gifted professional baseball stars among the alumni.

Waseda's four high schools varied in academic quality and in the percentage of graduates they sent on to Waseda University. At Waseda Koto Gakuen, the top-ranked Waseda high school, 100 percent of seniors went on to Waseda University; at Shunsuke's school, a little more than 80 percent did. Even so, teachers at Waseda Commercial insisted that the two schools were the same in quality. Students at all four Waseda high schools did have to take exams to enter Waseda University, but they were less competitive than those given to students from other high schools.

At Waseda Commercial, Shunsuke was a commerce student, a classification that further ranked him in the system. Commerce students were not considered as bright as those in the more difficult general course of study. Commerce students took more accounting classes and less math and science, and they usually went into the less elite departments at Waseda University: commerce, education, and social science. Of those taking general education courses, the best went on to the prestigious departments: law and political science. But Shunsuke was quite bright—he had finished fifth out of his class of ninety-seven in junior high—and although he had endured fourteen months of a cram school that kept him as late as ten at night, he had gotten into Waseda Commercial without doing any real studying on his own. He prepared for exams only on the night before the test, and Mariko always complained that he was lazy. Shunsuke had selected the commerce course—admittedly, it was easier to test into than the general course—because his dream was to be an accountant in charge of his own firm.

"I like sorting and arranging," he told me that fall, sounding quite directed for an eleventh-grade student. He also aspired to an adult life in which he would have a house of his own, a car, and other luxuries, but would not have to work very hard for a living. It was a dream that mixed bourgeois longing with standard adolescent fantasy, and it seemed far from guaranteed. That fall, after years of breezing through classes, Shunsuke's grades took a dramatic drop. His courses were difficult, and cramming the night before the exam was not enough. Further complicating matters was a new girlfriend, his first, who was taking up hours of his time on the phone each night. Suddenly, Shunsuke found himself in the bottom ten of the fifty students in his class. Mariko, who had never before pushed him to study, launched a nagging campaign. Shunsuke was her eldest son, and she had invested her greatest efforts in him. What a triumph it would be to have a Tanaka attend Waseda University! After all those years, how could he fail her now?

Saturday, September 21, Waseda Commercial High School, 8:45 A.M.

"While most people in Japan do their own gardening," a student in Shunsuke's eleventh-grade class read aloud, in slow but competent English, "professional gardeners are called in at least twice a year to keep their gardens in shape." Fifty boys, all dressed in the usual Prussian-inspired uniform of black trousers and black high-collared jackets, were plodding through a difficult and exceptionally dull passage in their English readers. The morning lesson was about the difference between Japanese and English gardens, not exactly a subject of burning interest to these sixteen-year-olds. The author seemed to be writing of the Japanese upper classes of a generation or two ago; twice-a-year professional gardeners were luxuries that now only the rich could afford. Most of the students in this class lived in apartments, or in houses too small for extensive gardens. But English as it is studied in Japan is an arcane subject, with little relevance to the real world. Like other schools, Waseda had in recent years added English conversation classes taught by an American, but the university entrance exams continued to test a student's mastery of the fine points of grammar, not the ability to speak. There was absolutely no incentive to learn the spoken word. This was the students' fifth year of English, and although they knew the difference between a restrictive and a nonrestrictive subordinate clause, few in the class could carry on the simplest conversation.

The teacher, an older, white-haired Japanese man in a gray suit, now launched into an explanation, in Japanese, of the grammatical points in the gardening sentence. To me, the grammar seemed so marginal and the style of teaching so absurd that it reminded me of a Japanese friend who told me he had spent an entire class studying the structure, themes, and historic significance of Beethoven's Sixth Symphony without ever actually listening to the music itself. Now the English teacher plowed forward. "In junior high you learned that the word 'while' means 'during,' " he said. "But here it means 'on the other hand.' " He went on to explain that the phrase "at least twice a year" was a way of counting, saying it was the same construction as such phrases as "three meals a day," or "seven days a week."

A hand went up in the back of the class. "Is it true," the student wanted to know, "that professional gardeners come twice a year?"

"I think it might be true in the spring and autumn," the teacher replied.

Apparently unsatisfied, the student persisted. "Even a family with a small garden will have a gardener twice?"

The teacher narrowed his eyes, clearly indicating that class time was not for asking irrelevant questions. "I have a small garden, but I don't like gardening," he snapped. "I don't want you to ask questions challenging the textbook. It doesn't make sense for you to ask me such things. It has nothing to do with English."

The class moved on. I was having a hard time staying awake, which I found embarrassing, given that I was an observer in what should have been an absorbing human laboratory. The entire day in Ken-chan's fourth-grade class had been interesting because the students had been so engaged, but here the passivity was stupefying. I had forgotten how tedious high school could be. The school would come alive only after three, when the students were let out for extracurriculars and sports—Shunsuke played what the school called American football—but now, to keep myself from nodding off, I shook my head and jotted down a few notes on the appearance of the room, a modern, characterless, grungy space, lit by fluorescent lights. It probably was built sometime in the early 1950s and apparently had not been cleaned properly since. There was no decoration and, in winter, no heat; Waseda, like other Japanese schools, believed that freezing classrooms built character.

"When a Japanese buys or builds a house," another student read aloud, now picking up with the next English sentence, "a gardener is called in to lay out the garden, no matter how small it is."

The teacher turned to grammar again. "No matter how," he said, in English. And then, in Japanese: "The meaning of this is 'even.' 'No matter how' also means 'however.' It is very important to remember this." Most of the students took careful notes in Japanese, although one napped. Shunsuke was at the back of the room, not too far from Sachiko and me, trying to ignore the unspeakable embarrassment of having two friends of his mother's in class.

The morning continued to creep along. Before English, we had already endured an excruciating health lesson that reminded me of the worst hygiene classes of my youth. The instructor had opened the class with an admonition about the weather. "Because of the influence of typhoons, the weather is not good for your health," he began. "So you have to keep yourselves clean, and change your underclothes." He asked the class to turn to the lesson "The Application of Values" in their health books. Then, for the next forty-five minutes, he presented an ominous and disjointed lecture in a monotone about the pitfalls of adolescence.

"When you are faced with a problem, you have to endure suffering," he said. "So endurance is the most important thing. If you don't have this endurance, you will end up as a delinquent, running away from home or refusing to attend school. Already, I have seen some students like this. . . ." Aside from the Japanese emphasis on endurance and suffering, I noticed, Mr. Kubo was beginning to sound strangely familiar. Had my own high school health teacher been reincarnated in his body? Or maybe all high school health teachers were the same. Not surprisingly, more students were napping. Finally the bell rang and we were relieved of our misery.

Saturdays were always half days, and Shunsuke's last class, around noon, was world history. Today it would be held in the audiovisual room because Eiichi Kojima, the teacher, was showing *Night and Fog,* a French film about Auschwitz. For the next half hour, the horrors of the German concentration camp flickered before us in grainy black and white. There were scenes of bulldozers shoving bodies into mass graves, of laboratories where medical experiments were carried out, of hollow-eyed children, of ovens. Shunsuke's generation is only vaguely aware of the Holocaust, and some of the students, Shunsuke included, put their heads down and fell asleep the minute the movie started. Others, however, were watching intently. I wondered what was going on. It was only September, and the school year did not end until March. I knew that world history had begun in August with the Sumerian civilization around 2700 B.C.—how could the class have reached World War II already? I also knew from Shunsuke's textbook that Auschwitz was not part of the curriculum. Where was Kojima going with this?

He stopped the film and flicked on the lights. The class was silent.

"Maybe you have looked at worse pictures in the Hiroshima museum," he began, referring to the scenes of death and destruction after the Americans dropped the first of two atom bombs that ended the war with Japan. "And people do have a tendency to compare Auschwitz and Hiroshima. But the important thing is this: In

Japan, in the case of Hiroshima, we really think we are the people who received damage from outsiders. But in Germany, in the case of Auschwitz, the Germans see it as something they did to themselves. They really regret that this happened."

Now I really wondered where he was going. Kojima began talking of the 1937 Nanking massacre, when the Japanese army swept through the city during two days of rape and murder, killing what the Chinese say were hundreds of thousands of innocent civilians—a number never mentioned in Japanese school textbooks and still routinely disputed by Japan's right wing. "It is important for the Japanese to recognize that we also did this thing," Kojima said, although it was unclear whether he agreed with the Chinese count of the dead. But the principle was there. "We are not only the receivers," he said. "We did the same thing to the Chinese people that the Germans did to the Jewish people. But only a few people in Japan recognize the fact that this happened in Nanking. It's exactly the same as concentration camps in Auschwitz. We Japanese always try to exaggerate what happened to us in Hiroshima."

Kojima then passed out a Japanese translation of a speech in 1985 by German president Richard von Weizsacker, who stunned the world by going further than any German leader before him by calling on all Germans, not simply those directly involved, to accept the reality of the Holocaust. Weizsacker declared that "all of us, whether guilty or not, whether old or young, must accept the past" and "keep alive the memories" of the war, a statement that no Japanese leader made until Prime Minister Morihiro Hosokawa was elected in 1993. "The important thing is that people have to look at the facts of the past," Kojima said. "Because of the concentration camps, each German has a responsibility. Weizsacker admitted the German responsibility, and really clarified it. This is the mentality among the German people. But in Japan, General Tojo was convicted as a war criminal, and yet we've enshrined him in Yasukuni shrine." (He was referring to the shrine in Tokyo built to honor the Japanese who died in the battles of modern Japan; it is the subject of continuing controversy since it deifies not only Tojo but eight other A-class criminals of World War II. Every year, China and other Asian nations indignantly protest when the Japanese prime minister or members of his cabinet visit the shrine to pay their respects.)

Kojima then sounded Weiszacker's theme, saying that while the Japanese of today have no direct responsibility for the events of the past—much as contemporary Americans have no direct responsibility for slavery—they still must accept the reality of the past, and remember and teach it. The Japanese have not done this at all. "You don't have any responsibility for the war that happened," Kojima told his students. "But you have a lot of responsibility for the future. And in order for people to have responsibility for the future, they have to know about the past. History is not just learning about the date that something happened."

Suddenly Kojima stopped and called me to the front of the room. He had known I would be sitting in on his class, and I now understood that perhaps the morning film and lecture were not meant entirely for the students. So much for being an unnoticed observer. Kojima asked me to tell the students my impressions of the class, in very slow English, so they would understand. He then invited the class to ask me questions.

A boy raised his hand. "In America," he asked, "do teenagers who are not Jewish know a lot about Auschwitz?"

I told him I thought so, but admitted I wasn't completely sure. (I later learned that some polls in the United States have indeed found considerable ignorance among Americans about the extermination of Jews by Nazi Germany.) The students asked a few more questions and then, mercifully, the bell rang. I was now intensely curious about the purpose of the Auschwitz lesson and about Kojima himself, who seemed to have the leftist critical bent of many Japanese historians and teachers. (It has always been a source of irritation to the ruling elite that Japanese teachers are stalwarts of the Socialist Party.) I went up to Kojima after class to learn more. He was an open and affable man of thirty-five, an alumnus of the school and a graduate of Waseda University, where he had received a master's degree in modern German history. His thesis was on the diplomacy of Konrad Adenauer, the chancellor who led the rebuilding of West Germany after the war. Kojima had studied in West Germany from 1981 to 1983 and now taught world history at both Waseda Commercial High School and Waseda University. He was a member of the private school teachers' union but was not a particular admirer of the larger, heavily politicized, left-leaning public school teachers' union, which he dismissed as pathetically weak. He was the father of two, and he and his wife and children lived with his parents. He said he did not like drinking after work with his colleagues but instead went home every evening before five to study, prepare for his classes, and help take care of his children. He seemed proud that he did not follow the typical Japanese salariman's routine.

Kojima was an interesting character to me, not least because he was like the high school teacher that every student remembers—demanding, strict, a little eccentric, perhaps, but with strong views and a passionate commitment to teaching. Although Shunsuke was not a particularly good student, he liked Kojima and often quoted him. Certainly Kojima proved that not all Japanese men were as conservative as Mariko's husband. He was different, but, as was so often the case in Japan, he was different in a typical way.

Over the next few months, I interviewed him a few times and sat in on two more of his classes, both of them more standard history lectures. He later admitted that the Auschwitz lesson had been introduced partly for my benefit, partly for the students, and partly to relieve himself from the monotony of the textbook. Once, during a lecture on Catherine the Great, Kojima departed abruptly from the text and sped nearly two hundred years forward to World

War II, the Baltics, and Hitler. The leap was interesting and made historical sense, but I noticed that no one took notes because they knew it was a digression that would not be on any exam. "The tests have to be based on what's in the textbook," Kojima told me later, "so all that the students have to do is study the book. But just sticking to the book is too boring for me."

Kojima was a part of the system but nonetheless was critical of his own role within it. "In the class it's all one-way," he said. "The teacher provides something to the kids. There's no feedback, they wear uniforms, they look the same, there's too much control." In a different conversation, he went further. "We are very good at teaching fundamental things, but not creativity," he said. "Our students are not very logical, and they are not good at discussion. We have not been trained to discuss at all. Did you hear when the students said something to me? They were all questions. Nobody said, 'I think this way.' The situation continues through college and when they enter society. Then it's easy for companies to handle these people. They have been trained to follow the guidelines. They make very good salarimen."

He told me he sometimes felt out of step with his own country. "I studied a lot of Western history, and I lived in a foreign country, so I'm in the position of a foreigner when I look at Japan," he said. Politically, he was an admirer of Western European social democracies and, not surprisingly, no great fan of the Japanese government. In this he reflected the views of the tiny leftist minority in Japan, whether Socialist or Communist, which tended to see the nation as a repressive, hierarchical society where the rules were enforced by social pressure and economic incentives. People on the left were often active in the environmental and antinuclear movements and adamantly against any use of Japanese troops overseas, even in United Nations peacekeeping operations. "We are very close to being a republic that has a constitution and an emperor," he said. "But we are not a democracy." He told me he liked living in Japan

—there was good food and it was safe—and yet, "I live every day feeling so many contradictions. Like in politics, the atmosphere has not changed at all. The same party has had power for so many years, which is partially our fault. The scandals haven't changed things at all. People forget easily."

One day Kojima gave a lecture on the American Revolution. He had only one class—fifty minutes—to cover it, so he jumped in at a dizzying speed, rapidly writing "1763" on the blackboard, the year of the conclusion of the French and Indian War. It was his way of introducing the idea that the Revolution was simply the culmination of a series of wars on the American continent. As I was soon to see, Kojima was not going to take a romantic approach to the birth of the United States.

"During these wars, the colonies and the British cooperated," Kojima said. "But after 1763, the colonies and the British began fighting with each other. To understand why, there are two things we have to know. The first is that the British imposed taxes on the colonies, and the second is that they banned people from moving westward. Today, we will talk about how the British imposed the taxes, and how the Americans reacted."

Kojima raced through the Sugar Act, the Stamp Act, the Townshend Acts, and the Boston Tea Party, explaining that "radicals" dressed as Indians attacked a ship and threw 340 chests of tea into Boston Harbor. The British, he said, responded by closing the port, and the colonies united in battle against them.

Kojima's lecture was a neutral, tempered review of the events and their context, assigning no praise or blame. I was impressed by the amount of detail he was teaching, and was interested that he was presenting both the British and the American points of view. When he summed up, for example, he explained that the British felt the colonies should help the mother country pay the cost of administering and protecting the vast new territories won in the earlier wars, when both were on the same side. He then went on to give what in a traditional American high school class would have been a wholly unsentimental explanation of the seeds of American democracy. He talked, for example, of Thomas Paine, but instead of sounding declarations about "the rights of man," he taught a lesson in economic determinism. In Kojima's telling, Paine's *Common Sense* was the rallying cry for the revolution within the colonies, while the Declaration of Independence was written to demonstrate to potential allies in Europe that the colonists' goal was true independence, and not just a better economic deal from Britain.

"The other European powers saw the battle as the British people fighting each other," Kojima said. "They did not want to intervene. They thought that even if they supported the thirteen states, after the war the British and the colonies would still be together. And the European powers would have lost a lot of money. So the colonies had to strongly display the attitude that we want independence from Britain."

Now Kojima was warming to the subject. "When you look at the Declaration of Independence, it looks great," he said. "But the background is that the colonies couldn't get the support of the European countries without it. So while *Common Sense* served to unify opinion within the colonies, the Declaration of Independence served to unify opinion outside of the colonies. As a result, England became isolated, and was defeated."

The class was over, on a note that would have made any American revisionist historian proud. There had not been a word about the ideals of democracy, only about economic interests. After class I asked Kojima why he had presented the Declaration as a pragmatic document and had not mentioned the ideals of self-government that American high school textbooks hold dear.

"Other teachers teach ethics," he replied agreeably. "In the ethics class, the teacher is supposed to teach the principles of democracy. He will also teach the French Revolution. So I think it's more important for me to tell them about the other factors involved."

Leaving aside the accuracy of Kojima's presentation, what struck me most was how little passion there was in it. Even a Japanese student could be taught the American Revolution in the context of the Enlightenment of the eighteenth century and the birth of the ideas of freedom and the rights of the individual. But Thomas Rohlen, in his study of the Japanese education system, says that Japanese social studies textbooks ignore such important subjects, not only in American history but in other areas of study as well.

"The first and most basic quality of Japanese social studies textbooks is their studious attempt to avoid explicit interpretations and evaluations," Rohlen writes in *Japan's High Schools*. "Extraordinary individuals like Gandhi and Stalin, great events like the atomic bombing of Hiroshima, and powerful movements like Fascism or Communism receive only passing mention as part of the march of events and historical details." Rohlen finds this all of a piece with the way Japan itself is discussed in schools—as a neat and clean system, free of class conflict; there is little or no mention of discrimination against the low-caste group known as Burakumin, corruption among the political elite, and the ban on immigrants. Japan, like history itself, is presented as bloodless. "The inspirational side of social studies is largely neglected," Rohlen writes. "Few images of national heroics or social injustices are conjured in the minds of Japanese high school students. . . . Great historical figures stare out, expressionless, at the reader."

Nine-thirty in the morning, on a brilliant autumn Sunday. The sky was a deep blue; the leaves were turning; Tokyo was at its best. None of that mattered, however, to the thirty-two fourth-grade students who were spending their one day off that week inside an antiseptic, fluorescent-lit cram school classroom working out math problems. "A boy named Hasegawa ate 5,760 roasted rice balls in three hours," the teacher said. "How many rice balls did he eat in twenty minutes? How long will it take to eat 16,000?"

A boy had his hand up. "But usually people eat roasted rice balls very fast in the beginning, and not so fast at the end," he said, obviously wanting to be helpful.

The instructor offered a pained smile. "Don't worry about that," he said. "Hasegawa can eat them all right away."

None of Mariko's children happened to be in cram school that fall, so I took up an offer from Sachiko to go to the cram school her own son attended, comparable to the ones Mariko's children had gone to in the past. Sachiko's son, Yota, a ten-year-old, was there that morning, in a sweatshirt and shorts, head bent over his notebook. The school was in a second-floor walk-up off a busy side alley of coffee shops and video rental stores in the business district of a suburban neighborhood near Mariko's house. The classroom itself was new and modern, like a computer training center, with none of the smells and texture of Ichomachi Elementary. On one wall was a list of the students from this cram school who had passed the 1991 exams into some of Tokyo's most prestigious junior highs.

The instructor this morning was a Mr. Ito, who, I noticed, was different from the authoritarian types I had seen in public schools. He was talking to the students as a friend and was dressed with a little more style—longish hair well over the back of his collar, aviator glasses, a pin-striped shirt, and a tie. Cram school instructors made more money than public school teachers, and many parents considered them better at educating their children. Ito was forty-three, had been with the cram school for two decades, and made $80,000 a year teaching and administering this particular branch, more than half again as much as he would have made teaching public elementary school. He told me, disingenuously, I thought, that his cram school did not push its students, but it was a claim echoed by Ken-chan's public school teacher, who told me she thought cram

schools were a good influence in general because they made students "more willing to study."

But what was the use in criticizing? Cram schools had become
so pervasive in Japan that they were operating like a parallel school
system. In the early 1990s, Japan's Yano Research Institute found
that nearly 4.4 million students were enrolled in as many as 60,000
cram schools nationwide; they represented 18.6 percent of elementary school students and 52 percent of those in seventh through
ninth grades. In Tokyo the percentages were even higher. Most
educators I talked to traced the beginning of the cram school boom
to the 1970s, when Japan's growing affluence enabled more parents
to afford college for their children—and a cram school education to
make sure they got in. Around the same time, public schools were
perceived to be growing less academically rigorous, ironically
because education reformers were trying to downplay the importance of entrance exams.

Parents constantly complained about cram schools, but sending
a child to one was still the most powerful way to reassure themselves they had tried their best. In Tokyo, where the pressure to get
into a good private school was the most intense, not sending a child
almost implied negligence. Every parent knew it was impossible to
get even a highly intelligent child into one of Tokyo's elite junior
highs without several years of cram school—a claim I at first dismissed as hyperbole. But as the academic race intensified each year,
with more and more cram school–prepared students competing in
an overheated system, elite private schools were forced to make
their entrance exams increasingly difficult to weed out all but the
very best. Even the cram schools themselves were becoming selec-
tive. Nichinoken, one of Japan's largest and most successful cram
school chains, with 30,000 students in 49 schools nationwide, had a
tough entrance exam of its own. Nichinoken also functioned as an
adviser to parents by directing them to the private schools whose
exams their children had the best chance of passing; only the most

stellar performers were encouraged to take the tests for the most competitive schools. In 1991, for example, only 320 out of 10,000 Nichinoken students took the exam for the elite Azabu Middle School. A little more than half got in. "It's impossible to pass Azabu without going to cram school," declared a Nichinoken official, Yoshito Higuchi—a comment supported by Azabu's headmaster, Takeshi Oga. "All of our exam-takers have gone to cram school," Oga confirmed. When I asked him if *any* student in recent years had passed the Azabu exam without going to cram school, he had to think. "Ten years ago," he finally said, "one student who passed had not gone to cram school. But his mother had graduated from the education department of Waseda University. She taught him at home. She was the cram school."

Just as the Nichinoken cram school measured its success exclusively by how many of its graduates got into the most prestigious private schools, so the private schools measured their success by how many got into Tokyo University. Of its 300 graduates each year, Azabu sent about 100 to Tokyo University, a phenomenal percentage to be sure, though not as impressive as the 190 graduates sent by Keisei, another elite high school. Because of this, Azabu had slipped in recent years from its position as the number-one private boys' school in the Tokyo area to the number-two spot. Azabu officials claimed they were not alarmed and insisted that Azabu produced more well-rounded students than the grinds at Keisei. "And the Azabu student," Oga added, smiling, "appeals more to girls than Keisei students do." I was not sure what to do with this piece of information, although perhaps it was reassuring that Azabu did not want to be famous for its nerds.

Mariko had sent both Chiaki and Shunsuke to cram school in junior high. Both children looked back on it as a bleak period in their lives, a trauma they had somehow survived. Hearing their schedules made me shudder, and I understood why in Japan there were advertisements for caffeine drinks for kids. In ninth grade, for example, from Monday through Friday, Chiaki went to her public school from 8:20 A.M. to 3:00 P.M., came home to study for a few hours, then went to cram school from 6:00 to 10:00 P.M. When she got home, she had dinner and a bath; she was in bed around midnight. On Saturdays she went to junior high from 8:20 A.M. to noon and to cram school from 3:00 to 6:00 P.M. On Sundays she was exhausted. "I stayed at home all day," she recalled. "I studied for two hours, and I watched TV."

She called it the worst year of her life. She worried constantly that if she failed her exams she would have to try again—after another whole year of studying—or worse, find work. That was a terrifying prospect. "I knew that a junior high school graduate would not have an opportunity to work at a good place," she said. She explained that she had tested into only a "midlevel" high school, but after her onerous year, she was just relieved she had gotten in at all.

Chiaki's schedule, as awful as it was, could not compare with that of Aya Shimada, a student whose mother I met through Sachiko. Aya was eighteen and attended the prestigious Gakushuin University, the school favored by the Japanese imperial family. Aya's mother, Hideko Shimada, was one of Sachiko's college friends. Sachiko insisted I meet Hideko as an example of a true education mama, a species she felt I should encounter before leaving Japan.

In fourth grade, Hideko's daughter, Aya, began attending cram school twice a week for two hours. By sixth grade Aya was up to five times a week for three hours. In the final three months before the exam, Aya began attending another cram school for an additional three hours on Sunday afternoon—*after* she had taken a weekly practice exam at yet another cram school at eight-thirty on Sunday morning. That made three cram schools and more than twenty hours of class in all, plus regular school. At the age of twelve, Aya Shimada devoted her entire life to three activities: studying, sleeping, and eating.

Aya's mother was her full-time coach. She ferried her to and from cram school, attended a special class for mothers on Sundays to learn how to help Aya with her lessons, made nutritious meals and box lunches, and made sure Aya got as much sleep as was possible. But of course she had misgivings. "My daughter began to be very nervous around December, up until she took the entrance exams in February," Hideko said. "She had a slight fever every day. I took her to the doctor and he said it was a cold. But the fever went away when the entrance exams were over."

Fortunately, Aya and Hideko's all-out assault was successful. Aya was accepted at Gakushuin Junior High, which assured easy passage into Gakushuin High School and then Gakushuin University. After the nightmare of her sixth-grade year, she never had to take an entrance exam again and was, according to her mother, really enjoying herself in college, where she was free from the arduous life she once led. College students in Japan generally work far less than their American counterparts, not least because they're finally on R&R from the examination war. This causes some people to observe that Japan's entire education system is upside down, and that students are so burned out from high school that they have no energy to take advantage of what should be a truly creative period of their lives—college. The falloff in work is so dramatic that the educator Hidetoshi Kato compares Japanese college in Japan to amusement parks. "These young people have four years to spend at Disneyland, so to speak," complained Kato. "If they're serious, they can go to class every day and improve themselves, but fifty percent of the students are lazy and do nothing."

Some students actually start cram school as early as kindergarten. "They don't feel any pressure to come here," insisted one kindergarten cram school instructor, Masako Karaki, another model of either blindness or disingenuousness. Sachiko and I were at her cram school, called Moroki Kai, off an alley in one of Tokyo's commercial districts, watching six children between the ages of four and five cut out identical pine trees from green construction paper along predrawn lines—a practice session, evidently, for the scissors proficiency test that is part of the private elementary school exams. It was four in the afternoon, already dusk in the short days of Tokyo's autumn. The students had already spent three to four hours in a private kindergarten, which is available to Japanese children as early as age three. This cram school added another hour and forty minutes to their day. The cram school called the group the Small Fish Club, and it met only once a week, on Thursday. But by the following fall the sessions would be increased to four times a week as the November entrance exams loomed. Outside the class in the school's reception area was a list of Tokyo's top twenty "Famous Elementary Schools." As I looked at the children, barely four or five years old, all working industriously at desks pushed together into a horseshoe, apparently perfectly happy in the windowless, characterless room, I thought it was one of the most depressing things I had ever seen in Japan. About the only positive thing to be said was that these children would never have to take an entrance exam again if they passed the tests into any of the Tokyo schools that went from first grade through college. As awful as kindergarten cram school was in the short run, parents argued—and I did see their point—it was more humane in the long run because it spared the children from "examination hell" later in life.

Karaki, the cram school instructor, told me that every one of the twenty students from her school who took entrance exams each year got into one of Tokyo's "famous" elementary schools. And in 1991, she said, three of her students were accepted at the elite Keio, affiliated with Keio University. "Keio took a total of ninety-six boys and thirty-six girls for first grade this year," she said. "So one hundred thirty-two got in. But thirteen times that many took the test. It's the most competitive in the city. But if you get into Keio, you can go all the way to college. Once the children pass, there are no more tests. It's a big advantage."

Not surprisingly, Karaki claimed the atmosphere in her classroom was relaxed and congenial because she avoided the excesses of other institutions. "I have heard of some children getting bald spots and nervous tics at the age of five because of cram school," she said. "Some cram schools provide only paperwork"—that is, just problems to solve on paper, and no artwork—"and some use a stopwatch." (The schools do not require children to be literate for the entrance exams, so questions are oral. An examiner, for example, may tell a room full of test takers that a mother gives a child three apples, plus one more, and then will ask how many apples there are in all. Students answer by circling the correct number of shapes on a paper before them.)

Karaki showed me a previous test from one of the most competitive elementary schools in Tokyo, in which the students had been asked to string beads in the order of the colors announced by the examiner: red, blue, white, yellow. Then they had to knot rubber bands in a given order of colors. They also had to tear along the dotted lines of a star with their fingers. So this is where it begins, I thought to myself—a life of learning how to follow instructions precisely. I asked Karaki if such tasks determined real intelligence.

"The schools are not concerned with intelligence," she answered brightly. "They're concerned with how the children can concentrate on the teacher's instructions."

She turned her attention back to her students and the pine trees. Everyone had finished cutting, and now it was time to put on ornaments. She brought out stickers in the shape of red circles, all identical. "You put them on the front and back of the tree," she said, demonstrating. Each sticker had to go on exactly the same place on each tree, with no variation. The students turned to their task with great concentration.

"The schools all require three-minute one-to-one interviews," Karaki continued, turning back to me. "Although at Futaba"—an academically rigorous and socially elite girls' school, known for its *ojosan*, or "young ladies," from the city's upper-middle class—"a student has to go with her mother. The interviewer will ask, 'What is the meaning of your name?' Then she asks the mother to please explain the meaning of her daughter's name, but to the daughter. The interviewer watches the conversation and the relationship between the mother and daughter. She checks the attitude of the daughter, and whether the daughter is good at expressing herself. If the daughter cries in the interview, or doesn't answer, she fails."

Now a teaching assistant was leading the students in putting identical stars in the identical place on the top of each tree.

"This *juku* does well," Karaki continued. "But mothers play the most important role. We teach for only two hours. So we tell the mothers how to deal with their children during the rest of the time." That of course meant that a diligent mother should practice the test questions with her child at home. For example: There are two identical tubs of hot water. A fat person enters one tub, and a skinny person enters the other. Which person will cause the tub to overflow more? Or: Here are three cups of coffee—big, little, and littlest. You put two teaspoons of sugar in each cup. Which one is sweetest?

As Sachiko and I got ready to leave, the students were handed sheets of paper with a row of pictures that included a broom, a dust pan, a pail, a feather duster, and a cooking pot. "Please circle the thing in the row that doesn't belong," Karaki instructed. Sachiko and I walked out the door, leaving the four- and five-year-olds in their horseshoe to ponder the problem.

Officials at the Ministry of Education deplore cram schools, as well they should, since their growing importance means that education policy is increasingly set by institutions whose main motive is profit. (In the early 1990s, the average monthly fee for cram schools during the junior high years was $175, but the best charged many times that amount—some schools cost $5,000 a year or more.) In addition to depriving young people of their childhoods, the schools undermine the goals of a supposedly egalitarian society and the mandate of the Education Ministry itself. The ministry has tried to improve public schools by reducing class size and upgrading teacher training, but education officials acknowledge they have failed. Despite Japan's soaring success in teaching its children, it is hard not to see the spread of the cram school as a sign of a fundamental breakdown in the education system and society itself. For three years in Japan, I heard endless talk of education reform, but I left thinking that the only way to stop the insanity was for the government to ban all cram schools and entrance exams overnight. Then it could start over somehow. The idea was of course absurd, and when I went on in this way to Mariko and Sachiko they would turn to me and say, "Well, if *you* had to educate a child in Japan, what would you do?" I honestly don't know. Send my child to cram school, I suppose.

Cram schools and their competitive pressures are also partly responsible for one of the biggest recent problems of the Education Ministry—that of the growing number of students who simply refuse to go to school at all. The Japanese call this the "school refusal syndrome," and they apply the term to a student who refuses to go to school on more than fifty days of the year. The number of such students is small by American standards, less than 1 percent of the total student population, but it is growing at a rate that is uncomfortably rapid for the Japanese. At the least, like the phenomenon of bullying, it represents a fraying at the edges. "Even in our affluent social environment, these numbers are increasing," Koichi Sakauchi of the Education Ministry told me. "Education should teach students to live in society after they graduate. We have to enrich both their minds and their hearts, and we need to create a more flexible education system. This can be changed."

Then what, in the end, can Americans learn from Japanese education? Merry White, an American scholar and the author of *The Japanese Educational Challenge*, says that we can pay more attention to "commitment and effort." She argues that the only time these two qualities are brought to bear in our schools is in sports. She overstates it, perhaps, but her larger point is well taken. "So we can do it," she writes, "even though our society does not value endurance for its own sake. Knowing what the Japanese do, we might also begin to ask more from children, parents, teachers, and schools. Expectations matter."

Even Mariko's daughter, Chiaki, believed in the value of an exacting system. Although she once told me she was very envious of American high school students because she had heard they did not have to study so hard, in the end she looked back on the nightmare of cram school and entrance exams as one of the great triumphs in her young life. "I made it somehow," she said. "So it was very good for me."

7

NEIGHBORHOOD POLITICS

The Ichomachi shrine

OCTOBER

In the beginning of October, after the typhoons had blown out over the Japan Sea and Tokyo was once again baking under a summerlike sun, Sachiko and I went along with Mariko one morning to her part-time job for the water department. Mariko was a meter reader, and Sachiko predictably complained that my enthusiasm for exploring every nook and cranny of Mariko's life, no matter how banal, was wearing her down. Sachiko had not, after all, spent years in expensive interpreting schools just so she could follow around a Japanese housewife who shoved trash aside and shooed gecko lizards out of the way to read water meters in the Tokyo suburbs. To be honest, I was also expecting a tedious morning. How enlightening could meter reading be? I asked to go only because the job took up a lot of Mariko's time—four hours a day, sixteen days a month—

and as her biographer for a year, I felt an obligation to experience it with her.

At least it was a gorgeous day, warm and breezy under a brilliant blue sky. I was as happy to be out as Mariko, who liked her job enormously. It was decent money, about eighty dollars a day, and along with that she got some exercise outdoors and a chance to meet people and peer a bit into their lives. Finding the positive aspects in meter reading was typical of Mariko's enthusiastic response to almost everything, but I soon came to understand what she saw in this job as we explored Tokyo's back alleys and popped in on sleepy, distracted, or lonely souls as they went about their daily routines. Meter reading with Mariko turned out to be one of the more pleasant and oddly intimate experiences I had in Japan. So much of what has been written about Japan in the West is cataclysmic: Japan is number one, Japan is an enigma, Japan is invading Hollywood, Japan must be contained, Japan is in collapse. All of that may or may not be true, but to knock on doors with Mariko was to be reminded how little time ordinary Japanese spend worrying about the portentous big picture and how much time they spend, like anyone else, simply getting to the market or taking the dog to the vet.

Sachiko, Mariko, and I were to meet around ten in the morning in a neighborhood not far from Ichomachi, yet another suburban hodgepodge of ramshackle old Japanese homes wedged alongside the white-tile eyesores of the newly rich. Mariko and I arrived first. I had taken the train, but the connections for Mariko were so complicated that she found it easier to make the three-mile trip from her house by bike. She arrived, sweating, in a uniform of sorts: jeans, a short blue jacket issued by the water department, white cotton gloves like those taxi drivers wear. She had a metal rod for opening up the lids of the meters that were set in the ground, and in her pocket were computer cards with the name and address of each customer in the area. Her readings would be the basis of people's bills, as in the United States. Even in this minor uniform, she suddenly took on a new dimension in my eyes—as not only a housewife but a working woman. I was glad I had come.

"Good morning," she said cheerfully. We started to chat. As often happened when Sachiko was not around, I spoke to her in rudimentary Japanese and she to me in English. This exercise involved its own rituals, requiring that we lavishly compliment each other on our incredible language skills, no matter how abominable our speaking abilities. I could see that the beautiful day had put Mariko in a good mood, although I knew she had a lot on her mind. Her biggest worry at the moment was Shunsuke, whose grades were continuing to plummet. At this rate, how would he ever get to Waseda University? Chiaki was a problem too. After the tortures of cram school the year before, the private high school she had worked so hard to get into was not all she had hoped. Although Chiaki had not told her in so many words, Mariko knew her daughter was feeling out of place among the girls from rich families who had the money to shop every weekend in the boutiques and department stores of Shibuya. Meanwhile Takeshi was as moody as ever, and was more and more miserable at work. Mariko had a vague idea of the problem—it had something to do with that delayed construction project in Kawasaki—but she had had neither the time nor the interest in the last few weeks to ask much about it. After twenty years, she had lost most of her patience with her husband's complaints about work and what she saw as his defeatist attitude toward himself and his life.

Sachiko arrived and the three of us were off. We headed up a small side street to our first stop, a traditional wooden Japanese house, shabby around the edges, and rang the bell. A sleepy and rumpled young woman in bare feet came to the door. "I'm going to read the water meter," Mariko told her in a singsong voice. The woman nodded distractedly, gave Sachiko and me a curious look, then closed the door. Mariko jotted down the figures from the meter on an outside wall and quickly moved on to the next house. There she had to push aside a garbage can full of empty beer cans, pass through a veranda strung with damp underwear hanging on a line, then duck under a barbed-wire fence into the chest-high weeds of an empty lot. She knew the meter was somewhere in the undergrowth, but she had to spend a few minutes wrestling with the vegetation before she finally found it under a persimmon tree. "Ahhhh!" she called out in victory. As we moved on, I heard a dog barking from a nearby balcony; he sounded strange, as if he had laryngitis.

At the next house, another sleepy, barefoot woman came to the door. Inside I heard the sounds of a television set. It was eleven in the morning, a Friday, a working day. I wondered what all these solid citizens of Japan Inc. were doing at home. What kind of superpower was this? This block of the neighborhood did not seem to be doing its part to make Japan the economic powerhouse of the world. We moved on again, this time coming to a house where a crabby old woman answered the door. She peered suspiciously at Mariko and then at Sachiko and me. Mariko introduced us as "researchers," without elaboration, which evidently did not satisfy. "I don't know who you are, because you're with *them*," the woman groused at Mariko. We continued on our way, through another small alley, which had a ripening Japanese orange tree and a little border garden in seasonal transition. Its dark orange zinnias and marigolds were past their summertime prime, and some healthy-looking chrysanthemums with lustrous leaves were not yet in bloom. We turned right, past a dreadful new house made of what appeared to be white bathroom tile, with two modern stained-glass windows. Where did people get the ideas for this stuff? Across the street, as a counterpoint, was an old wooden house with a small tasteful garden of bamboo, pine trees, and azaleas out front. Mariko asked a man to move his car so she could read the meter beneath it. The man seemed agreeable. "There are two types of people," Mariko observed. "Those who are happy to move their cars, and those who aren't."

While she read the meter, I watched a Mercedes glide by. The driver, a heavyset man wearing lots of gold jewelry, had a little girl in a frilly dress with him in the front seat. Were they going to a birthday party? At the end of the street was a large parking lot filled with vintage MGs, owned by a family that had a large car dealership nearby. Sachiko and I stopped to browse, admiring a dark green 1970 model in good condition. The son of the owner came out, and I idly asked the price of the car. He said $16,000, so we moved on.

We were now on a busy street, working our way up the outside terrace of a three-story apartment house. On the second floor, where there was a strong smell of mothballs, Mariko had to move a child's bike to read the meter; on the third floor, as she took the lid off the meter, a frightened gecko lizard darted out. Mariko let out a tiny scream and we all laughed. Up at this height, I looked out over the vista of suburban Tokyo: telephone wires, television antennas, and boxy ferroconcrete apartment buildings bathed in a warm, yellowish haze.

When we were back down on the street, a well-dressed woman opened her door as a small brown dog yelped around her heels. I immediately recognized him as the beast with laryngitis, and I asked what was wrong with his voice, saying I had heard him bark pathetically from down the street. "It's a sore throat," the woman replied genially, as if it were the most natural thing in the world that an American should turn up at her door inquiring about her dog's health. "I've been taking him to the vet. It's very expensive."

On the other side of the street the houses were bigger, farther apart, and more modern. We passed large homes of tile and brick and a parked Jaguar. Mariko's work took longer here, but there were only a few houses to visit, and by the time the sun was hot and high in the sky, her meter reading was done. It was time for lunch, so we decided to head into the trendy neighborhood nearby, home to import boutiques like Charles Jourdan, Yves St. Laurent,

Laura Ashley, and the only L. L. Bean store in the world outside of Freeport, Maine. As usual, Sachiko knew of a good restaurant. It specialized in roasted eel, and it was airy and cool, the perfect place to relax after the morning's wanderings. The eel was tender and sweet, and we ate with gusto. Mariko, her work over, was in a good mood. "One man left me a nice note, saying thank you for moving all the stuff on top of the water meter," she reported proudly. In his meter box she had found a gift he had left for her: coupons for six bottles of beer. It was just a small gesture, she knew, but it made her happy. Yes, meter reading was a very satisfying job indeed.

That fall, Mariko's neighborhood held its own local festival, a more relaxed but no less inebriated version of the Sanja Matsuri the previous spring. On a hot Sunday afternoon, the soul of the god worshiped at the Ichomachi shrine was taken out in a *mikoshi*, or portable shrine, for a tumultuous ride through the streets. Mariko's husband and a group of his friends had made the *mikoshi* themselves: a palanquin of rough keyaki wood with garish orange and red flashing lights, considerably less elegant than the glittering chariots of the Sanja Matsuri but perhaps more pleasing to the god in its homemade appeal. Mariko loved this neighborhood bacchanal. It was more manageable and more intimate than the extravaganza of Asakusa, where, for all the thrills, she was still a visiting outsider. Here she would always be an insider, enjoying the sense of security that came with living in the same place since birth.

Mariko's roots in the neighborhood were deep. Her side of the family had been in Ichomachi for two generations; Takeshi's family traced its ancestry much further back, to the Kamakura Era, the twelfth century, when the Tanakas owned huge tracts of land, or so the family lore had it, stretching from Ichomachi all the way to what is now downtown Tokyo—parcels worth billions of dollars today. In the nineteenth century the Tanakas were still one of the three big landowning families in Ichomachi, employing laborers and farmhands to work the rice paddies in the low-lying areas near the river. Dramatic change came in the twentieth century, when the Tanaka family holdings shrank because of the land reform following World War II. Takeshi's father's share of the family land, after generations of subdivision, was a quarter of an acre. When he died in the early 1970s, that quarter acre was further subdivided among Takeshi and his siblings, leaving Mariko and Takeshi with their two thousand square feet. Two families were living in two houses crammed on two-thirds of that property, paying a small land rental fee that was about equal to the property tax paid by the Tanakas. The arrangement left Mariko and Takeshi with less than seven hundred square feet for their sliver of a house, which covered virtually every square inch.

I had been looking forward to the Ichomachi festival for a long time because I knew it would give me a chance to meet more of Mariko's neighbors, many of whom had known her since birth. I also wanted to use it as an opportunity to tour the streets of Mariko's childhood, past the homes of friends and the Buddhist temple and the Ichomachi shrine, which might open up some of her old memories. Officially the neighborhood was called Ichomachi's District Number Two; in essence it was a mile-square village of some seven thousand people. Ichomachi had six districts in all, home to about twenty-five thousand people; Districts One and Two were densely packed with middle- and working-class flats, while Three, Four, Five, and Six were up in the hills and were the preserve of the affluent.

Another reason I wanted to make the tour was that I was hoping to loosen up Mariko's husband so I could ask if I might visit him at work—a request he had turned down several times, saying his office was boring and that my presence would be disruptive and embarrassing. I knew from Mariko that he was beginning to complain about me, asking why a book about his wife was now reaching into all aspects of the Tanaka family and the community beyond. He did have a point. I suspect that seven months before, when Mariko asked his permission for the project, she had presented it in the least threatening way, probably as just a handful of interviews with her. But now the project probably seemed to him to be spreading out of control in numerous directions, going far beyond what I had told Mariko and anticipated myself. Even so, Mariko remained cooperative and bemused about where her life was leading me. It was she who suggested I ask her husband at the festival about the office visit, guessing he would say yes if he got sufficiently drunk.

By late afternoon the festival procession, some twenty-five strong, gathered at its usual starting point on the street outside the big house of the local contractor, a friend of Mariko's from elementary school, who had grown fat and rich building homes in the suburbs in the boom years of the 1980s. Mariko and Takeshi and the others were dressed as everyone had been at the festival in Asakusa, in straw sandals, the tight-fitting cotton pants called *momohiki*, and short, indigo-blue kimono-like jackets. I had brought Steve and Madeleine with me, plus an old friend from Bangladesh, Arshad Mahmud, who happened to be visiting Japan on a fellowship. Sachiko would join us later. She had called to say she was in the emergency room with her son, who had fallen off his bike and had hurt his arm.

Mariko greeted us exuberantly, introduced us to a few friends, and then asked us to come with her. "I have a surprise for you," she said. We followed her through a back alley to her old house, the one she had moved from to be with her parents. Once inside she brought out a toddler's festival outfit for Madeleine. As Mariko took charge of the dressing, I looked around. The house was much smaller than that of her parents, no more than a single room wide, but the design was a pleasing, stylish mix of traditional Japanese tatami rooms with modern bathrooms and an updated kitchen.

Mariko's children often complained about having to live in the creaky old house of her parents, and now I could see why. My eighteen-month-old daughter, meanwhile, now looked like a miniature Japanese waiter in her own tight-fitting indigo-blue pants with a matching top and headband. We all clucked over her, then headed back to the clutch of shrine carriers. Soon they hoisted the *mikoshi* up to their shoulders and were off, grunting *uh UH, uh UH, uh UH*, as the drunken and sweaty celebrants had in Asakusa. Steve, Madeleine, Arshad, and I followed behind, goofily waving to people in the afternoon's fading light. We passed houses with red tile roofs, yellow brick apartment buildings, camellia bushes, bamboo hedges, parked bikes, motor scooters. It was that beautiful time of day when the sun bathes everything in a warm golden glow. I can think of few times when I had more fun in Japan.

The procession jerked merrily along, past a neighborhood bar, a barbershop, then a plant shop with dozens of potted ivys spilling onto the street. After fifteen minutes the shrine carriers, all now sweating and red-faced, lowered the *mikoshi* to a wooden stand in the middle of the street and took a break for some chilled barley tea. Then they were off again, careening past an electrical appliance shop that sold lightbulbs and rice cookers, past a traditional Japanese house with chick blinds and a luxurious growth of pink bush clover out front—its bursting blossoms promised that the cooler days of autumn were ahead—then past an especially ugly stucco suburban box, one of the first modern houses to go up in the neighborhood. "They built it when I was in high school," Mariko recalled later. "I thought it was so modern and wonderful—and now look."

We turned left and came to a stop on the street outside the Buddhist temple. This time cold beer was brought out, and the shrine carriers, their jackets soaked with perspiration, guzzled it down. Some of the carriers wandered up the long stone walk leading to the temple, past the old cemetery on the left, where Mariko had played hide-and-seek as a child. The temple, a small, 150-year-old wooden structure, was topped with an elaborate tiled roof and sat alongside the home of the priest, a beautiful old wooden building with mythical birds carved in the transom above the front door. Mariko often said she thought the setting looked like Kyoto, Japan's ancient capital, and it did, down to the prodigiously pruned trees that had been clipped into submission by compulsive Japanese gardeners over the years. "The trees were exactly the same size and shape when I was a child," Mariko recalled.

Nearby were a half dozen small stone statues, like little round-faced dolls, called *mizuko jizo*. Found at Buddhist temples all over Japan, they are effigies in memory of aborted, miscarried, or still-born children; mothers typically gave money to the temple priest, said a silent prayer in front of one of the statues, then left behind heartbreaking gifts—stuffed animals, bottles of apple juice, pacifiers—to keep the soul of the dead child content and amused. One after-noon a few weeks after the festival, when Mariko, Sachiko, and I walked over to the Buddhist temple, we all noticed that a chocolate bar and a lollipop had been left beside one of the statues. Mariko then told me something she hadn't mentioned before, which was that almost twenty years earlier, the year after she was married, she had a miscarriage when she was three months pregnant. "I am very sorry for the baby I lost," she said quietly. Presumably like this woman, she had gone to make her offering—not at her own neigh-borhood temple but outside Ichomachi, where she was not known and where people would not talk.

The procession was up again, this time going left around the corner and on past Mariko's house, where Mariko's mother was sitting up in bed, watching the crowd with Saburo through the open door. We waved and moved on, beyond the house of the coach of Ken-chan's softball team, past an old photo studio. Mariko had pictures of herself taken there as a child; today in the window was a photograph of the man in charge of the festival posing proudly with his plump new grandson. The procession inched forward, then rested at the end of the street, near the wooded hill leading up to the Ichomachi shrine. The thirty gingko trees, chopped down by the crew of workers four months before, still lay in the shadows at the base of the hill. Even though the plans for the parking lot were temporarily stalled, I was surprised to see that the gingkos had not yet been moved. What did this mean? Mariko herself didn't know.

By now it was dark. Sachiko arrived and said her son was fine. Through the remaining trees on the hill we could see just a bit of the Ichomachi shrine at the top, all lit up like a beacon in the balmy night. The *mikoshi* carriers popped open more beer, and Mariko, laughing, passed out yakitori as the men began to drink in earnest. The smell of the succulent grilled chicken and cold beer was as luscious as ever. The *mikoshi* carriers seemed to be settling in for an extended rest stop, so Steve, Arshad, Sachiko, and I decided to head up the steep path to the shrine. At the top, the first thing we saw was a carnival in progress. Paper lanterns bobbed in the night breeze as hundreds of people milled around food stalls offering fried noodles and freshly roasted corn on the cob. We found Ken-chan there, sampling the treats. Then we watched as worshipers approached the shrine through the pair of elaborately carved stone watch dogs flanking the entrance. Each worshiper tossed a coin into the cash box, clapped hands to waken the god, then prayed—for healthy babies, for prosperity, for sons to pass entrance exams. The shrine itself, bathed in light for the festival, was beautiful, but almost off-handedly so. With its dark carved wood, vermilion edging, and gabled roof with the upward sweep at the eaves, it was as exquisite and ordinary as every other neighborhood shrine in Japan.

There had been a Shinto shrine on this site for nearly a millennium, but Mariko told me that now the shrine, like so many others in Japan, was struggling financially. Although the Ichomachi shrine made money from the usual sources—soliciting contributions from

the neighborhood, cash-box collections at the New Year's celebrations, the priests' blessing of babies—the income could not keep up
with the soaring costs of maintenance. Many Buddhist temples
made money from running businesses like cram schools and
kindergartens, and now the Ichomachi shrine was also seeking some
outside income. This explained why it wanted the parking lot.
Mariko, like so many others in Ichomachi, was appalled that the
trees had been cut, but she was also keeping her distance from the
organized neighborhood protest. "Those people are too aggressive,
and I don't like the way they talk," she told me. So far, she said, she
had hung back from joining in.

Steve, Arshad, Sachiko, and I headed back down the hill, to find
the *mikoshi* carriers ready to leave again. By now all the men were
happily drunk. Soon the procession was lurching across a busy
street, past the shop of the neighborhood rice merchant—"He's too
expensive and he never stops talking," Mariko grumbled—and
then into a winding narrow alley, where it made several sharp
turns before coming to another stop. This time I was told it was my
turn to help carry the shrine, so I was given a short blue jacket, and
we were off: *UH uh, UH uh, UH uh, UH uh!* One of the big planks
that supported the shrine dug into my shoulder, but I found it all
completely enjoyable, except for the drunk behind me, a typical
festival hazard, who breathed fumes down my neck and pushed up
against me the whole time.

At last we came to our final stop, an alley outside the home of
the neighborhood grandee, a Mr. Yukio Tanizaki, widely acknowledged as the unofficial mayor of Ichomachi. Mariko and her husband had known him all their lives and dutifully supported him
every four years when he ran for reelection to his seat on the local
ward council, a position he had held for three decades. Mr. Tanizaki
was in his sixties, had a fuel-oil business, and sold kerosene to all
the elementary schools in the ward. People assumed he got the
kerosene contract through his political connections. He was spo-

ken of as a kind of affable operator, part of the natural order of the neighborhood, and if he was not particularly loved in Ichomachi, he was at least respected. People were obsequious around him because they thought it prudent to be on his good side.

"We need him," Mariko's husband once told me.

"For what?" I asked.

"Small things, like getting road clearances for our festivals," he said. "We could do things properly without him, but it's good to have his help." He thought for a moment. "There is no place for people in Ichomachi to gather. Mr. Tanizaki has land and provides his place. He also lets us use his warehouse. He won't rent it to people he doesn't know." Mr. Tanizaki was also the sponsor of various softball teams in the neighborhood, including Ken-chan's team, the Junior Wets.

The festival had now moved inside a tent set up over a small parking area across from Mr. Tanizaki's house. Mr. Tanizaki owned both the property and the tent, but we were told that he was out attending a softball game. His absence did not seem to dampen anyone's spirits, which were running high from the beer and dinner, a Japanese stew called *oden*, plus the last boiled and salted soybeans of the summer, all served at long tables in the tent. It was now around seven and Takeshi, fueled by beer, was in a good, loose mood. "Go ask him now about visiting his office," Mariko whispered. Sachiko went alone to work him over. I watched as she talked nonstop, laughing and teasing, telling him it was time to tell his side of the story. Finally she returned triumphant. He had agreed, and we would see him in a few weeks.

My only disappointment at the festival was that I did not have a chance to meet Mr. Tanizaki, who seemed too intriguing a personality to be missed. Soon afterward I asked Mariko if she could put me in touch with him, and a few weeks later there were Sachiko and I, parked in his kitchen. Mr. Tanizaki was short and round and had a shock of white hair and eyes that crinkled up at the corners when he laughed. He was talkative and eager to please. I felt as if I had encountered Mr. Tanizaki many times before—on city councils in the United States, on village councils in India, in the halls of Congress in Washington. If this had been a small town in the United States, Mr. Tanizaki would have been president of the Rotary Club.

"You must stay for lunch," he insisted. "I'll order in sushi." He picked up the phone at the table in his kitchen, the fantastically cluttered heart of the house. Spilling off the surrounding cabinets and shelves were bowls, dishes, plastic souvenirs from various tourist spots around Japan—did the Tanizakis watch *Dreamy Trip* too?—pots, pans, kitchen appliances, stacks of old papers. It looked like a household of busy pack rats. Mr. Tanizaki's wife stood at the stove heating some miso soup to accompany our sushi. There was none for her—as a woman, she would not eat with her husband's visitors—but she served it to us in what appeared to be a sullen, hostile silence. I wondered what was going on. Had life with Mr. Tanizaki, the generous soul of the community, perhaps been more difficult and trying than the neighbors might suspect? Was she tired of the constant stream of supplicants to the house? Or had she always been like this?

Whatever the case, Mr. Tanizaki seemed not the least bothered by his wife's mood and cheerfully told us a little about himself. He had lived in Ichomachi since he was an infant, and after the war he began helping out in the family coal business, since there was no one else; one of his two brothers was killed in the battle for New Guinea and the other died of tuberculosis. In the 1950s the family began selling kerosene, and in 1960 Mr. Tanizaki took over from his father as president. Three years later he was elected to the ward council and in 1977 served a term as its chairman. Neighbors said he owed his political fortunes to a powerful friend in the long-ruling Liberal Democratic Party, and there was a time when the people of

Ichomachi expected that Mr. Tanizaki would end up with a seat on the Tokyo Metropolitan Assembly, the city legislature. But for reasons unknown, Mr. Tanizaki had never left the small pond of Ichomachi. He remained for twenty-seven years on the ward council, longer than any other elected member and longer than any of the professional staff too. His seniority alone brought him a measure of power over the years, but so did his labyrinth of contacts, business dealings, and involvement in the history of the area.

Curious about Mr. Tanizaki and his world, I asked if I could attend a meeting of the ward council, and he agreed. He suggested a good day, and two weeks later Sachiko and I found ourselves observing Japanese local democracy in action. We were in a newly built auditorium with beige carpeting, tawny walls, and recessed soft lighting, all far more luxurious than what I had seen in local government offices in the United States. The ward of which Ichomachi was a part was one of the biggest and richest in Tokyo, with a population of almost eight hundred thousand. Mariko lived in a middle-class area, but the ward's boundaries also included some exceptionally expensive residential neighborhoods where the price of a tiny parcel of land could go as high as $10 million. Not surprisingly, the ward had few people on welfare—just over a thousand, most of them handicapped or chronically ill.

On stage this morning in the auditorium sat the ward mayor, the most powerful elected politician in the ward, plus a phalanx of bureaucrats in charge of the various government departments. They faced an audience of fifty-five elected members of the ward assembly, including Mr. Tanizaki. The ruling Liberal Democratic Party dominated the ward council, but it was short of an absolute majority by one vote and so belonged to a "majority coalition" of other parties. On the morning's agenda was a kind of open discussion, what Mr. Tanizaki had described to me as a chance for council members to air problems and ask questions of the mayor and the bureaucrats. Oddly, or so I thought at the time, no members of the public were present. Mariko told me she had never been to a meet-ing and could see no point in ever going.

First up was one of the eight women members of the ward council, newly elected the past spring; she seemed to be about forty and had a businesslike manner. Reading from a prepared speech, she stood up at her seat and began a formal presentation about the difficulties of women in the ward. "There are still not enough opportunities for them as part-time workers," she said. She sug-gested that the government could help organize part-timers to work at after-school groups for children of full-time working mothers, but only if the salaries were better; then she mentioned a recently opened center run by the ward to assist women in re-entering the labor force after having children. "But no one knows about it," she said. "There need to be materials advertising it."

The woman's presentation seemed well thought out and rea-sonable, but it was obvious that despite giving lip service to the idea, few men on the council took women in public office seri-ously. Mr. Tanizaki confirmed as much when I saw him later, com-plaining that the women on the council only cared about a few issues. It was true that women in local politics tended to view themselves chiefly as experts on women, education, aging—and food. Later I talked to the woman who had made the presentation that morning, and I learned that like a growing number of women in local government, she owed her political success to a vocal net-work of food cooperatives run by housewives, the Seikatsu Clubs. The clubs buy organic food in bulk for distribution to some two hundred thousand members nationwide, and in recent years they have tried to bring their opposition to food additives and pollu-tion, along with vague calls for world peace, into local politics. More than a decade earlier, the first Seikatsu Club member was elected to Tokyo's Nerima Ward Council, helped by a get-out-the-vote effort among the clubs for one of their own. By 1991, the

Seikatsu Clubs had thirty seats on Tokyo's ward councils and one seat in the Tokyo Metropolitan Assembly. Two years before, a club member ran for Parliament, supported by the Socialist Party. She lost, but the Seikatsu Clubs have grown in strength. "We are a grass-roots organization, and it was too early for us," she said. Still, their successes showed that women were likely to remain a force in the restive Japanese electorate.

The ward's response to the woman's speech came first from the deputy mayor, who read vague remarks from his own prepared text about the need for a more favorable environment for working women. He obviously knew in advance everything the woman was going to say; the woman had submitted her question beforehand, a practice often followed in the Japanese Parliament. The artificial and ritualized quality of the proceedings was, of course, exactly what the leaders of the ward council wanted. The real decisions are made behind closed doors by professional bureaucrats, who usually then dictate their decisions to the elected leaders. The Japanese sometimes call their tradition of powerful bureaucrats a consultative democracy, more efficient and less messy than unseemly public squabbling. The open meetings were a formality—or a charade, depending on one's point of view. With the exception of very senior council members like Mr. Tanizaki, most elected ward council members had little power. I now understood why few ordinary citizens attended the meetings.

After his prepared remarks, the deputy mayor passed the ball to the director of the civic affairs department, a bureaucrat who read from *his* prepared text. "There are many pros and cons to part-time work," he observed. "On the positive side, you can choose your own time. But on the negative side, the salary is low." Moving on from this revelation, he said the ward had issued a booklet about the women's center, and promised to have more information available by the end of the year. Next up was the personnel affairs manager.

"We are trying to expand opportunities for women," he began, once again reading from a prepared text.

The meeting went on in this vein until, mercifully, at 11:55 A.M., precisely on schedule, it adjourned. Mr. Tanizaki, Sachiko, and I repaired to a large ceremonial office, where Mr. Tanizaki introduced us to the chairman of the fifty-five ward council members and also to the mayor, an up-and-comer of about forty, who seemed to be on his way somewhere else. He chatted with us briefly and then departed, leaving me to be interviewed by the young representative of the official bulletin of the ward government. When the reporter asked my opinion of the ward council proceedings, I decided to get into the polite spirit of things. "They were very interesting," I said. By now Mr. Tanizaki was summoning us for lunch, exquisite sushi again, this time laid out in a corner of the office.

Over salmon eggs and tuna, I asked him the point of the scripted nature of the morning proceedings. "It's a way for the ward to let all the council members know where it stands," he said. "It's for clarification." We also talked about the big issue in the ward, garbage, which Mr. Tanizaki had mentioned briefly in his kitchen. Trash was accumulating at an alarming rate in Tokyo's landfills, and in a classic not-in-my-backyard battle, the ward was fighting the plans of the powerful Tokyo metropolitan government to build an incinerator in one of the ward's most prized parks. Mariko did not live near the park, but those who did were in an uproar, and talks between the two sides would soon be under way. Unfortunately for the ward inhabitants, Tokyo had jurisdiction over the park, as it did over most other big parks and major roads in the ward, which left the ward with very little power within its own boundaries. The ward usually took orders on most issues from Tokyo; the garbage fight was the first time in recent years that the ward had begun to show some independence and fight back.

Lunch over, Sachiko and I made plans with Mr. Tanizaki to attend another council meeting a few weeks later, this one a kind of budget hearing. As Mr. Tanizaki explained it, council members would have the chance to question the ward's bureaucrats about expenditures. On the appointed day, though, it turned out that there were almost no queries on the budget itself. Instead members used the session to press for money for pet projects and to air suggestions, some of them exceedingly marginal.

The first council member to speak, for example, suggested putting the mayor's face on the ward newsletter. Another council member deemed this inappropriate. Then a council member requested bus service from a local park to the ward's art museum, pointing out that it held thirty-six hundred artworks, many from area artists, and was a great treasure. The response from the ward's general affairs manager was, in summary, "Kento shimasu"—literally, "Let me explore it"—which everyone in the room seemed to think was favorable. Another member got up and informed the room that the ward had sent one hundred cherry trees to Vienna, where they had been planted along the Danube River, the sister river of the Ichomachi River. Unfortunately, ninety-five trees had died. There was then a discussion of having a sister-city celebration with Vienna, the kind of thing that Japanese love. Subsequent topics meandered from plans to improve local train stations to reconstruction of a junior high school, improving a shopping area, and rebuilding a collapsed bank of the Ichomachi River.

The meeting ended at lunchtime. We said good-bye to Mr. Tanizaki, but I had a feeling we would see him again.

8

SCENES FROM A MARRIAGE

Mariko and Takeshi's wedding, 1971

OCTOBER AND NOVEMBER

At the end of October, Takeshi Tanaka's troubled year at his company, Nippon Electric, grew even worse. In a disastrous setback, a $2 million contract for the electrical work in a new apartment building in a suburb of Tokyo abruptly fell through. The construction company overseeing the project informed Nippon Electric it was obligated to award the wiring subcontract to another electric firm with which it had close relations. Doling out business contracts on the basis of maintaining relationships with a variety of companies was standard in Japan, particularly in the construction industry, where much of the competitive bidding for big government-subsidized construction projects was a charade. Takeshi, like everyone else, knew that contracts were quietly awarded before the formal bidding even opened. Competing companies simply got together behind closed doors, much like the ward bureaucrats, and decided among themselves whose turn it was for a job. Spreading the wealth in an orderly manner made planning possible and kept the industry stable, or so the theory goes; the Japanese greatly prize predictability in business. But in this case, Nippon Electric had been led to believe this particular project, a nongovernment deal, was theirs. Takeshi was angry and upset.

Four months earlier, when Sachiko and I visited Takeshi at the construction site in Yokohama, he was in a frustrated mood because his work was already sluggish. Now the loss of the $2 million job meant that Takeshi would continue to languish as he had for the past two weeks, sitting gloomily around the office with nothing to do. It was another sign that Japan was going through hard times as the inflated real estate and stock prices of the 1980s were collapsing. It was also the longest period of time Takeshi had been idle in his twenty years at the company. The work on the much-delayed Kawasaki City Hall was still stalled, and money would not start coming in for years. What Nippon Electric needed now was a quick job with a fast infusion of cash; the $2 million apartment complex in the Tokyo suburb of Hino City, which would have taken a year, was ideal. When the bad news came, on Monday, October 21, Takeshi chose not to sink deeper into self-pity. This time he stalked furiously out of the office in midafternoon. For once he managed to avoid the bars, and instead took a train to Shibuya to see an afternoon showing of *Terminator II*.

"It's a very busy movie," he told me afterward.

On Tuesday, he got drunk, but not too badly, at least in his opinion. Mariko did not bother to complain when he staggered home that evening. Later he could not remember whether he had told her then about his problems at work; usually he did not. "She wouldn't understand," he said.

It was now Thursday, cold and cloudy, and about the only thing that would have put Takeshi in a more sullen mood was a visit from

Sachiko and me. Unfortunately, it was the day for the long-awaited interview that we had arranged the previous month, when Sachiko had cornered him in a happier mood at the Ichomachi festival. As we drove toward his office, we talked about how hard it would be to draw Takeshi out, laughing about the comical aspects of trying to get a classically taciturn and preoccupied Japanese salariman to be forthcoming about his business problems. I had a lot of questions, almost all of them the kind that Japanese men don't like to answer—especially when the questioners are women, who could not possibly understand. But what I really did not understand until much later was how difficult Takeshi's problems really were.

Nippon Electric was south of the city, in a dirty white building in the bleak flatlands of an outlying industrial area of Kawasaki. Like most Japanese offices, it consisted of one large room, with gunmetal-gray desks pushed together into little clusters of six or more, all utterly functional, like an office from the 1940s in the United States. Of course, it was no more seedy than the interior of the Ministry of Finance. In Japan, a drab office means you are properly spartan and serious; decorated suites are for decadent American corporate executives.

As Takeshi had predicted, his office was almost entirely empty, and I wondered briefly if he had somehow arranged this. A solitary man worked at one of the desk clusters, and a supervisor in the front of the room officiously shuffled papers. On Takeshi's desk were drawings of a project, but he was making no pretense of being busy. Instead he was sitting at a table in a corner near the television, watching the Hiroshima Carp play the Seibu Lions in a championship baseball game of the Japan Series. We sat down awkwardly at the table with him. He didn't bother to introduce us to the supervisor or the other employee, and said that everyone else was out. He was obviously uncomfortable having us at the office; in two decades of marriage, Mariko had never been there herself. (This was typical, and it reminded me of something that once happened at my husband's office in Tokyo. A secretary employed by *The New York Times* had to pick something up at the Finance Ministry, where her husband held a prestigious position after many years of service. She was amazed to find that he worked in such squalor.)

Mariko rarely called Takeshi at his office, avoiding what would only be seen as wifely pestering about household and personal concerns. A man could get a reputation if that happened too often. One person Takeshi did talk to during the day was a drinking buddy, a man five years his senior at the company. When the two went to the bars together, Takeshi unloaded all of his frustrations about work. But never, even when drunk, did he talk about anything more personal than that.

"Sometimes I do want to talk to somebody about those worries," Takeshi told me over the din of the baseball game. "But I don't think talking to somebody about my worries makes the worries any easier."

I asked about Mariko. "I only talk to her when I'm drunk," he said moodily. "And then I complain."

He was in a terrible funk, and most of all mad at the company. "The management is not good," he said. "The chairman is the emperor. There are many voices from the employees, but the chairman doesn't listen."

I noticed that the supervisor was still shuffling papers at his desk. Could he hear what was going on? Did Takeshi want him to hear? The Carp and the Lions were still making a racket, but otherwise the office was as still as an abandoned ship. How had I found a place of such apparent ennui when all over Japan people seemed to be bustling purposefully about, making perfect cars, attending meetings, sweeping sidewalks? Maybe this sort of lassitude and disgruntlement was more widespread than people thought. Whatever the case, the atmosphere in that office was so stifling that I suggested we move to a coffee shop.

Around the corner was Jonathan's, a Western-style restaurant chain, where Takeshi ordered coffee and continued his complaints. First he told us bitterly about the problems of losing the apartment-house job, but then he turned to the big disappointment of the year in his office, the Kawasaki City Hall project, which was now at an impasse. The problems began right at the start, when the foundation of the project was flooded and had to be drained. As a result the building was delayed two years, and now Nippon Electric was losing so much money that it wanted to withdraw from a part of the contract. As Takeshi explained it, Nippon Electric's partner on the project also wanted to withdraw, and the two firms were at a standoff with the construction company in charge. A year before, Takeshi had been going to the Kawasaki site every day, but Nippon Electric had decided the best strategy for the moment was to stay away from the job entirely—so Takeshi was in limbo, forbidden by his superiors to go to the site until the dispute was resolved. It seemed an oddly discordant note, at variance with the myth that all Japanese industrial problems are settled in an atmosphere of harmony. Here there were no big confrontations or lawsuits, just a quiet stalemate that froze everything in place and left everyone unhappy. "It's irritating," he said. "I haven't been to Kawasaki for one year, but I still have a desk there, and a locker with my working clothes in it. I can't even go there to take my clothes home." Forced to sit at the office, he stewed. "I have a tendency to think of unproductive things," he said. "Like I'd rather switch to another company." And yet he told me he'd had a worse year, his third at the company, seventeen years earlier, when he had problems with the contractor on a project and the clients complained about the electrical work. "I was almost ready to quit," he said. "I hated the job."

I asked him what was more important to him, his company or his family. "If you had asked five years ago, I would have said the company," he answered. "But now I won't say that. For me now, the company is not so important. But also the family is not so important either. If I had to take either of these, I would say maybe the family. But these are things you can't compare. The question is like 'Which do you prefer—Papa or Mama?' "

I was nonetheless impressed by how much the company meant to him, and so I asked what had changed in the last five years. "I used to have guts," he said. "I had more energy. I wanted to change the company's way of management. But now I know that even if the management is changed, the style won't be."

I asked him who he was closest to. "My wife," he answered, surprising me a little. For "wife" he used the informal *nyobo*, rather than the more official *kanai*, brought out when introducing a wife to business colleagues and superiors. Like most traditional Japanese men of his generation, Takeshi never called his wife by her first name. "It's very embarrassing to use it," he said. In high school, like all the other boys, he had called Mariko by her family name with a *-san* at the end for respect; like all the other girls, Mariko had called Takeshi Tanaka-kun, the *-kun* being a masculine diminutive. After they were married but before the children were born, he adhered to traditional Japanese custom by calling her Oie, which roughly translates as "Hey!" She called him Anata, a polite and—in this context—intimate form of "you." After the children came, she called him Otosan, for Father, while he called her Okaasan, for Mother. These honorifics are the traditional forms among the Japanese, although many in the younger generation now tend to use first names.

I asked Takeshi if he had any goals or dreams, or anything he looked forward to.

"I don't have a dream," he answered sourly. "I live as it goes. Life goes on, and I go on."

Over the past months, I had begun to think of Takeshi as little more than a one-dimensional figure, an alcoholic who made life miserable for Mariko. Now I was beginning to see beyond the stereotype, and for the first time I realized that he was trapped by his society in a way that Mariko was not. Unhappy in his job, emotionally cut off from his family, Takeshi went blindly through the paces expected of a salariman. No wonder he drank. For all her complaints, Mariko was in charge of her life. She was the authority at home and had her children, her jobs, her friends, her hobbies, her dreams—a life, she said, of real meaning. It was then that I began to see at least some wisdom in the Japanese belief that married women, for all their secondary status, are ultimately more free than men.

I was curious if Takeshi acknowledged Mariko's dominant role in their lives, so I asked him who ran the family.

"*Are*," he answered, using the word for "that" in Japanese, a curt, shorthand reference to his wife. Then he amended his answer with a metaphor, saying that "*teki*"—the Japanese word for a rival or competitor—ran the family. "She nags the children a lot," he said. "And me, too. But I deserve to be nagged. She nags when I arrive home drunk, which is justified. Unfortunately, I'm a very selfish person."

Sachiko, tired of his sullen mood and self-pity, spoke up.

"Please tell us what the good parts of you are," she said.

"I don't have any," Takeshi replied morosely.

Takeshi may have been having a bad year, but it turned out to be a good month for his sixteen-year-old son. On October 6, Shunsuke met his first girlfriend at his high school's Culture Festival, a celebration of student plays, music, and art exhibits, and within a few weeks, in the stomach-churning manner of teenage love, he could think of little else—least of all his grades, which continued their downward spiral. Shunsuke's girlfriend lived in a prosperous suburb to the northwest, and went to another private school. So far they had been on three dates. One was to play pool, another was to get together and talk, and the third was to see *Terminator II* in Shibuya. "Hmmm," Sachiko said when Shunsuke told us about it. "So now two people in this family have seen that movie recently." Shunsuke had no idea what she was talking about—his father obviously had not told him about stalking out of the office in the middle of the afternoon—so I let it pass.

In any case, Shunsuke was too wrapped up in his love life to pay much attention. His new girlfriend was quite modern and had twice called him at home. Each time they talked from eight-thirty until ten at night, driving Mariko to distraction. She needed the line to make calls for the PTA and to her own friends, and evening was the one time she could reach everyone. "Get off the phone!" she yelled at Shunsuke. But even Mariko was no match for the tenacity of a lovesick teenager. As it was, she hardly approved of a girl who called a boy, even in the 1990s. And she definitely did not approve of Shunsuke's skulking in from a date at ten on a weeknight. "How does she have time to study when she's seeing you so much?" Mariko demanded.

Chiaki, at the age of fifteen, also had a boyfriend that fall, and she was doing her best to keep him a secret from her mother. Mariko of course had suspicions, which is no doubt why she insisted on sitting in on a conversation I had with Chiaki one night in November—one of a series of interviews with the three kids. In the months up until then, my only contact with Mariko's children had been saying hello to them as they floated in and out of the house. Although I had been to school with them, and I had seen Chiaki snap at her mother, most of what I knew of their problems and aspirations came from Mariko. When I told Mariko that I wanted to speak to them individually, she readily agreed and, in typical, efficient Mariko fashion, set up the next Friday, after eight, as interview night, saying that was the earliest all the kids would be home. Shunsuke had football practice and didn't get back until six-thirty most days, while Chiaki's volleyball team kept her after school from two to seven-thirty five days a week.

The kids came downstairs for their interviews one at a time, in reverse order of age because of bedtimes. When Ken-chan was done, he went upstairs and sent Chiaki down, and when Chiaki was done, she summoned Shunsuke. Each child sat at the *kotatsu*, with Sachiko and me on either side. It was not, to say the least, a particularly relaxing experience, and a few months later I had more revealing conversations outside the house with both Chiaki and Shunsuke about school, friends, and their parents. But these first talks were a start.

Ken-chan, the first down the stairs, told me he wasn't sure what he wanted to be when he grew up, but pro wrestling looked good. His friends, however, thought he should be a sumo wrestler. "They only tell me that because I'm fat," he said a little sadly. "I run ten minutes every day, up and down the street, to try to lose weight." Ken-chan answered my questions with both the sweetness and great seriousness of a nine-year-old, and was quite poignant when he talked about his relationship with Takeshi. "I don't tell my father anything," he said. "Mommy tells him what I said." But he spoke matter-of-factly, as if his remote relationship with his father was normal. Perhaps it was. I suspected that many of his friends felt distant from their salarimen fathers too.

I was curious about what a fourth-grade Japanese boy had learned of the outside world, so I next asked Ken-chan what he knew of America. He said he only knew what he glimpsed occasionally on the morning news. "Seventy percent of the residents of New York City are not Americans," he informed me, obviously influenced by a report on immigration. "They have American nationality, but they come from somewhere else. They were not born in America. They're Americans—but not truly Americans." His comment, of course, was typical in a country that has no concept of nationality other than one based on race.

As we talked, Mariko rattled around in the kitchen, but from time to time she came in and took a seat at the head of the table, where she smoked a slow cigarette and listened carefully. It was too awkward to ask her to leave, and I'm not even sure that's what the kids wanted. In any case, I don't think Mariko cared whether her presence might embarrass or inhibit them. She was simply curious. She did show remarkable restraint, at least for her, by keeping mostly silent during my talks with Shunsuke and Ken-chan. But when it came to her daughter, who was next down the stairs, she couldn't control herself.

It happened when I asked Chiaki if she had a boyfriend. Yes, she said, she did, a holdover from junior high. The two now went to different high schools but still met once a week in the early evening on a bench in the woods below the Ichomachi shrine.

"I didn't know that boyfriend was still around," Mariko interjected.

Chiaki looked at her mother accusingly. "How did you know he was a boyfriend?" she snapped. Turning to Sachiko and me, she added: "I don't like my mother's attitude. She makes fun of me." She said her boyfriend "used to call here, but I told him not to because my mother is so nosy."

Mariko blew smoke from her cigarette and chuckled. "Chiaki thought I asked too many questions," she said. "Like, 'When are you going to see him? Or where?' "

"You really *did* ask those things," Chiaki said.

Silence. Chiaki fumed. Mariko refused to budge from her position at the head of the table. I awkwardly changed the subject and asked Chiaki whether she would prefer to live in a Western- or a Japanese-style house when she grew up.

"The bigger the house the better," she said, ignoring my lame attempt to defuse the situation. "And if I don't get married, I don't want to live with my parents anyway."

I was clearly glimpsing the intense, nonnegotiable opinions of a rebellious fifteen-year-old who enjoyed rejecting the life her mother had led. Earlier that evening, when I had asked Chiaki whether she wanted to marry or have a career, she answered without hesitation. "I want to work," she said, as Mariko listened quietly. "I don't want to have children, and if possible, I don't want to get married. I'm selfish. Looking at my mother, I know it was very hard to raise me. I don't want to spend that kind of time."

Mariko smiled. "I've heard this many times from her," she said, dragging on her cigarette.

Chiaki's attitudes were a window into generational shifts in Japan that were not so different from what my own generation had experienced in the United States. In this case Chiaki saw her mother's life as exhausting and wholly organized around others. And yet I knew that if Mariko had worked full-time, Chiaki would have felt neglected. Maybe then she would have wished that her mother had stayed home with her children. I was beginning to realize that Mariko's children were already like their parents, vaguely wanting something different from what they had. I don't know whether Chiaki understood that Mariko's marriage lacked intimacy; her negative feelings about marriage are embraced by many women of her generation.

Chiaki was a good student at her new high school, but she wasn't sure what kind of work she wanted to do. For a while she thought about becoming a cartoonist. She knew for certain that she did not want to be an office lady, like some of her friends. "An O.L.'s life seems boring," she said. "Every day is the same. They make tea and photocopies." She had also considered being a veterinarian but had rejected that as too difficult.

"She doesn't know what jobs are good," Mariko interjected. "I keep telling her she should be a pharmacist. She can keep working if she marries. And if she quits, she can always return."

Chiaki had no reaction, so I tried to move things along by asking about a career in business. She seemed to withdraw a little, and it was at this point that Sachiko embellished my question by telling her that being a businesswoman meant wearing beautiful suits and high heels. "And you would walk quickly and be very nice to look at," Sachiko added. This was hardly what I had meant, but Chiaki now loved the idea. "And at the office you wouldn't have to flatter the men," Sachiko added.

It was ten P.M. by the time it was Shunsuke's turn to come down from upstairs, blowing in like a thunderstorm. "I've been waiting two hours!" he said brusquely. Sachiko and I had had no idea he was simmering upstairs. I was feeling so guilty for inflicting myself on the kids so late on a Friday night that I was ready to reschedule our talk and go home. But then Sachiko smoothed things over by apologizing for the delay. Mariko stayed out of it. Like everyone else in the family, she knew Shunsuke's bad moods would pass. Chiaki, who got along with her brother well on his good days, told me that she had two theories about her brother's moodiness, both linked to his volatile teenage self-esteem. The first was that Shunsuke might have had an argument some time before with friends, and that led to a permanent anger he carried into the house. "The second," Chiaki said, "is that home is the only place he can be arrogant."

Shunsuke sat down grumpily. Dispensing with small talk, I asked him what he wanted to do with his life. "I want to be a CPA," he said. "I've wanted to be one ever since I was in high school. I like sorting, and arranging. And I really liked my accounting course." His dream, he said, was to have his own accounting firm.

"My work would not require me to get up early," Shunsuke said, cheerful now and relishing the thought. "But my basic aspiration is to work when I want to work. And I want a house, not an apartment, with my own study, and a room for each kid. The bedrooms should be upstairs and a cozy living room downstairs. I want a Western house, with one tatami room. Also I want a car for the family, and a sports car for me. And the last thing: I want to become skinnier, a little."

Shunsuke had just described a lifestyle impossible to sustain on a mere accountant's salary. "It will be difficult," he admitted, dismissing the thought as quickly as he entertained it. "I also want to be able to afford to go to the Super Bowl every year in the United States. And after that I want to see the Pro Bowl."

I knew that Shunsuke's grades were a sore point with Mariko, and he acknowledged that they had dropped. It was a new situation for him, since he had always been at the top of his class. "When I was in junior high school, I was tenth in a class of ninety-seven," he said.

"Fifth," Mariko corrected.

He was now in the bottom ten out of the fifty in his class at Waseda. Mr. Kojima had spoken to him about his poor performance, to no avail. Shunsuke said that his courses had become more difficult and that he was not studying enough. "I've never really studied, except the night before the exam," he explained. "But that doesn't work anymore."

It was getting late, but I had one more question, about the upcoming fiftieth anniversary of Pearl Harbor and the newly revived debate about whether schoolbooks whitewashed the history of Japan's aggression. Shunsuke's world history text contained one sentence about the Pearl Harbor attack. I was curious to know how much he had absorbed from Mr. Kojima's lecture on the subject two months earlier, so I asked him now what he thought led to the war.

"There was the Pearl Harbor attack in 1941," he said, then fast-forwarded six years to the American Occupation. "Japanese chased after chocolate bars given out by the American troops. It was a bad scene."

I asked him again why he thought the war started. "When a country gets very strong, it has the desire to take over a weaker country," he said. "Japan misunderstood its power and picked a fight with the United States. It was stupid."

He then had a question for me: "Is it true that the reason for the Persian Gulf War is that America wanted to revive its military industry?" Shunsuke had watched the top-rated show *News Station* every night during the Gulf War the year before and had been fascinated by the host's diatribes against the United States. I sidestepped Shunsuke's question, telling him that Americans generally supported the war, although many had been critical.

"Maybe America doesn't know about the terribleness of war because your mainland has never been attacked," he said. I was happy to see he was now at least in a feisty mood.

A few days after Sachiko and I met Takeshi at his office, he arrived home well after midnight "half drunk," in the words of Mariko. Years of experience had taught her that he had two kinds of drunks, cheerful and arrogant, and as she lay on the futon she wondered which it would be. But when he walked into the room, Mariko noticed with some alarm that he was neither. Instead he seemed unusually tired and depressed.

"I'm a failure," he told her. "It's not good for you to be with me."

Mariko, taken aback, said nothing. "But I thought to myself, This is going to be very bad," she told me later. Preparing to listen to his story, she told him to come to bed, and surprisingly, without argument, he lay down next to her on the futon.

"I don't have any reason to work," he said quietly. "I want to be free from everything. I want to cut off my life."

Mariko's body went cold. Incredibly, it sounded as if he wanted to kill himself. Was he really that depressed? He had been complaining about work more than usual the past few weeks, but she had been too busy to pay much attention. Now she was scared.

"Tell me what the problem is," she said softly.

So Takeshi began to talk about Kawasaki, about his frustrations, about how he went to the office but had no job. For the first time in years, Mariko listened intently. It was rare for a man like Takeshi to unburden his soul like this. Mariko found herself asking real questions about his projects and the people at his office, trying to be a partner who understood his worries and fears. Takeshi, savoring his wife's sudden attention, talked for an hour, until close to two in the morning.

"You're not really thinking about committing suicide, are you?" Mariko asked.

He started to laugh. "How can you think that way?"

"I was shocked by what you said," Mariko answered. She was exhausted now. "If you're tired, let's go to sleep."

He agreed. Mariko told me later she thought her listening to all his troubles had been good for him.

"Even if you have lots of problems," she told him before dropping off, "you still have to move forward in life."

"You're very strong," Takeshi sighed, resigned.

I did not learn of this conversation until ten days later, in early November. By then the crisis had eased and Mariko seemed only mildly worried. But I wondered how much of a role Sachiko and I might have played in bringing Takeshi to talk so intimately to his wife. Whatever the case, I didn't say anything to Mariko, who, I think, viewed Takeshi's confessions as the natural progression of his mounting problems. "For years he has complained about his low salary," she said. "He'll tell me, 'I don't want to be an electrical engineer, and I want to quit.'" Mariko typically tried to find something positive to say, like suggesting that he take an examination for an additional certification, and higher salary, as an electrician. "Maybe you should get the book for the exam and study," she would say.

And Takeshi, in his typical fashion, always brushed her off. "I'm not a person who makes efforts," he would say.

Mariko sighed. "It's true," she told me. "Whenever a job is there, he does it. But he is not a self-starter."

He never had been. Back in high school it was Mariko who pulled Takeshi's hand when their bus was late to make sure he got to class on time, and the pattern never changed. "But these days I don't have the same maternal instinct toward him," she complained. "I'm too busy. And he's forty-four. He shouldn't have to depend on me."

The night before, Takeshi had again come home late, at one A.M., drunk and morose. He started to complain about work. "Again?" Mariko asked with impatience. It was the first cold night of the season, and Takeshi did cheer up a little when he saw that Mariko had assembled the *kotatsu*, the table heater, in the living room. "It made him feel that I was concerned about the family and the household," she said. "He really doesn't appreciate what I do for this family."

From what I could see, Mariko did everything, and I told her so. "But he thinks that is the normal obligation for a housewife," she said. "He thinks it's natural that I do these things. That's the problem." On the other hand, she felt he was less critical of her than in the past. Right now, for example, she was in the middle of changing the closets from summer to winter clothes, and everything was out on the floor. A few years ago he had yelled about the mess, but not now. To Mariko, this was a real improvement.

At this point Sachiko took the conversation in a different direction. "Mariko's husband is known for being very feudalistic,"

Sachiko offered, in English. "When he was younger, he was very popular outside the house." I caught her drift.

"He had a girlfriend?" I asked Mariko.

"Of course," she said, surprised that I needed to ask.

She told me then about the woman he had seen seven years before. The woman worked in the bar where Takeshi stopped on his way home from work—just a friend, he told Mariko. Mariko didn't completely believe him but was too distracted by the demands of three children and her part-time work to pay more attention. Occasionally he would drop hints, as if he wanted her to know. "I went to a movie," he would say. "With who?" she would ask. He wouldn't answer, but later he would drop other hints—taunts, really. "I took a taxi and someone put a head on my shoulder," he once told her. "Who put a head on your shoulder?" Mariko demanded. Again there was no answer, and no confrontation, as if neither of the two cared enough to fight. They simply retreated silently into separate worlds.

But one day, when Mariko was in what she described as a foul mood, she looked through her husband's datebook. And there it was, the woman's name and telephone number. Mariko snapped. "Around that time I was very tired physically, and also very tired of not having enough money," she said. "I became very emotional. I asked him, 'What are you thinking when you do something like this?' He couldn't answer. One day, I even called his office, crying, and asked him to please come back early."

Mariko said Takeshi's relationship eventually ended when the woman moved away some months later. The crisis was over, and Mariko and Takeshi fell back into routine. Mariko was detached and casual as she recounted the events. She seemed to have made peace with at least this disappointment in her marriage, and viewed Takeshi's transgression, however painful at the time, as the normal behavior of a Japanese husband.

To a large degree it was. Before World War II, Japanese wives were for procreation and mistresses for pleasure; society admired a man rich enough to maintain a long-term relationship with an expensive geisha, provided he handled his affair with propriety and discretion. Things have changed some in modern Japan, but not as much as might be expected. When Prime Minister Sosuke Uno was forced to resign in 1989 after his relationship with a geisha became public, most Japanese were more offended by the geisha's description of Uno's loutish treatment of her than by the affair itself. A visit to a prostitute is still considered a male prerogative, and longer-term extramarital affairs are commonplace. Surveys show that most Japanese men and women do not regard sexual fidelity as crucial to a good marriage and that one in six Japanese wives has had extramarital sex; for those wives born before 1945, the rate is one in four. *More*, the respected women's magazine, found in 1989 that of 1,400 married women, 30 percent said they had "boyfriends," which in most cases meant lovers.

Certainly Mariko understood the temptations facing her husband. "If I see an attractive man, I feel the same way," she said. "But the difference is whether I'll take any action. I don't mind if he is attracted by a woman. But I do worry about it. If he starts seeing someone else, he's the kind of person who will take it seriously and fall in love."

Mariko always surprised me a little with how bluntly she complained about her husband. Once, when I asked if she thought she had made a mistake in marrying him, she so clearly understood my question, and was so eager to answer, that she gave me an emphatic "Yes!" before Sachiko had time to translate. Another day she complained that her husband always wanted to make love, but she had long since lost interest in him. They had sex once a month, Mariko said, if she was in the mood. "It's based on my cycle, like an animal," she said. "It has nothing to do with love." About the only good thing she had to say about Takeshi was that he brought his whole salary home, although from time to time she did tell me he was "very kind."

Eventually I came to see that Mariko was fairly typical in her criticisms of Takeshi. Once, when I was describing my work on this book to two Japanese married women who were friends of mine, I asked if they thought it unusual that a wife was so open about her problems. "But that's normal—we all talk about our husbands like that," one said, referring to conversations among close women friends. I was beginning to learn how different the Japanese view of marriage is from that of Americans. While the family is sacrosanct in Japan, the relationship between husband and wife is not. Wives of Mariko's generation often say that a good relationship should be "like air"—vital but scarcely noticeable. Marriage is not something to work at or worry about. Marriage is for children, for security, for settling into a proper niche in society. By and large it is not for romance or even much emotional intimacy. In her book *The Japanese Woman*, Sumiko Iwao underscores the differences by calling Japanese marriage a "rather cool, practical relationship" in which the "verbal expression of feelings of affection or attachment is practically taboo." She is describing the reluctance of the Japanese to express feelings, especially innermost ones, in marriage—a trait that goes beyond marriage, she might have added. But Iwao argues that this kind of marriage is actually liberating because it lets couples relax and "tacitly and effortlessly" depend on each other free of the formal rituals of other Japanese relationships. Iwao does admit that the relationship between a Japanese husband and wife "is almost too distant," but she then contrasts this with her observation that relationships between husbands and wives in the United States "may be too close." In her view, American couples invest too much in marriage, wanting to "know and understand what the other is thinking, feeling, and doing—*all the time.*" Such intimacy, she says, can breed tension, stress, and exhaustion. Iwao can never resist a good swipe at American social problems, but she does make a good point about the unrealistic expectations many Americans have for marriage. Certainly her views about American obsessions with sharing and intimacy are consistent with what I heard from other Japanese. One married woman I know told me that Japanese women are stronger because they don't have to hear "I love you" from their husbands all the time.

To me it always seemed that Japanese husbands and wives were simply making a virtue of marital detachment. How many spouses would choose lack of intimacy in a marriage as a kind of ideal? Perhaps on some levels it was liberating, much like an arrangement between an American husband and wife who have agreed to go their own ways, but to me it sounded lonely, a denial of passion and life. Yet lonely or not, most Japanese couples do lead independent lives, like Mariko and Takeshi. Women are said to find their emotional intimacy with long-time friends in their neighborhoods, men with colleagues at the office.

Like most young Japanese women, Mariko did harbor some romantic notions as a newlywed, and luxuriated for a time in the fantasy of being a Japanese wife who flawlessly served her husband tea or handed him his underwear as he stepped out of the bath. "When I first got married, it was very fresh for me," she said. "There were so many things I didn't see. I thought, I will follow him. It was very different from the idea of equal marriage in the United States. We've always been told to follow three steps behind." When Takeshi came home in those days, Mariko would even kneel and put three fingers on the floor as she bowed, the traditional, submissive welcome of a wife for her husband.

She was soon disillusioned. The first year of her marriage, she said, was by far the worst. Takeshi was starting out at Nippon Electric, and there was very little money. The two took a tiny Ichomachi apartment without a bath, not unusual at the time, and had to wash at Takeshi's elder brother's house nearby. They could have used the public bath, a pleasant place of neighborhood gossip, but turning down Takeshi's brother's invitation would have been rude. Worse than the lack of privacy was Takeshi's drinking, which was actually heavier in those days. "It was a very hard time," Mariko said. "He was twenty-four and he could drink a lot. Whenever he was invited for drinking, he'd go. Before we got married, he wasn't a bad drinker. He was a happy drinker. But he changed."

Even given the low expectations of Japanese couples, I wondered sometimes how Mariko had come to terms with her marriage. Her separate existence from Takeshi freed her, it was true, but I could not understand how Mariko—or any woman in Japan, for that matter—was supposedly so accepting of the kind of remote marriage that Sumiko Iwao described as the norm. Western revisionist historians and journalists often write of the Japanese as culturally almost alien, with thinking processes and feelings unlike our own, but I learned something different. I came to see that Mariko was human in a universal way, and that she had longings for intimacy and hopes for her family like anyone else. Now, on this cold November day, as we finished up another interview in her living room, I asked why she put up with it all.

"What else can I do?" she answered, frustrated. "Can you tell me? Divorce is impossible. I really care about myself. I don't want to break up my life. I have established my position in this neighborhood, and if I got divorced, I would have to start from the very beginning. I would have to change everything. And even though I don't like my parents so much, I wouldn't want to upset them with a divorce."

"Have you thought about divorce?" I asked.

"Many, many times," she said.

"What would your ideal life be?" I asked.

"I want a husband who respects me," she said. "I want our children to have a spirit of independence. And in a job, I want to be able to use my ability." Her dream was to study when Ken-chan was old enough—she had already bought a book—and become a travel agent.

And what of her husband?

"I don't want to be with him," she said. "If he won't change his inflexible attitude—yes, I don't want to be with him." Like everyone else, Mariko was reading the stories in the newspapers about the small but increasing number of Japanese women divorcing after decades of marriage. With their children grown, they could no longer face living alone with their retired salariman husbands for the rest of their lives. "There are so many women getting divorced after twenty or thirty years," Mariko said. "Finally these women will be freed."

A little more than a week later, nine months after I started my project with Mariko, I learned for the first time that my presence in her life was causing talk in the neighborhood. Mariko didn't seem too upset, and in fact I think she saw our interviews—and the inevitable gossip—as part of her growing independence. The subject came up when I asked Mariko about the magazine, *Croissant*, that she had bought in Asakusa a few months before. The copy was still in a corner of the living room, and I knew Mariko had by now read the article, "I Can't Be Someone Who Is Loved by Everybody," that had caught her eye. The story was obviously aimed at Japanese women like Mariko who had been raised to please, and I asked her if she saw herself as such a person—a woman who could not be loved by everybody.

"I've thought about that all my life," Mariko said. "I'm always regretting what I said, and worried about what people think of what I've said."

I assumed she was talking about the kind of directness that from time to time annoyed her friends, yet Mariko took a different tack.

"For example, in our case, in these interviews, people might not understand why I am doing this," she said. "People are puzzled.

They might find it a little strange to do this kind of interview. But when I accepted your proposal, I thought it would be nice to recall my memories. I decided that I didn't care what people said, because it was a good way for me to open myself up. Some people said, 'Why is it good for you to reveal the secrets of your life that way?' Everyone has an opinion." Mariko didn't elaborate who such people were, but I assumed she meant her husband and friends in Ichomachi. "In my mind," she concluded, "I know that I cannot be a person loved by everybody."

The article, written in the patronizing style of the traditional Japanese women's magazine, consisted of ten profiles of successful women who had ignored the restraints of Japanese society and bulldozed ahead. *Croissant*, despite its tone and its strange name (the French was thought to add sophistication), did contain some relatively serious articles. Mariko, I thought, probably looked on the characters in this particular story as role models.

The best-known woman among them was an academic, Keiko Higuchi, a professor in the school of literature of Tokyo Kasei University, who had become a ubiquitous television commentator on women's issues and was the author of a book about raising children without gender stereotypes. She offered this advice to women speaking out against the system: "You will need a support group whose members will lend an ear. Your ideas need a place to be forged and polished. And you must believe that facing the biting head wind is the spice of life."

Another woman featured was Kuniko Tanioka, the president of Chukyo Women's University. Tanioka, who was single, had had a baby, which caused much comment in the press, focusing on her refusal to have an abortion or give up her child. Instead, she raised the child on her own.

There were also profiles of an antiwar cartoonist, a poet, and a lawyer, Mizuho Fukushima, who was working to change the law requiring Japanese women to adopt the surnames of their husbands.

"No matter what people say, if you yourself are satisfied, then fine," Fukushima said. "You shouldn't fear the public eye and worry that people are going to gang up on you."

Another woman, Yoshiko Tsujimoto, was the founder of an unusual Osaka consumer organization that handled grievances from people about their medical care. Japanese doctors are treated as omnipotent and malpractice suits against them are rare, but Tsujimoto, in a bit of radical advice, told patients to shop like consumers for the best medical services they could find. "I was once the good wife and wise mother who deserved to be awarded a medal," Tsujimoto said, explaining that in the old days she had baked her own bread and made handknit sweaters. "I was so attuned to the needs of my husband that I knew immediately what he wanted long before he finished speaking." It was no wonder, then, that her husband did not speak to her for three months when she moved to Osaka for her job, leaving him behind in Tokyo with two sons. But she came back on weekends and the family adjusted, and after six months her husband told her he would no longer complain. "I think what I do is a good reason for my husband to divorce me," Tsujimoto admitted. "He never expected I would be so determined to leave the family behind."

As it turned out, Mariko did not identify with these women at all. She saw them, I think, as aberrations, and they reminded her of her own obligations to her family, and how traditional she actually was. Although she liked Tsujimoto of the consumer organization because she seemed to respect her husband—and was on the side of the patient—the other women were another story.

"They're too far out for me, and too headstrong," Mariko said. "All these women are too free. They're living too much the way they want. They're too selfish, and they don't care about the people around them. Sometimes I'd like to change my life too, but I don't because of my family. If I wanted to be like one of those women, I'd have been out of here a long time ago."

9

THE GINGKO TREES

Mochi making

DECEMBER

The department stores of Ginza were packed on the first Saturday in December with holiday shoppers buying such treats as smoked Scottish salmon, imported $300 honey-cured hams, and thin silver bracelets nestled in baby-blue boxes from the Tokyo emporium of Tiffany. It was the day of Mariko's big samisen performance, and as I made my way through the festive sidewalk crowds toward the Ginza concert hall where she was to play, I found myself on the front lines of Japan's year-end gift-giving frenzy. The Japanese exchange presents during two seasons, winter and summer, complaining each time that *this* year the gift-giving has finally gotten out of hand. Families give dozens of presents to friends and business associates, largely because they must reciprocate for every one they receive. Some people are known to buy extra refrigators to store all the steaks and muskmelons delivered to their doorsteps. Paralyzed by fear that someone might actually give them something without receiving a comparable gift in return, the Japanese are unable to stop a buildup that always struck me as a kind of benign nuclear arms race. Christmas was coming, too, and although a Shinto and Buddhist nation did not celebrate it as a religious event, in recent years the imported holiday had become still another opportunity to shop—particularly for romantic gifts for young lovers, as it was the fashion when I was in Tokyo to designate Christmas Eve as the ideal night for assignations in expensive hotels.

On my way through the streets I passed several Santa Clauses, a nearly elephant-sized Babar promoting his books, and numerous expensively dressed women picking at French pastries at tea salons. The day was clear, crisp, and gorgeous, a jewel of the winter season. The huge Mitsukoshi department store banner, advertising the Christmas items inside, flapped importantly in the breeze, while down the street the Itoya stationery shop was doing a brisk business in New Year's greeting cards. Millions of such cards are sent throughout Japan at the end of December. Itoya sold beautiful Christmas cards, too, including the ones I could never resist, with the Kabuki actors in scarlet and gold finery. (The Japanese tended to select those with snow scenes from Vermont.) I admit I was more enticed than repelled by all the consumption and the earnestness of the buying. Shopping seemed nothing less than the Japanese national pastime.

Mariko's concert was at the regrettably named Gas Hall, pronounced Gas-u Hor-u—its benefactor was a utility. Situated close to the Matsuzakaya department store, it was a handsome space with some two hundred seats, about half of them occupied by friends and family of the performers. Mariko had two old pals from high school in the audience, as well as three colleagues from meter reading, but no one in her family was there. The kids were in school for their Saturday half day, and Mariko had not bothered to ask Takeshi, who was not a big fan of samisen music. The only time she had ever invited him to a concert was two years before, when she had performed at the Kokuritsu Gekijo, Tokyo's prestigious National Theater. "Once he came, he enjoyed it," she said. "But he really doesn't like that kind of thing."

At 1:15 P.M. the curtain rose, revealing fifteen somber men and women kneeling in kimono on a bare stage. The musicians were in two rows, seven in front, eight in back; behind them were two golden folding screens gleaming under the lights. I picked out Mariko in the back, fourth from the left, in a dusty-pink-and-mauve kimono. Near her was a striking young woman in a sea-green-and-turquoise kimono—an authentic geisha, Mariko told me later. Mariko's samisen teacher, her aunt, was also playing, as was one of the women who had gone with us to the karaoke box the past summer. I smiled now to think of that beery afternoon of cigarette smoke and trashy love songs. Here they all were in their kimono with their eyes cast down, looking serious, grave, and modest—and so Japanese.

The musicians turned together to their samisen, and soon the metallic, twanging music filled the hall. It was a selection from the Kabuki play *Kanjincho*, or *The Subscription Scroll*—the same piece I had heard Mariko's class practice the previous May. The music was as wistful and sad as before, but this time I recognized small parts of it and broke into applause with the rest of the audience after one particularly beautiful passage. Halfway through, Mariko had a short solo, about thirty seconds long. She seemed to do well, and I thought as I looked at her face that I had never seen it more serious and focused. She told me later she was nervous before the concert, but as she started to play the familiar passage from *Kanjincho*, her concentration elevated her into a trancelike calm. "I loved the tension of the stage," she said afterward. "It's hard to explain, but the sound of playing onstage is entirely different from the sound of practicing."

It was around this time that I realized I had never seen Mariko in a kimono, the traditional, formal robe of Japan, which is tied at the waist with a wide sash called an obi. Not only did she look different, she seemed to have transformed herself into a person I didn't know. Like most Japanese women, she wore a kimono only a few times a year, for weddings, holidays, or samisen concerts, always aware that it changed her manner and the atmosphere around her. "I feel like a very quiet woman," she said. "The kimono is feminine. I have to move differently in it, and I feel less casual. When I wear a kimono, I'm in a different world. Actually, I feel unreal, and warm. The time goes very slowly."

Mariko's aunt had given her the kimono as a gift a few days before the concert. The aunt knew that money was tight for Mariko, and Mariko was indeed relieved not to have to spend twenty-five hundred dollars on a new hand-dyed silk kimono suitable for a concert. (Kimono are a major investment, and many cost much more than twenty-five hundred dollars; brides rent wedding kimono for as much as one thousand dollars a day.) The only problem was that the kimono was too big to take home on her bicycle, so Mariko had had to ask Takeshi to drive her over to her aunt's house in his company car. The trip prompted an uncomfortable conversation about the extravagance of Mariko's samisen lessons and concert fees.

"Did you give money to your aunt for this kimono?" he asked on the way home.

"I think she used the money from the fees I paid her," Mariko responded.

It was more or less true that there was no extra payment for the kimono, but Mariko didn't elaborate. The less Takeshi knew, the better. In fact, the fees that Mariko had to pay for the Ginza concert came to twelve hundred dollars. The total included a gratuity to her aunt as the teacher, plus a portion of the cost of the stage rental. Mariko explained to me that since admission to the concert was free, there would be no way to defray expenses from ticket sales. "Our group is not good enough to charge money for tickets," she said. The gratuity to the teacher was traditional. "We would never make it without her," Mariko explained. "The teacher is like a god." All the fees were on top of the twenty-five hundred dollars Mariko spent each year on lessons alone.

In any case, it turned out that Takeshi was less interested in the cost than Mariko had feared. Changing the subject, he had turned solicitous and asked her, perhaps out of guilt over his own inattentiveness, if she would wear a kimono more often if he bought her one. "If you were to wear a kimono all the time, like your aunt, very neatly, I'd be happy to get one for you," he said.

Perhaps he meant to sound conciliatory, but Mariko grew irritated listening to him, and she wondered how he could say something so . . . well . . . out of it. What century was he living in? Did he have any idea of how hard it was to move around in a kimono? She suspected that he even enjoyed the idea of her wrapped up like an immovable doll.

"I can't do it," she had said curtly, cutting him off.

Mariko's solo was followed by a much longer solo by the geisha, who played the samisen as part of the entertainment she provided at the private restaurants of Tokyo's business and political elite. Geisha are a dying breed—there are only about a thousand left in Tokyo—and few modern ones study the samisen at all. Those who do play the instrument take pride in keeping up the rigorous traditions of a profession that emphasizes arts and performance, not sexual favors. Serious geisha serve as hostesses in a handful of private restaurants in town, where they engage in flirtatious conversations and sing and dance for the wealthy clientele. In spite of their image, serious geisha are not prostitutes, and although affairs with longtime customers are always possible, they occur only after elaborate and expensive courtships that none but the richest men in Japan can afford.

After the concert, I went backstage to congratulate Mariko. She was flushed and happy, with beads of perspiration glistening on the small triangle of throat that the high V-neck of her kimono laid bare. Her friends surrounded her with gifts and flowers, fussing and cooing. Mariko introduced me to one of her high school friends, then excitedly pointed out the pretty geisha. She was wearing ordinary makeup, not the traditional geisha whiteface and lacquered wig, but her presence had added a touch of glamour and prestige to the event.

Relief swept over Mariko after the concert. She stayed for a few more hours to hear some other students play, then headed home by subway. She reached the house at six, in time to serve dinner. Her husband wasn't home, and her children didn't even ask about her concert. But Mariko hardly expected questions—the concert was another of the private moments she did not share with her family—and in any case she was on too much of a high to care.

Three days later, I reached a turning point in my understanding of what I came to think of later as the mystery of the gingko trees cut down at the Ichomachi shrine. I also began to understand a bit more about Mariko and her relationship to her community. The improbable setting for my education was a fractious meeting of the so-called action committee of the Ichomachi Elementary School PTA on Tuesday, December 10. There I first came across two women, both strong personalities, who were on opposite sides of a set of conflicts whose levels of emotion, suspicion, and complexity surprised me. Anyone who called Japan a harmonious society clearly had not met the good women of the Ichomachi PTA.

Everything began innocuously enough at 2:15 P.M., when Mrs. Yoko Mori, the president of the PTA, a tall, elegant woman with excellent posture, called the gathering to order. Mrs. Mori was dressed in the usual conservative suit, and Mariko spoke of her with the respect befitting her status at the PTA and as an important person in the community. Mrs. Mori, it turned out, was also the wife of the priest of the Ichomachi shrine.

"I welcome everyone to the last meeting of 1991," she said in a formal tone that reminded everyone that the PTA was serious business. Mrs. Mori was seated behind a table at the front of a classroom, flanked by the members of her board. The other members of the action committee—the culture representative, the public relations representative, the classroom representatives, some twenty-five in all—sat at student desks arranged in a horseshoe facing the board. Mariko was there as a member of the Bellmark committee, the source of the controversy. Most of the mothers (there was not a father in sight) wore nearly identical knee-length gray or brown wool A-line skirts, although a few were in jeans. One woman stood out, however, because she was wearing a pea-green sweatshirt that said, in English, "Nukes No Thanks!" on the back. Wrapped around her hair, like a small turban, was a green, yellow, and purple paisley scarf from India. There was something of the aggressive nonconformist about her, and sure enough, Sachiko pointed her out as the troublemaker of the group.

After the chairwoman's greetings, Mariko got up and introduced Sachiko and me, elaborately apologizing to everyone for the inconvenience of our presence at the back of the room. Everyone inspected us, then smiled tautly. We smiled weakly back. Sachiko, needless to say, was feeling self-conscious. She almost never went to PTA meetings and was grateful that her career as an interpreter had rescued her from such things; now here she was, trying to decipher what she viewed as the muddled ramblings of housewives in the middle of the afternoon. "I'm allergic to these meetings," she said.

The first order of business was a report from the Ichomachi assistant principal, who told everyone that a building employee had quit because of ill health, and also that a thief had been arrested for stealing five hundred dollars from the school. Neither announcement elicited much reaction. In other news, the assistant principal announced that a disabled child at the school needed help climbing the stairs. He reported that the school had a new jungle gym but no money for a sandbox, and that several children had broken bones in recent bike accidents. "I want you to think about menus that make bones stronger," the assistant principal admonished the mothers, deftly shifting the blame onto them.

After this came a report from an action committee member about what other schools did about *shudan toko,* a system set up so students could walk to school together in groups. Mothers generally liked it, because it helped ensure that their children would not wander off, but its pros and cons were a matter of dispute. There was obvious safety in numbers, but some mothers thought crossing the streets in large groups was dangerous.

"We reviewed this system ten years ago, and decided to keep it," Mrs. Mori observed.

The proceedings continued to crawl along at a Zen-like pace. PTA meetings were always held during the day, although there had been talk of switching to seven in the evening to accommodate working mothers. But since fathers were never home that early, who would look after the children while the mothers were at the meetings? Baby-sitters were scarce and expensive, so in the end, the idea of evening meetings was rejected. PTAs were introduced after the war, when the U.S. Occupation authorities imposed American practices on Japan in the hope that a more democratic participation by parents would serve as a counterweight to the education bureaucracy. Four decades after the Occupation, the PTA was still referred to by its American name. To me the Ichomachi meetings seemed to be from a bygone era. Even Mariko, a big PTA supporter, was irritated by the time it took to make and receive "chain calls" passing on news of board meetings and announcements of films to be shown at the school. Such bulletins were almost always included in the papers the students brought home, but the mothers were expected to make the calls anyway, invariably during the early-evening chaos of trying to get hungry and irritable children bathed and fed.

At 2:45 P.M., the women reached the agenda item that was causing all the fuss, and an anticipatory hush seemed to settle on the classroom. A woman stood up near Mariko. "The Bellmark committee wants to buy one unicycle and one unicycle stand," she said quickly. "Please clap to show your approval."

I had learned from Mariko that Bellmark was the name of a company that put a small logo, a bell, on products such as Kewpie mayonnaise, Fuji film, and an array of junk food. Consumers cut out the little bells, collected them, and sent them in for prizes, much as Americans used to do with S&H Green Stamps in the 1950s and 1960s. Collecting Bellmark logos was a big activity for PTAs in Japan, and the Bellmark company was aware of it. Over the years, the members of the Ichomachi PTA had pooled enough Bellmark emblems to buy the school five unicycles, difficult to learn to ride but popular among the Ichomachi students. Saving them was a minor nuisance, but Mariko and most others felt it was an excellent example of the importance of thriftiness. As a member of the Bellmark committee, she had proposed the previous July that the PTA buy a sixth unicycle and a stand for all the unicycles with its latest collection. The matter was approved, or so she thought.

But at the November meeting, one month before the one I was attending, a member of the action committee forcefully objected. She called Bellmark awards a dubious bargain that forced up the prices of foods with Bellmark emblems, and she charged that Bellmark foods contained harmful chemical additives. She also said it was not the job of the PTA to meet the students' needs; the ward, which collected taxes, should bear the responsibility. Mariko was so stunned by the hostile presentation that she initially didn't know what to say. The action committee chairman, anxious to make peace, did what she always did in a PTA crisis, which was to table the issue until the next meeting.

When Mariko told me about the controversy afterward, she described the Bellmark objector, Yumiko Sato, as a notorious malcontent who sat on school groups like the action committee and did little but complain. Then Mariko told me something more interesting: Mrs. Sato was also a leader of the protest against cutting down the trees at the Ichomachi shrine, and was one of those who had helped collect eight thousand signatures nationwide. I remembered that Mariko found the protesters too aggressive, even if she agreed with them in principle, and now I could see that the Bellmark matter had made her react strongly. I understood why Mariko felt the way she did, but Mrs. Sato was beginning to intrigue me. Protesters of any kind are rare in Japanese society, and I wondered if Mrs. Sato could be as insufferable a woman as Mariko seemed to think. In any case, Mariko knew that something had to be done to deal with Mrs. Sato before the next meeting. She picked up her phone and called the members of the Bellmark committee to make sure they were all on the same side—the side of the unicycle.

Now, here at the December meeting, the members seemed not to be discussing Bellmark at all. As instructed by the Bellmark committee representative, the women clapped to show their approval of the unicycle purchase.

"So we have decided to buy one unicycle and one stand," the representative said. That was it. The matter had been decided in fifteen seconds.

And yet, all eyes moved silently in the direction of the woman in the "Nukes No Thanks!" sweatshirt—Mrs. Sato, of course, the agitator Sachiko had pointed out to me at the beginning of the meeting. To my disappointment, she sat silent.

A board member at the front of the room spoke up. "If anyone has any questions about Bellmark, please let us know," she said.

She did not look directly at Mrs. Sato, but everyone knew who she meant.

Mrs. Sato and two friends seated beside her began murmuring among themselves.

The board member tried again, making a painstaking effort to solicit every possible point of view. "Are there any questions about Bellmark? If something is not clear, please let us know. Is there anything else anyone would like to raise? Any other topic?"

Mrs. Sato said nothing, and an uncomfortable silence hung over the room. I was a little mystified by the board member's comments; it seemed to me that she was needlessly inviting more second-guessing.

Finally, a woman in blue jeans broke in with a banal digression. "The mothers' volleyball team used to be enjoyable," she said, "but now it has become so competitive."

No one seemed perturbed by this irrelevant comment, which provoked a halfhearted discussion. "We've never thought we had to win," a woman in a green sweater commented.

Then the talk turned to the cherry blossom festival scheduled for Ichomachi the following spring. The assistant principal said the school would participate because it was a community event, and a board member said the PTA would lend its support.

Suddenly it was three o'clock, and the room filled with the sounds of school letting out. Kids could be heard running and screaming in the halls. Just as I was wondering whether anything would come of the issue of the logos, Mrs. Sato spoke up.

"I am very confused," she said, angrily letting loose what were obviously pent-up thoughts. "The way you have made the decisions about Bellmark and the cherry blossom festival is very confusing. This meeting should be a place for us to exchange opinions. But the Bellmark issue was already decided before the meeting began. The cherry blossom festival was decided the same way. Everything has already been determined in advance by you. This action committee is so bad."

A member of the board spoke up. "We didn't decide in advance about the unicycle," she told Mrs. Sato. "The membership clapped and approved it."

"But it seems like everything was already decided," Mrs. Sato asserted again. "And I was going to make a proposal today."

"But we've already talked a lot about this," another board member pointed out.

Mariko, hearing her own work criticized, maintained a silence at first. Then she stood up, her face flushed. What I didn't realize at first was that the mere expression of dissent by Mrs. Sato had now torpedoed the decision that had just been impeccably approved with democratic clapping. Unaccountably, the issue had now been reopened. So there it was, right before my eyes, an example of Japan's great fear of discord. Mariko understood this too, but it did nothing to placate her. "I told everyone at the July meeting how I thought we should use Bellmark—and I thought you approved," she said forcefully. "We reached a consensus, and we made a big effort to collect Bellmark stamps. Now I have a complaint against all of you."

I knew Mariko was furious with Mrs. Sato, but I could tell she was also angry with the board for inviting Mrs. Sato to speak up after the case was closed.

Another board member sounded the toll. "We need to have another opportunity to talk about Bellmark," she said. "The point is—should we continue Bellmark itself?"

Amazingly, not only was the board caving in on the unicycle issue in the face of dissent, it was questioning whether Bellmark should be used at all. I glanced over at Mariko. She was sitting sternly with her arms folded across her chest.

"Bellmark is for us to buy something for the children," a woman said innocuously.

Mariko could take no more. "We have twenty-three unicycles at this school," she said. "We bought five of them with Bellmark. We need a stand for the unicycles. The school doesn't have a good one. And only one of our unicycles can be used by first- and second-grade students."

One of the board members turned to the assistant principal. "We have to have a new unicycle for next year," she said. "But we don't have the money from the ward. If we didn't get the unicycle through Bellmark, how would you get the money?"

The assistant principal responded with something vague and inconclusive.

Mrs. Sato continued to murmur with her minions and then brought up another matter entirely. "We need to create a better environment for disabled people," she said. "We only have one disabled student at the school, but there is the possibility of more."

"Can he walk by himself?" Mariko asked, her anger subsiding a little.

"Yes, he can," the assistant principal said. "But he has trouble on the stairs. The principal is working on it." He then excused himself to meet someone outside the room, no doubt relieved to make a getaway. The session quickly ended, leaving the momentous Bellmark issue up in the air once again—until the next meeting. Democracy Japanese-style had triumphed. I now knew that PTA meetings were susceptible to the same odd rules that have led to paralysis over legislation in the Japanese Parliament, even when there is a majority to pass it. Unanimous consent is something Japanese politicians on every level make every effort to achieve.

As the room cleared out, I went up to Mrs. Mori, the action committee chairperson, to ask her about Mrs. Sato's behavior. I expected a brush-off but instead Mrs. Mori responded with some relish.

"She's very touchy—and radical," she said. "She thinks everything about Japan is bad. And her husband is a Communist." I asked about Mrs. Sato's three friends, and Mrs. Mori gave me an ominous look. "They're Soka Gakkai," she said, referring to the lay organization based on Nichiren Buddhism that has become a major political force in contemporary Japan. Among other things, the group controls one of Japan's minor political parties.

It was obvious that there was something going on here besides the ordinary business of the Ichomachi PTA. Mrs. Mori, as the wife of the Shinto priest at the Ichomachi shrine, naturally looked upon a member of the Soka Gakkai Buddhist sect as a member of a fringe element with its own political agenda and ambitions. Their proclamations of idealism were not to be taken too seriously. I was determined to find out more, not only about Mrs. Sato but also about Mrs. Mori, who was figuring as an interesting force in the neighborhood. Like Mariko, Mrs. Mori was bound to resent Mrs. Sato not only for stirring up trouble at the PTA but also for helping to start the agitation in Ichomachi over the gingko trees.

I asked Mrs. Mori about Mrs. Sato's charges that the action committee made decisions, like the one about Bellmark, behind closed doors, and was startled to hear her acknowledge the truth in her claim. "Sometimes we agree with her opinions," Mrs. Mori answered. "But when she's too radical, we do get together before the meeting to decide how we will handle her." She smiled sweetly. I smiled back. Mrs. Sato had been on to something after all.

Three days after the meeting, on December 13, Mariko saw Mrs. Sato outside the school. Mariko tried to say something to her, but Mrs. Sato turned abruptly away.

"I was too amazed to be furious," Mariko said.

To me, the great Bellmark debate at the Ichomachi PTA was at first baffling because of the great passions vented over such minor stakes. But of course the stakes weren't small at all, as I came to learn. The PTA was merely a stage for acting out the deeper resentments and cleavages in the neighborhood, and if the fight hadn't been about Bellmark, it might well have been about something else. The most immediate battle was, of course, over the gingko trees and the future of the Ichomachi shrine, but the larger war was a conflict over differences in political beliefs and social class.

Looking at the geography of Ichomachi and the setting of the shrine was in itself telling. On the top of the neighborhood's highest hill lived Mrs. Mori, the PTA president, wife of the priest, and chatelaine of the shrine. Her house on the shrine grounds was in an aerie of moist woodland and cool breezes, protected from the summer sun and the noise down below. At the base of the hill was her tormentor Mrs. Sato, who lived in a cramped apartment that had a view, at least until recently, of the thirty gingko trees. Now her heart sank every time she looked out her window and saw the denuded hillside with the thirty dead trees piled up on the ground.

Mariko, like everyone else, inhabited the streets down below, but had never made common cause with Mrs. Sato. She thought her as odd as she was contentious, and disapproved of her rough, masculine way of speaking. (Mrs. Sato used neither the formal form of verbs nor the honorific *o* in front of nouns, both expected of women.) Mariko was especially puzzled by her head scarf, which Mrs. Sato changed daily to match her clothes. There was talk in the neighborhood that Mrs. Sato was bald, but Mariko had run into her one sweltering day without her scarf and saw that she had plenty of healthy shoulder-length hair. Simple, neat, perhaps a little eccentric, the scarf had become an irritant to the other women in the neighborhood over the years, a symbol of Mrs. Sato's insistence on remaining different. There is an old Japanese saying, "The nail that sticks up must be hammered down," that illustrates the Japanese discomfort with those who are different. The scarf, trivial as it was, also fed dark rumors that Mrs. Sato was part Korean, or was related to the Ainu, descendants of the people believed to be the original inhabitants of the Japanese islands. The Ainu are said to have lighter skins and more body hair than the average Japanese; certainly they are longtime victims of discrimination and are among the poorest minorities in Japan. Mrs. Sato told people she had no Ainu blood, but she seemed to take perverse pleasure in saying that she wished she did because she so admired the culture.

I was beginning to think of Mrs. Sato as a "resister," a word the author Norma Field applies to those Japanese who pay a heavy price for dissent. Field's 1992 book, *In the Realm of a Dying Emperor*, explores Japan through the lives of three extraordinary rebels—a supermarket owner who burned the Rising Sun flag as a symbol of Japan's militarist past; a widow who objected when her husband, a member of Japan's defense forces, was enshrined by the military as a god; and the mayor of Nagasaki, who set off a nationwide furor when he said Emperor Hirohito bore some responsibility for Japan's role in World War II. The three were treated as outcasts, and the mayor was shot in the chest outside the Nagasaki City Hall in an attack by a rightist. I admired them as noble symbols of dissent in a nation that has no obvious tyrant but nonetheless suppresses nonconformity in subtle ways. I happened to be reading the book when I first met Mrs. Sato, and although I had to agree with the other PTA women that she was a pest—and something of a knee-jerk iconoclast—I wondered nonetheless if I wouldn't find something admirable about her independence.

Meeting her was complicated, because I worried that Mariko would see my interest in Mrs. Sato as disloyalty. So I waited for tempers to cool after the PTA meeting and then casually mentioned to Mariko one day that I was curious about Mrs. Sato's background and the influences that had shaped her. Mariko seemed untroubled, and Sachiko called Mrs. Sato, whose only objection was that her children were too noisy and her apartment too much of a mess for an interview at home. We met instead, on two afternoons, at Sachiko's place, a small fourth-floor walk-up in one of Ichomachi's back streets. There we ate Napoleons from a nearby French bakery and drank too much coffee as warm sunshine poured in through the windows. In the cozy atmosphere of Sachiko's living room, Mrs. Sato, perhaps because she had my sympathetic ear, seemed more vulnerable than the parent who had vented her ire against the PTA.

"When I heard that people thought I was part Korean or Ainu, I felt they were looking down on me," she said softly. "It meant they didn't think of the Ainu or Koreans as human beings. At first, I cried. And when my two daughters went to kindergarten, I heard that people were criticizing my turban and the direct way I talk. I was so upset, because it was hurting my children. But I think the people who say, 'If you take off your turban I can be your friend'— well, they aren't real friends. The turban is an expression of my resistance."

"To what?" I asked.

"To all the Japanese who try to be the same. Everybody has a television set and a family computer. Everybody sends kids to cram school. If yellow is in fashion, everybody wears yellow."

Mrs. Sato told me she had a part-time job working to expand the membership for an organic-food cooperative. To me, it was appropriate that she was part of the mostly female army opposed to pesticides and food additives. But even such progressive causes are not free of the nation's oligarchic tendencies, Mrs. Sato said. "It's really a pyramid-shaped company," she explained. "Men are in authority. It's a scaled-down Japan." Mrs. Sato's activism was nonetheless more fulfilling to her than teaching cooking and corsage-making at home, her previous pursuits.

Her real love, of course, was trying to bring about social change. Her causes were the favorites of the Japanese left, and she was a regular at the weekend demonstrations at the big open plaza in Shibuya. The past February she had protested the Gulf War, and more recently she had marched against sending Japanese peace-keeping troops to Cambodia. She also marched with the Korean "comfort women" who had come forward with tales of their forced sexual service to Japanese troops in Korea in World War II, and who were now demanding reparations. And on the April anniversary of the Chernobyl disaster, she demonstrated against nuclear power plants.

There was little in her background to explain why Mrs. Sato became such an impassioned leftist, although she suggested it was because of her birth and upbringing in the northern island of Hokkaido. Mrs. Sato, the daughter of a civil servant, said that the Japanese of Hokkaido were forthright and open, and that she naturally absorbed the values of the frontier from them. But in the mid-1960s she moved to Tokyo to major in home economics at a junior college—"a school for princesses," she told me dismissively—and she watched the student riots on other Tokyo campuses from afar. "My friends were involved," she said. "I really admired them, but I couldn't do it. Maybe I was afraid." In recent years she had made up for that reticence with her activities in Ichomachi, where she told me she felt like a minority, not an outsider. She was grateful that her husband, a salariman for an engineering firm, supported her protest activities and stayed out of her way. "We don't concern ourselves with each other a lot," she said simply.

Getting down to the subject at hand, I asked Mrs. Sato why she objected so strongly to Bellmark. Collecting stamps for a good cause did seem old-fashioned, I commented, but how could it hurt? Mrs. Sato expanded on the argument she had made at the November meeting, that Bellmark was a scheme of the food industry to take advantage of naïve housewives. She argued that even if two yen (a few pennies) were given back to consumers through the Bellmark stamps, the industry had previously increased the price of the product by two yen or more. "So we pay school taxes, and we pay the higher cost of Bellmark products," she said, adding that she felt the authorities were placing too much pressure on the mothers to give gifts to the school. The previous November, she complained, the assistant principal said he would greatly appreciate a new unicycle for the fourth grade. "Why does the PTA have to buy it?" she asked. I thought she made a good point, though she was being a little doctrinaire in a case that was essentially harmless. PTAs are not revolutionary bodies. What was wrong with using the Bellmark money for something undeniably beneficial?

It was perhaps inevitable that Mariko and Mrs. Sato would be on different sides, or at least have different perspectives, when it came to the gingko trees. For one thing, Mariko lived far enough from the shrine so that she was not reminded daily, as Mrs. Sato was when she looked out her window, of the devastation of the chain saws. Mariko's life had not changed, but for more than six months now a large part of Mrs. Sato's activities had been defined by the gingkos. In May, Mrs. Sato recalled, she had been shocked to discover that they had been cut. By June, she and other protesters had moved with astonishing speed to collect their eight thousand signatures on a petition demanding that thirty new trees be planted. The demand was presented to the ward council and the protesters met with a council subcommittee in September. I assumed the matter was still up in the air, but I was intrigued by this rare case of an authentic neighborhood protest.

"More than a year ago, I saw a sign at the shrine saying that trees were going to be cut for a parking lot," she said. "But we weren't told which ones." When she and a few friends asked about it, they were informed that the shrine needed the income from the parking lot.

"We thought the shrine was something that belonged to the community, not just to the people who own it," Mrs. Sato said. "Our attitude initially was: 'How can we help you find a way to raise money without cutting down the trees?'" She and her friends suggested, for example, that the shrine ask for larger voluntary cash contributions, called *ujiko*, from local residents, who traditionally paid small amounts to ensure that the shrine's deity protected everyone from misfortune. In Ichomachi the payment was only eight dollars for a single-family home, forty dollars for Mrs. Sato's entire apartment building. The protesters thought residents would pay more without complaint, especially to save the trees. But the shrine leadership wanted a more reliable source of income, Mrs. Sato said. Half of the new parking lot was to be for shrine worshipers, the other half for people renting permanent spaces. The parking-lot scheme would no doubt prove lucrative in a city where monthly parking charges can run into thousands of dollars. In Tokyo, no one may buy a car until an inspector makes sure the purchaser has a place to park it off the street.

Mrs. Sato and her friends had three meetings in all with the shrine leadership, but they came to realize that the leadership was not going to back down. As time began to run out, Mrs. Sato and her group took their campaign public. A Communist Party newspaper ran an article taking the protesters' point of view; after the trees were cut, the mainstream establishment press and television news shows picked up the story. The residents of Ichomachi were, like Mariko, sorry and angry to see the trees go, but few actively joined in the protest once the gingkos were down.

"We have it in our culture that so many people think we should follow authority," Mrs. Sato said. "But we had to make our voices heard." She dismissed most of her neighbors, including Mariko, as politically naïve. "It was very hard for people who lived in Ichomachi to actually understand our movement," she said.

I wasn't sure I understood everything myself, but Mrs. Sato offered a new insight into the dispute when she said in passing that her campaign to save the trees was backed by Komeito, or the Clean Government Party, the political branch of the Buddhist sect Soka Gakkai, which has grown popular and powerful in the last half century. Now I saw some light. Shinto shrines, like Ichomachi, are generally tied to the conservative elite, usually including sup-

porters of the Liberal Democratic Party. I realized then that the battle over the trees was also a fight between temple and shrine and
the opposing political parties they backed—a local version, in fact,
of what was occurring in Japanese national politics. Clearly the tree
advocates' ties to a political party that shrine supporters disliked
escalated the conflict, but Mrs. Sato evidently felt it was worth it.
"I think having Komeito on our side really provoked the shrine
against us, but we needed help," she said. She said she was not a
member of Komeito but leaned toward the Socialists. Her husband,
she said, favored the Communists—which was just what Mrs.
Mori, the wife of the shrine priest, had told me at the PTA meeting.

The story of the trees took on still another dimension when Mrs.
Sato mentioned another character I had met before—Mr. Tanizaki,
the unofficial mayor of Ichomachi, and my host at the ward council
meeting. Armed with her petition, Mrs. Sato had gone to him for
help in blocking the parking lot. "We told him that if he supported
us, we would support him in the next election," Mrs. Sato said. "But
he said he was caught between two forces and didn't know what to
do." Unmoved by his predicament, Mrs. Sato left with the feeling
that he couldn't have cared less about her precious trees because of
his closeness with the shrine leadership and their allies. She even
suspected that he had operated behind the scenes to make sure the
trees were cut. Her allegation made me wonder why Mr. Tanizaki
had supported such an unpopular affront to the neighborhood. He
was a local stalwart of the Liberal Democratic Party, of course, but it
occurred to me that there had to be more to it than that. Sachiko and
I decided we would have to schedule another visit to Mr. Tanizaki.

First, though, we paid a call on Mrs. Mori, the PTA president,
up at the top of the hill, to hear her side of the story. She received
us for tea at her home, the large but creaky residence of the priest,
in a characterless Western-style sitting room obviously meant for
visitors. Down the old wooden hall were the family's private quarters, traditionally Japanese and far more interesting to me, with

their damp tatami mats, sliding doors with paper screens, and verdant views from the windows. By Japanese standards the place was enormous, but like the homes provided for diplomats, university presidents, and rectors in affluent parishes, Mrs. Mori's house had a slightly sterile, institutional feel.

Mrs. Mori was gracious and correct, very much in tune with her role in the house and the community. I did not have high hopes that much would come of our talk, other than comments about how hard all the lovely mothers were working to improve the school. But Mrs. Mori turned out to have a certain conspiratorial view of the world beneath her hilltop and saw the PTA and the gingkos as interconnected battlegrounds of the political and religious groups of the neighborhood. And no wonder. The trees were in fact the cause of a highly unpleasant anonymous phone call she had received some time back.

"A few months after the trees were cut, a woman called me up and didn't identify herself," she said. "She told me the shrine had created a big controversy with the trees, and she wanted to know when I would resign as PTA president. I asked, 'Who is this?' But the caller hung up."

Mrs. Mori did not have to think hard about the identity of the crank caller, of course. "Mrs. Sato and her group make trouble," she said, shaking her head and smiling stiffly. She noted that they were part of the small group of dissident Japanese who did not like to have the Rising Sun flag at the school's graduation ceremony, because of its lingering symbolism left over from World War II. "And they don't like to sing the national anthem," she said, referring to a song that many object to on the same grounds. As for the trees, Mrs. Mori said, there was no other choice. The shrine needed the money. "I didn't want to cut the trees, but it's done," she said, adding that the only thing the protest had accomplished was to prevent the gingkos from being carted away, stalling the parking lot. "We need to proceed," she said impatiently.

From Mrs. Mori's point of view, the main culprit in the tree controversy was Soka Gakkai. "This shrine is Shinto, and Soka Gakkai doesn't like Shinto," she said. She knew that Soka Gakkai, through the Komeito political party, had supported Mrs. Sato against the shrine. Even worse, she said darkly, was her strong belief that Soka Gakkai had actually infiltrated the PTA. She reminded me a little of an American parent worried that religious right-wingers were going to take over the school district.

"When I was the vice-chair for two years, the chair was a member of Soka Gakkai," she said. "I had a terrible time with her." Mrs. Mori proceeded to tell me that the Soka Gakkai chairwoman had committed the grave offense of privately suggesting to the school principal that the action committee should support the neighborhood cherry blossom festival. Soka Gakkai ran that festival, Mrs. Mori said ominously, and in order to pull people in, they offered free sake and popcorn. "It's not obvious that Soka Gakkai is involved, but it's true," she said.

Of that I had no doubt, although it was unclear to me why the cherry blossom festival, even with the supposed collusion of Soka Gakkai and the PTA, was such a malevolent event. Festivals, cherry blossoms, shrines, even gingko trees—they were all such benign, sentimental symbols of Japan, yet here in this little neighborhood they were the weapons in a seething power struggle. Perhaps, then, I should not have been surprised when I learned that the world of the decorous PTA president had been even darker than I had imagined. In a fit of reflection and confession, Mrs. Mori proceeded to tell some of the secrets of her life, including accounts of an unhappy marriage, depression, and eventual solace found in, of all places, the Ichomachi PTA.

Mrs. Mori's parents died when she was young. In addition, she stood five feet seven inches tall—a giantess in Japan—which made it hard to find a husband. Both factors contributed to the lateness of her arranged marriage, at the age of thirty-nine, to the priest, a widower with three children. "When we were introduced, I was told he had only one child," Mrs. Mori said pointedly. After a few dates she was startled to learn that there were in fact three offspring, and after more dates came the truly alarming news that her potential husband lived with his mother. At this late stage, however, Mrs. Mori felt it would be rude and unfair to break off the relationship. "So I got married," she said. "It was a big mistake."

She and the priest had two children of their own, but the pressures of her marriage and of living with her mother-in-law sent her into what she described as five years of near mental breakdown. She became dizzy in department stores, was nervous around people, and sometimes had difficulty breathing. A doctor prescribed tranquilizers, and she lived in seclusion. Then one day a friend who was a member of the action committee called her up and issued a draft notice for the PTA. "It seems you haven't done anything," said the friend, which was true. Backed into a corner, Mrs. Mori offered to be one of the treasurers—an easy job, she thought. But at the next meeting she was elected a vice-chair, and there was no looking back. The position forced her out of her house, and she found that she enjoyed people once again. Her mother-in-law died soon after, relieving some of the tension at home, and suddenly Mrs. Mori found herself running as president of the entire PTA. When she won, she knew the dark years were over.

"It was a big victory for me," she said.

I walked away a little dazed. The interview had started with Bellmark stamps and chopped-down gingko trees but had ended with the story of the collapsed marriage of one of the pillars of Ichomachi. I could not understand why Mrs. Mori should offer to a stranger the private details of her marriage, particularly since I told her I would be using her real name. (I changed my mind later and am using a different name to avoid embarrassing someone who had never before talked to a journalist.) As Sachiko and I left the grounds of the shrine, I thought about something Mariko had told me that fall. People in the neighborhood were talking about my interviews with her, she said, and were wondering why she was revealing her secrets. Did Mrs. Mori somehow think that she should tell me her secrets too? Or was she just happy to get something off her chest? Whatever the case, I was reminded that people are not always what they seem, and that even exemplary lives are rarely tidy in private.

On the night of December 25, Takeshi Tanaka never made it home. Christmas was not an issue—like most Japanese, the Tanakas hardly took note of it—but Mariko was once again upset and angry. When I saw her late the following afternoon, on December 26, Takeshi still hadn't surfaced. Mariko had last seen him at eight the morning before, when he left for work. She knew Takeshi had been paid on the twenty-fifth, and she suspected that he had stopped at a bar, then slept in his car. But not even a phone call? I asked why she wasn't worried that he had hurt himself in an accident.

"The police haven't called," she said curtly. "I'm tired of waiting for him." She told me then about some of the previous times he had pulled the same stunt. I, of course, remembered that night in June, on the banks of the Arakawa River. But now I learned that one night in October he hadn't come home at all and had eventually turned up the evening of the following day. Mariko thought it disgusting that he slept in his clothes and went to work without bathing, using only an electric shaver he kept in his car. But what could she do? His work was still going badly, and his unhappiness got the better of him from time to time. A month before, he had had a company health exam, and the results showed his liver was weak. Mariko knew from the experience of her younger brother what a weak liver could lead to, and she warned Takeshi to be careful. "We'll help you, but you really have to do it yourself," she told him, hoping sympathy would work better than anger.

As Mariko expected, Takeshi dragged himself home on the evening of the twenty-sixth, remorseful and exhausted. Mariko was over the worst of her ire, and there was no blowup, or at least none she told me about. In any case she was too busy preparing for the New Year's holidays to focus much on Takeshi. New Year's is the biggest holiday in Japan, a time when millions of Japanese visit shrines and temples to expunge all the bad fortune in the previous year and pray for good fortune in the new one. The holiday runs through the first week in January, when Tokyo weather is usually magnificently clear, cold, and bracing. Mariko's elder brother, the one who lived in a bordering prefecture, was bringing his family to the house for a big lunch on January 1, and there was a mountain of food to be made. Mariko planned to serve everyone at two low tables in her parents' room, so that her mother could participate in the gathering from her bed. The guests were invited for two in the afternoon, and Mariko expected them to stay no more than three or four hours; given the strain she felt around her brother, she was not counting on a lengthy family gathering. "I'm going to try to enjoy it," Mariko said, with a weary smile. "But I probably won't very much. It's just a ritual." Mariko had last seen her elder brother in April, at the memorial service on the anniversary of her younger brother's death. She had never been close to her elder brother, and though the two had a workable relationship, she could not forget what he said when he moved away from his own parents to be closer to the family of his wife. "When he walked away," Mariko told me, "he said very bluntly that his wife's family was of a much higher class than ours. It was humiliating."

Mariko also had her hands full getting ready for the family's annual *mochi*-making party. She was again making the heavy, chewy rice cake served at New Year's at home, and she invited me over for the festivities on December 30. I arrived in mid-afternoon to see a gaggle of friends and neighbors drinking beer and sake in the street outside her house. Mariko was bustling around in a big blue cotton apron, looking as if she meant business, while the men were collected around a makeshift brazier, nothing more than a large overturned can with a side opening for wood scraps. As a hot fire burned inside, sending tendrils of smoke into the crisp winter sky, Mariko steamed two round containers of rice on the can's top surface. When the rice was ready, she removed the container from the brazier, then placed the lump of hot, steaming rice into a heavy wooden tub. Takeshi sprinkled the mound with cold water, then grabbed a big wooden mallet. He swung the mallet over his shoulder and with a series of loud whacks began pounding the rice into a gooey white paste, making the job look like hard work but fun. When Takeshi got tired, one of the other men took over, and soon the paste became transformed into a plump, sticky rice dough. Mariko dusted the stuff with white cornstarch, divided it into fat little apple-sized balls, then flattened each one slightly and placed them side by side on a large tray. "Try one," she insisted. I did and found it chewy and bland; I would not have gone out of my way to eat any more. But I could see that for the Japanese, *mochi* was a great comfort food, with its distinctive texture and soothing associations with holidays and childhoods past.

The following night was December 31. After dinner I went back to Mariko's with Sachiko to watch *Kohaku Utagassen*, Japan's annual New Year's Eve television show. In the broadcast, a brassy Las Vegas–style variety show, two groups of singers and celebrities—organized as the Red Team and the White Team—competed in a singing contest. The singers performed in front of a live studio audience while a sensor, attached to a UFO-like contraption that floated over the crowd, supposedly measured the intensity of the applause for each performance. At the end of the show, each team's score was reached by totaling up the applause and factoring in votes from viewer call-ins. Like the Academy Awards in the United States, the show brought torrents of complaints from viewers, and the audience had declined a bit in recent years, but it remained a New Year's tradition. The show started at seven and ran until midnight, and although nobody could sit through all five hours, people kept it on as background noise. Mariko, an avid follower of celebrity gossip, never missed it.

"I enjoy the clothes and the special effects, but not the songs," Mariko told me that evening. Sachiko and I were with her in the living room, drinking beer, with our legs warming under the *kotatsu*, as we watched the show on the big television set in the corner. The household was otherwise quiet. I noticed that on top of the set Mariko had put a small vase with a few branches of shiny green leaves and red berries, called *senryo*, a New Year's flower that was supposed to bring riches in the coming year. Takeshi, who hated the New Year's show, came into the room to say hello but disappeared to help make *soba*—hot Japanese buckwheat noodles in broth—at the neighborhood Buddhist temple, where New Year's revelers would be thronging at the stroke of midnight. Ken-chan was already there, and Shunsuke and Chiaki had gone with friends to the hip precincts of Harajuku to cram in with the tens of thousands of people at the enormous Meiji Jingu, one of Japan's largest Shinto shrines, an immense wooden structure deep in the woods of central Tokyo and a popular destination for teenagers and dates on New Year's Eve.

We turned our attention to the show as a Japanese pop star called Kan, inanely dressed as Mozart in a white wig and blue velvet (the show was celebrating the composer's two-hundredth birthday), sang "Love Wins," one of the hits of the year. "Bad song," Mariko said. It was true Kan could barely sing, but he was earnest and cute. The same was true of one of the show's two hosts, Yuko Asano, an actress who was famous for her work in TV's trendy dramas and who, by my count, changed her clothes during the course of the broadcast at least a half dozen times; her outfits ranged from a red-and-white kimono to black taffeta and leather, my favorite. She was the cheerleader for the Red Team and introduced all the team's performers, including one famous singer who appeared on stage in a pink Cinderella ballgown and tiara.

"Bad taste, everything," Sachiko observed with a laugh.

"She changed her man, and now she's changed everything," Mariko agreed, who had read about the latest gossip of these stars somewhere.

Another memorable performer from the Red Team was a singer who wore a birdlike costume of black sequins and white feathers with a conical gold headpiece. At the conclusion of her number she spread her wings and, suspended by wires, flew off the stage. "I heard on the radio that her costume cost nearly one million dollars," Mariko said. The birdwoman was followed by a well-known *enka* singer. "She's thirty years old and divorced, and she has a child," Mariko reported. "One of my friends from work once read her water meter."

By the end of the show, the Red Team had won, which was announced to much mirth. Streamers fell from the ceiling, cheerleaders shook pompoms in the aisles, and Yuko Asano, weeping tears of joy, spouted banalities. "I'm very happy," she said. "The Red Team was perfect. I'm so happy. Thank you very much."

It was just a few minutes before midnight. Sachiko went home to be with her family, but Mariko and I put on our coats and headed over in the cold to the Buddhist temple where we had stopped during the Ichomachi festival that fall. Tonight it was crowded with parents, children, babies, and family dogs, all there to ensure health and happiness in the new year. The temple was floodlit and full of cheer as the priests began to ring a huge bell 108 times; each stroke was meant to drive out one of the sins of man. Then people lined up to finish ringing out the number themselves. Takeshi ladled steaming *soba* from a deep vat, and other people passed out hot sake. Mariko, feeling relaxed and festive, spent the next two hours saying hello to neighbors and friends, her breath making white clouds in the crisp winter air. A new year had begun.

10

CRISIS

Salarimen going to work

JANUARY AND FEBRUARY

Mariko was absentmindedly watching a quiz show on the evening of Wednesday, January 8, when an "urgent news bulletin" ran across the bottom of the screen. She immediately perked up, as did Takeshi and the kids. They soon learned that President George Bush of the United States, who everyone knew was in Tokyo with three overpaid executives from Ford, Chrysler, and General Motors, had fallen ill and collapsed that evening at a state dinner. A U.S. spokesman said he was resting comfortably, but what the Tanakas saw next did not exactly match the upbeat line from the White House. The footage opened with a shot of frantic Secret Service agents crowding around the head table, where the president, out of camera range, was apparently flat on the floor. The agents managed to lift him up, exposing to the world an alarmingly disoriented and ashen-faced

George Bush. What television viewers couldn't see at the time was that the president of the United States had just vomited into the lap of Prime Minister Kiichi Miyazawa, who had cradled the head of his ailing ally.

The scene was broadcast again and again as the Tanakas watched, stunned. The symbolism would have been dismissed as heavy-handed in a novel or movie. But like everyone else in Japan, the Tanakas could not help but see President Bush's attack of intestinal flu—which is what the White House called it afterward—as a metaphor for a sickly America in need of help from a vigorous Japan. The Bush trip eventually came to be seen as a new low in postwar U.S.-Japan relations and a terrible setback for Bush's faltering presidency. The American press had already been portraying the visit as little more than an elaborate campaign photo opportunity to show Bush getting tough with Japan on trade barriers, and it was not hard for the Japanese to have the same cynical view. "He came for the purpose of his reelection," Takeshi told me afterward, repeating what he had read. "He wanted to show Americans that he was trying hard to rejuvenate your economy." But while Bush's gastrointestinal distress elicited sympathy from the Japanese, the three automakers, who were with him to pressure the Japanese to import more American cars and auto parts, were widely derided. "At school we laughed at them," Shunsuke told me. "Who would buy an American car? They break down easily, they get bad mileage, and they have left-hand drive." Shunsuke didn't yet have a driver's license but said he knew about the shoddiness of American cars from adults and from television.

Over the next few days, as the visit generated hundreds of thousands of ponderous words in newspaper columns about the U.S.-Japan relationship, Mariko got back into her routine after the long New Year's holidays. The family dinner with her elder brother had been more relaxed than she expected, although it was rescheduled for January 2 after he called and begged off for January 1, saying he wanted to unwind with his own family. As a result, on New Year's Day she found herself in the rare and luxurious situation of suddenly having nothing to do. "I ate and I slept," she recalled happily. The next day her brother arrived at noon with his wife, daughter, and two sons. The elder son, a twenty-three-year-old, delighted Ken-chan by playing poker with him while the adults sat with Saburo and Ito, Mariko's parents, and talked about Saburo's years in the war. The war was not something they normally talked about, but I suspect the memories had been revived by all the questions Sachiko and I had been asking, and perhaps by the publicity surrounding the recent fiftieth anniversary of Pearl Harbor.

The next day, Mariko and Takeshi went to a small party at a friend's house to see three other couples, all very close, some of whom had known one another since high school. The group always tried to get together during the New Year's holidays. Like most Japanese, the Tanakas paid special attention to friendships made in high school or college. The men, like Takeshi, were in solid middle-class occupations. One worked as a computer programmer for Fujitsu, another for a plumbing company, a third for a petrochemical concern. Mariko had been the *nakodo,* or go-between, for one of the marriages. Every year the four men took a trip together, usually somewhere in Asia; this year, in mid-January, they were going on a three-day package tour to China. One woman came to the party alone, saying she and her husband were having problems. The year before the two had come together, but both had used the occasion to confess that they weren't getting along. The woman was in tears. "This year they're sleeping on two futons, head to toe instead of head to head," Mariko reported. She and the other women had commiserated with the friend and tried to help her, but they were philosophical in the end. "Everybody has the same complaints about their marriage," Mariko said.

Mariko dragged herself back to meter reading on January 4, feeling sluggish but grateful she would be outside in the crystalline weather. A week later, Takeshi left for China. Naturally Sachiko asked Mariko if this trip or any of Takeshi's other Asian jaunts were sex tours—which were notoriously popular among Japanese salarimen looking for affordable prostitutes—but Mariko seemed taken aback by the suggestion and said absolutely not. In any case, Mariko was quite happy to be on her own and was looking forward to a few days of quiet, when a new crisis struck.

"Mariko!" her father called from the bathroom late in the afternoon on January 13. "Come look at this!"

Mariko, hearing the urgency in his voice, hurried in and saw a dark, dirty red in the toilet bowl. Alarmed, she went back to the living room and pulled her big medical textbook off the shelf. Blood in the urine had many causes, she read, but in the worst case it could indicate a malignant tumor. Her father, though seventy-nine, was seemingly in excellent health. Saburo called his doctor, who instructed him to go to a nearby clinic, where he was told to go to the hospital the next day for tests.

The following morning, Mariko left at nine-thirty for meter reading, knowing that her father would be finished at the hospital by afternoon. At two she called him at home.

"What happened?" she asked.

"I have to be hospitalized right away," Saburo said.

"Ehhhh?" Mariko replied, stunned. The worst possible thing has just happened, she thought to herself, frantic that this illness would affect his ability to care for her mother and force her to pick up the slack. She knew she was being selfish, but she couldn't help it. The person who took care of the sick person was now sick, maybe quite seriously.

Saburo told Mariko that the doctor at the clinic had found a tumor in his bladder. The doctor had not elaborated beyond that, and Saburo had not asked. This lack of discussion was standard in Japan, where doctors feel little obligation to inform patients of their true condition, believing that bad news will only depress them and weaken their ability to fight back—an old tradition that has been upheld by the courts. (In one well-known case in 1983, a doctor found gallbladder cancer but withheld the diagnosis, simply telling his patient to undergo surgery. Believing her case was not life-threatening, she declined. Six months later she died. Her family sued, saying the hospital should have been explicit about her condition. But a judge ruled that the doctor was under no such obligation, and he blamed the patient for not following the advice.)

In the case of Saburo, Mariko was informed that he would have to be hospitalized until his urine was clear of blood and he was ready for surgery. But who would handle the full-time care of her mother? Mariko knew she would have enough trouble looking after her father in the hospital and managing Takeshi, the kids, and her jobs as well. The only help she had was a woman paid for by the ward—the family called her "Helper-san," pronounced "Herupu-san"—who came to the house once a week and gave Ito a sponge bath as part of a government program for the disabled. But just as Mariko was beginning to panic, Saburo gave her some good news. Well aware of the problems his illness was causing for her, he had asked the hospital, a small, private institution only a five-minute walk from the house, if it could admit Ito and care for her while he was laid up. Ito did not require constant medical attention, but in Japan many elderly disabled are cared for in hospitals because of the shortage of nursing homes and the difficulties families have in looking after infirm parents themselves. In this case it helped that the Tanaka family had a long and close relationship with the hospital. Mariko was friendly with the chief nurse and had delivered her three children there. Two years before, Takeshi had been treated there for diabetes, and it was also where Ito had recovered after her stroke. Since the hospital had the room, it agreed to let Ito stay for a month; the hospital would be reimbursed by her national health insurance. Mariko was guilt-ridden about depending on the hospital to meet her family needs, but she was relieved nonetheless. The stay would buy her time and give her a chance to sort out the future should her father's condition prove to be more serious.

The next afternoon, January 15, Saburo checked into the hospital. Mariko, who had called the meter-reading office to ask for time off, remained at home with her mother, who would be admitted three days later, when a bed became available. Takeshi, meanwhile, was not due back from China until that evening. Here it was, a real crisis, and her husband was off with friends in a foreign country, no doubt drinking to all hours. But Mariko shrugged it off. She hadn't bothered to telephone him, knowing full well that the situation would not be very different if he were at home. "You can't depend on men in these kinds of things," she told me later.

Saburo had given Mariko a few quick instructions about Ito's care before leaving for the hospital. Now that he was gone, leaving Ito all alone in the big room, Mariko realized acutely how much she was saddled with. "It's like having two families," she said. In the past few years, Mariko had just begun to enjoy the relative freedom that came with older children. Chiaki was impossible, it was true, and Shunsuke was often sullen and didn't study, but the relentless pressures of toddlers and diapers and sleepless nights were long gone. Now here Mariko was, at the age of forty-five, caring for a mother who needed to have her adult diapers changed five times a day and could be left for only two or three hours at a time. It was a problem faced increasingly by women of Mariko's generation in Japan—it was always the women, never the men, who cared for the elderly, even elderly in-laws—but knowing that she was not alone scarcely made Mariko feel better. "My father was hospitalized last year for a blood clot in his leg, so I've known that maybe he would go first," she told me. "And I knew I would have to face this when I decided to live here. But now I'm confused. I want to help, but my body doesn't follow."

For the next three days, from the fifteenth to the eighteenth of January, Mariko worked virtually around-the-clock. "I barely had time to eat or go to the bathroom," she told me later. On Friday, January 17, for example, Mariko woke at seven and quickly got her husband and children fed and out of the house. She roused her mother at eight-thirty, changed her diaper, gave her a sponge bath, put cream on her bedsores, then cranked up the bed to a sitting position. She pulled Ito's frail body up so that her hips fit exactly in the bend of the bed, put a paper napkin on her chest, then brought her breakfast on a tray. Ito could use a spoon or chopsticks and feed herself, but her false teeth didn't work very well, so all her food had to be softened. She was slow in bringing the food to her mouth and sometimes missed her mouth entirely. Breakfast took a long time, which Mariko used to do laundry and clean out the small garden in back of the house. At ten-thirty, she cranked Ito back down, then made a half-hour phone call about one of her samisen lessons. After that she packed Ito's hospital bag for the next day.

At noon, she watched *You Can Laugh*, an hour-long talk-and-variety show starring the comedian Tamori, who always put her in a better mood. These days he was one of the few bright spots in her life. At one, she changed her mother's diaper again, cranked up the bed, and gave her lunch. At two-thirty she left to visit her father in the hospital. He was in no pain, just bored, which she hoped was a good sign. On her way back to the house she stopped at the bank and the grocery. Then she prepared dinner, a chicken stew with a white cream sauce, ahead of time. She brought in the clothes from the line, and just before four made tea for Sachiko and me.

We arrived a few minutes later. "Your face looks so beautiful and white!" Sachiko said immediately. To me, Mariko just looked pale and strained. At this point, neither Sachiko nor I knew what had happened to Saburo, but Mariko quickly filled us in. Then she told us something that she and Takeshi had talked about the night before. "We discussed putting my mother in a nursing home," she said. "But I feel sorry for her. And my husband said maybe we should keep her here. He feels it's too depressing for bedridden people to be in nursing homes. They can be very bad. They don't change diapers, and they're expensive." Mariko didn't know exactly what the family would have to pay, but in the early 1990s it cost around twenty thousand dollars a year to keep an elderly person in a nursing home. The government required that the family member charged with looking after the patient—Mariko in this case—be billed based on the ability to pay. Nursing homes were scarce in Japan, the fastest-aging society in the world, and those that existed often lacked adequate medical facilities and full-time doctors. Ito had a modest income from monthly government disability payments, and Mariko said her own salary might cover whatever else a nursing home would cost. But the family was already spending everything Mariko made. On the other hand, if Saburo was unable to take care of Ito after his surgery, keeping her at home would mean that Mariko might have to quit work entirely. "Economically we're going to have a very hard time," Mariko said.

Mariko took a drag on her cigarette and continued to think out loud, turning the possibilities over in her mind. "Maybe if I have a very hard time taking care of my mother, maybe we'll have to put her in a nursing home," Mariko said. "We'll have to see. Sometimes I wonder how much my mother really enjoys her life. But then she'll say, 'Don't leave me alone.' She really knows now that my father is hospitalized. She's always asking me, 'When will he come back?' I told her very honestly that he needs to be hospitalized for a while. I think she's very upset about it, but she's trying not to show it. These days she's been telling me that I can bring her dinner after the rest of the family is finished."

I asked if she was prepared to quit her jobs and take care of her mother indefinitely.

"I have to," she said. "My mother is still living, and I can't treat the living badly. But I also have to have my own life. So I'm thinking—how can we compromise?" She said that once everything was settled, when she got more efficient at taking care of her mother, perhaps she could create four or five hours out of her day for her own work. If she changed her mother's last diaper at midnight, she said, then maybe she wouldn't have to change it again so early the next morning. "But, oh, will I be tired," Mariko said.

She told us that Takeshi had suggested moving the whole family into Ito's room for breakfast. That way everybody could help, and Mariko would not have to wait on two families in two separate rooms. But Mariko knew it would make the children uncomfortable to have meals with an ailing grandmother to whom they scarcely spoke. "Right now they have a room to relax in," she said. "It's difficult for them to change."

That evening Sachiko and I took Shunsuke out for a long-planned dinner in Roppongi, Tokyo's restaurant and nightclub district. The idea was to continue in private the conversation about school, grades, and his girlfriend that we had started at the house in November, when Mariko had listened at the head of the table and no doubt cramped his style. Sachiko selected the restaurant, Il Forno, a trendy Italian transplant from Santa Monica, California. She had been an interpreter for the owner and was a regular there, and she thought a seventeen-year-old high school student would enjoy a taste of Tokyo's high life. But the crowd of beautiful young Japanese and American investment bankers in sleek black clothes seemed more intimidating than relaxing to Shunsuke, who was wearing a wool plaid shirt and was in a taciturn mood. The menu seemed to displease him—lots of tomato pastas, no big steaks—but after we ordered he settled in.

We started by talking about the recent departure of President Bush and the American automakers, and Shunsuke's comments about the sorry state of American manufacturing echoed the conventional wisdom I often heard in Japan. "America was number one in the fifties and sixties," he said. "But since then we have worked harder than you." He also acknowledged that the Japanese were great imitators and adapters but added that "we improved the technology we gained from you."

Actually, Shunsuke was less interested in talking about an America in decline than about sports figures and football, a new passion in Japan. "There are a lot of talented people in the United States," Shunsuke said. "Like Reggie White of the Philadelphia Eagles, Bruce Smith of the Buffalo Bills, and Deion Sanders of the Atlanta Falcons." He told me he had read about the sports stars in *Touchdown* and *American Football*, two Japanese magazines. He also religiously watched the one American football game broadcast in Japan each week, at one in the morning on Thursdays. "Sometimes I tape it," he said. "But I always see it. And I always tape the playoffs and the Super Bowl."

Shunsuke played center at Waseda, which was not known for its football team. "The number-one activity at Waseda is cheering on the baseball players," Shunsuke said, referring to the school's reputation as a hothouse for baseball players who go on to Japan's major leagues. "American football is not popular. Weird people play it, the kind of people who make lots of trouble. I wasn't ready to be a team member, but the captain talked me into it." The games were all played on Sunday mornings in front of a small sprinkling of mothers and friends. Cheerleaders, bands, and homecoming games were not part of the scene, at least not yet.

Moving on, I asked Shunsuke about his girlfriend, the one he had met in October.

"All the passion is gone," he said matter-of-factly.

"Already?" I asked.

"The crazy parts are gone," he said. "Like when I wanted to see her all the time." I casually asked if he had slept with her, since teenage sex is no less common in Japan than in the United States.

"It's a problem," he said, warming to the subject. "I have no encouragement. I'm afraid I'll be refused." He mentioned also that the two had no private place to go. Shunsuke's house was never empty, and he couldn't afford Japanese love hotels, the gaudy, campy trysting places with beds in the shape of Venetian gondolas, pineapples, spacecraft, and the like. What about his family's other house, the one the Tanakas had moved from a few years before? He brightened.

"Is there a futon over there?" he asked. Sachiko and I said we didn't know. "It's not nice to make love on a rug," he added, now absorbed in thought. Sachiko and I laughed, and the mood at the table lifted. Shunsuke had always seemed to me a big, surly bear, but now he came across as vulnerable, insecure, and charming in his own way. I was reminded of how hard it was to be seventeen, and I saw for the first time a sweetness in him. Not surprisingly, he told us he had not yet brought his girlfriend home to meet Mariko. "She's very critical," he said, stating the obvious. "I don't like the way she talks."

I knew Mariko was a nag, but I suspected she was easier on her elder son than she was on his younger siblings, and I told him so. Shunsuke agreed and offered an analysis of the shifting alliances and power balances within the family. "My mother is mad most at Ken-chan," he said. "Then Chiaki, and then me. Chiaki doesn't help around the house. She doesn't do anything. She's not like my mother. Chiaki doesn't like anybody in the family. She likes our father a little bit, but she doesn't like our mother. She hates me because I don't like her because she doesn't do anything. She doesn't like Ken-chan because Ken-chan doesn't listen to her. But Ken-chan doesn't listen to anybody. And he doesn't get upset when people get mad at him."

Shunsuke had opinions about his parents as well, some astute, others perhaps not. "My mother is cheerful and energetic about everything," he said. "It's true she gets angry, but overall she's cheerful. Sometimes, when I'm depressed, her cheerfulness is annoying." On the other hand, Shunsuke judged his father to be "calm and cynical." He added, "I think my father has been overwhelmed by my mother's cheerfulness. And he has trouble when he gets drunk." Nonetheless, Shunsuke said, Takeshi was a good father and his parents were a "good match" for each other. He admitted that it was hard to say precisely why. "Sometimes I'm puzzled by their relationship," he said. "But overall, they are a very good couple." I had to respect his opinion. After all, he lived there and knew things that I didn't. Or maybe it was just that his parents' marriage was the norm, repeated in the homes of his friends and all over Japan.

The next morning at eight-thirty a car came to the house for Mariko's mother and transported her to the hospital without incident. Mariko breathed a sigh of relief, but her reprieve was short-lived. Things were easier with her mother away, but Mariko soon realized how much time her parents demanded even in the hospital. Partly she was still nursing a sense of guilt. Since in her view the hospital had done the Tanakas such an enormous favor in taking in Ito (even though they were getting paid), Mariko felt obligated to help in her mother's care. The nurses changed her diapers, but every day from eleven-thirty to two Mariko was at the hospital to attend to her mother's other personal needs. She combed her hair, cleaned her ears, exercised her legs, and helped feed her lunch. Ito was as slow as ever and dropped her food as usual. Afterward Mariko washed out her mother's tea cup—Ito, like everyone else, had brought her own—then headed to her father's room on the floor below. Saburo still had blood in his urine but told Mariko he felt fine otherwise. Mariko stayed for only a few minutes. Invariably Saburo fussed that Ito's legs were not getting enough exercise, but Mariko reassured him she was fine.

In the evenings Mariko returned to the hospital to help her mother with dinner. Takeshi was still killing time at the office, morose over his lack of work, but at least he was home early most nights, at six-thirty or seven. The kids warmed up the dinners Mariko had prepared ahead of time, and sometimes Takeshi actually did the dishes. As remarkable as this was, Mariko refused to be impressed or grateful. "It's his minimum obligation in this crisis," she said. "If he didn't do even that, then he's not a human being. Besides, it's a good experience for him."

So engulfed was Mariko in the care of her parents that it came as a complete surprise to her a few mornings later that a major controversy was brewing between the United States and Japan. She was getting breakfast for the family, walking back and forth between the kitchen and the *kotatsu*, when at seven-thirty she saw a report from New York on *Zoom-in Morning*, the news show the Tanakas always watched as they started their day. It was hard to follow, but the announcer said that the Americans were again quite angry at the Japanese. A reporter was then shown talking to an American woman in an unemployment line, a union leader, the president of Toyota in the United States, and a spokesman for the Japanese consul general in New York City. The show also had an interview with an American autoworker in Detroit. Mariko didn't know it, but in the English-language version of the tape, which had been broadcast on ABC News, the autoworker called someone a "little Jap." The comment in which he used the epithet was translated on the show Mariko watched as "The Japanese could come to see us."

Mariko gathered that a Japanese politician named Sakurauchi had made a disparaging remark about American workers, but she couldn't tell for sure. "What's going on?" she asked her husband.

Takeshi couldn't believe his wife's ignorance. Where had she been? "It's been all over the papers for three days," he said.

True enough, the Japanese press had reported that Yoshio Sakura-uchi, the speaker of Japan's lower house of Parliament, complained that American workers were "too lazy" and that 30 percent of them "cannot even read." He referred to America as "Japan's subcontractor," and said that Japanese companies resisted buying American goods because U.S. workers "turn out so many defective products."

Mariko did not know what to make of the news report, and when I asked her what she thought about it, she became strained and silent. "Hmmmm," she said, at last. "Well, yes . . ." There was another silence, but finally she plunged in. "Since olden times," she began, "Japanese have been told that the Japanese and Germans are very skillful. I was brought up hearing it. I don't know Americans very well, but I'm wondering. Recently, on *Zoom-in Morning,* I saw some American children who had no educations. I felt very sorry for those children. It's not a matter of good or bad, just complicated."

Mariko was being polite, but she obviously shared the general Japanese disdain for the United States as a big, lazy crybaby whose best days were past. She had no firsthand experience with American products, since everything in her house—the stove, the refrigerator, the television set, the VCR—was Japanese. The only American she knew was me. Like her elder son, she associated American output with popular culture and sports. "I don't know a lot about cars," she said, "but for example, when I was meter reading, I found a broken water pipe. The faucet was American-made, and it was very difficult to get the parts to fix it. American parts are not the only ones that break down, but the service for American products is not adequate in Japan."

The next evening, January 24, as the debate over American laziness continued, Mariko's husband once again served as a paragon of Japanese work habits by spending another night in his car. Or so he told his wife later. He returned to the house about eight on the morning of the twenty-fifth and unfortunately pulled into the parking space the family kept next to their old house while Mariko was chatting with the neighbor across the street.

Mariko, seeing that he was disheveled and unshaven, looked at him with disgust. "I'm so happy you're safe," she said sarcastically, not caring that her neighbor heard. In fact, she was happy to have an audience, the better to shame her husband.

Takeshi gave her a pinched, embarrassed smile and crept home to change.

The following Monday, Sachiko and I went to visit Saburo in the hospital. Gifts were in order, and we had consulted with Mariko in advance. We brought him a bunch of apricot-colored tulips, a box of enormous, luscious strawberries—they cost twenty-five dollars at the gourmet fruit market in my neighborhood—and a pair of pajamas. These were as much a present for Mariko as for Saburo, since the hospital didn't provide any nightclothes and Mariko was constantly having to launder the few pairs her father had.

Saburo was sitting up in bed, unshaven but otherwise looking remarkably healthy. He was in a six-person room, separated from the others by a white curtain, in the bed nearest the door. The hospital itself was small, clean, and functional, with no extras like gift shops, visitors' lounges, and soothing artwork, which Americans have become accustomed to in the United States. Mariko was seated on one side of Saburo's bed. Sachiko and I sat down too, offered our gifts, and told Saburo he looked wonderful. He seemed happy for the company and told us that the next day the doctors would finally remove the tumor in his bladder. Saburo was of course intensely worried about the outcome, but at the time of our visit he seemed more fixated, understandably, on the mechanics of the procedure itself. To get to the tumor, Saburo said, the doctors were going to insert a small tube up his penis, which he referred to as *o-chinchin*, a cute, childlike word that, with the formal *o* translated as something akin to "honorable pee-pee." Talkative as always, Saburo imparted this information without the slightest embarrassment, and Mariko and Sachiko laughed. The three of us stayed another ten minutes, said our good-byes and good-lucks, then headed back to Mariko's. She fixed us tea, and we sat down in our usual places to talk.

"Tomorrow I'll know whether my father's tumor is benign or malignant," she said, speaking more frankly than she had in the cheerful atmosphere of the hospital room. The biopsy would take two hours, and she would talk to the doctor late in the afternoon. "But my father seems very healthy," she said. "Instead of worrying about it now, I'm going to think about it tomorrow." She was remarkably calm, given the circumstances, and the crisis atmosphere of the week before seemed to have passed. "The blood in his urine did seem very serious," she agreed. "I was also afraid normal life would collapse. The reason I feel a little more relaxed now is that my mother is hospitalized. It's hard, but it's still easier than I expected."

Late the next afternoon, Sachiko and I went back to Mariko's and heard the good news: Saburo's tumor was benign. The doctors had removed it, although they said there was a good chance it would grow back. Mariko, looking completely relieved, pushed that thought out of her mind. She told us she had gone to the hospital that morning around eleven-thirty to see Saburo before his biopsy. "He was very nervous," she said. Saburo was given an epidural block that anesthetized him from the waist down; the biopsy began about one in the afternoon, and at one-thirty Mariko went home to prepare dinner. At four, when everything was over, Mariko began calling relatives to tell them Saburo was fine. She was finishing up when Sachiko and I walked in an hour later.

"Now my father seems a little disappointed to be leaving the hospital so soon," she said with a weary smile, perhaps projecting her own feelings on him. She told us he had made friends with all the nurses, learned their ages, and wanted to be the go-between for the marriage of one of them. "What a crazy idea," she said, smiling and shaking her head. Mariko had also told the good news to her mother, still in a room one floor above Saburo's, who no doubt was the most relieved of anyone. "I feel much better," Ito told her daughter. That afternoon, Saburo had three visitors—Takeshi's mother and two neighbors—all of whom could see that he was in fine spirits and that the crisis had hardly stilled his loquaciousness.

Mariko sipped her tea and took a long drag on her cigarette. Now that her father seemed no longer about to die, she could complain about him again. "He talks all the time and says the same thing over and over," she sighed. "He talks about my mother's hip and fake teeth, and her legs. Three times a year his nephew comes to visit, and he always has to listen to my father talk about my mother's constipation. He always says the same thing, three times a year."

Mariko told us that both parents would be home from the hospital the following week. "With all of this happening, my father has begun to realize that things are very hard for him," she said. "It's very hard for him to take care of my mother, and I think he'll have less energy for it. So for a while I think I'll work at home." She told us the Japan Travel Bureau, where she still worked one week a month, would send paperwork to her, but that she wouldn't be able to read meters for some time. Her father, she said, had offered to make up what she was losing in salary with money from his savings and pensions. "Our money and your money should be the same," he told her. "We shouldn't separate it anymore." Mariko reluctantly agreed, although she insisted that he give her only what she would be losing in income during his illness, nothing more. They would somehow manage, in other words.

Takeshi, meanwhile, had not been to see Saburo at all. He told Mariko that since the family had been forced to ask the hospital for help with Ito, he was too embarrassed to go. The family should have tried in some way, he said, to handle her at home. His insistence sounded a little selfish to me, but Mariko agreed with him in theory; she just saw no alternative to the hospital, particularly since "the family" that would have had to take care of Ito at home meant her. So she continued to go on her own to see her father and, now that he was recovering, tend to the elaborate etiquette of gifts. Japanese custom required that she give reciprocal gifts to all the people who had given something to Saburo during his hospital stay, which was complicated enough. But by some mysterious and ironclad calculation in Japan, each return gift had to be one half the value of the original gift. Figuring out precisely what each gift should be was a terrible nuisance, but Mariko didn't mind, taking understandable consolation in the fact that the ritual meant the patient had recovered and was well.

That night it was Chiaki's turn to be interviewed by Sachiko and me at the restaurant of her choice, in this case the Red Lobster, an outpost of the American chain, which she had seen advertised on TV. As we walked in from the parking lot, I remarked that it was identical to the Red Lobsters in the United States. "But I thought it was Japanese," Chiaki said with some surprise, echoing what many Japanese also thought of the hugely popular McDonald's, pronounced "Maku-Donaru-doh." Strangely, her ignorance irritated me. Not only did the Japanese make perfect cars, I thought grumpily, but now they were taking credit for one of the brilliant American innovations of the era, the Big Mac.

Inside, as we ordered, I saw that Chiaki was relaxed, much less shy than before, and seemed happy to be out of the house. She told us she was working twice a week after school as a checkout girl at the neighborhood Marufuji, the supermarket where Mariko shopped. She made about seven dollars an hour, or a little more than forty dollars a week, all of which she saved. "I want to be independent," she said adamantly. "I want to live by myself, away from home. There are so many frictions at home. My parents really monitor me."

"But isn't that normal?" I asked.

"They're worse than other families," she insisted. "When I'm watching television, my mother always says, 'Did you finish your homework?' And later she'll ask again, 'Did you finish your homework?' And when I say yes, she just says, 'Well, why don't you help around the house?' She nags."

So far Chiaki was sounding pretty much like a typical fifteen-year-old. It was nice to know that for all the rigidity of Japanese society, teenagers could be as difficult here as anywhere, and that Chiaki had a mind of her own. Smiling, I asked Chiaki when her problems with her mother started.

"The first year of junior high," she reported. "I started rebelling, and that was when I started to see through my parents. It seemed to me that if they could do bad things, then I was entitled to do the same. My mother said to me that I had to take part in after-school activities, even though she told me that she herself had only done after-school activities for three months." Mariko, no doubt remembering how her own mother had forbidden her to play sports, had at first insisted that Chiaki keep up with volleyball, which had kept her at school until seven-thirty five days a week. But finally Chiaki prevailed. "The hours were too long," she said. "Now I get home before five o'clock, and I go to the library and read."

Chiaki's liberation from volleyball had not, however, made her look more kindly on Mariko. "My mother is very selfish," Chiaki said. "She says very nasty things, and they make me irritated." She said she told her mother "the absolute minimum" about school.

She had few good words for her siblings as well. "Ken-chan is very selfish," she said. "When he was born, everybody knew he was the last boy, so everybody really fussed over him. Ken-chan doesn't listen to me. But then, Ken-chan doesn't listen to anybody." She thought a moment, then changed her mind. "Ken-chan does listen to Shunsuke," she said. "Because Shunsuke is the owner of the family computer."

As we ate, I asked Chiaki how she thought her parents got along; I was curious to see if she would make the same happy assessment of their marriage as Shunsuke had. "I don't know," she said. "Both of them go their own way." When I asked if she thought they were happy together, there was a long pause, and I realized it was a difficult question for any daughter or son. "I think so," she finally said. "Because my mother is always saying how much she enjoys life. She's optimistic."

And yet again she said, as she had earlier in the fall, that she would not choose her mother's life for herself. "My mother is nagged by her children, and she's nagged by her husband, and she can't say anything about it. Even after my mother sits down, my father asks her to bring water from the kitchen. Nobody resists my father at home." Chiaki's words startled me, because I had not yet seen that side of Mariko; I thought of her more as a prod to her kids than as their doormat.

Now I asked Chiaki about her father, since Shunsuke had told me she got along better with him than he or his brother did. "The longer I live with him, the less I understand him," she said. "He's a person who doesn't say anything about himself in front of us." Once, she recalled, he took her to his office when she was small. "But he never asks anything about me," she said. "He's old-fashioned. He's one generation behind." Her blunt comment made me sad, but I also wondered how much of her hurt feelings were simply part of growing up anywhere. A recent survey in the United States, after all, showed that almost half of American teenagers think their parents don't have enough time for them, and the percentage was the same whether one parent or both parents worked. Takeshi would hardly be a model parent in America, but in Japan he seemed typical of his generation. When I offered that observation to Chiaki, she disagreed. "Other daughters are better friends with their fathers than I am," she said. She turned to look over at another table in the restaurant, where two girls, both about twelve, sat with their mother and father, a young-looking man in horn-rimmed glasses and a preppy blue sweater. "They seem very happy and nice to me," Chiaki said wistfully. "That man looks like a father who would really listen to my problems."

"He's a 1990s father," Sachiko offered sympathetically, as if to console Chiaki by telling her that the problem wasn't her father but the generation that shaped him.

We moved on to the subject of Chiaki's boyfriend, whom she was still seeing once a week on a bench in the park. She was keeping Mariko in the dark about it as much as she could. "That kind of thing gets her very excited," she said. Chiaki and her boyfriend had been to see the American movie *Ghost* in Shibuya, and lately he had been pressuring her to sleep with him. "But I don't want to," she said. "In junior high, sleeping with a boy was a scandal, and nobody did it. But at my new high school, girls sleep with their boyfriends and talk about it." She went on to say that the girls were so forward they thought nothing of sitting crosslegged in short skirts. "They're from very rich families," Chiaki reported. "Some of their fathers are presidents of companies." Although Japan is more genuinely middle-class and egalitarian than most other industrialized democracies, there are economic differences, and Chiaki was well aware of them. ("There are *many* classes in Japan," Mariko once said to me quite pointedly.) Japan's growing consumer culture probably played a role in Chiaki's feelings too. The girls at her high school, she said, got $150 a month in allowance, had part-time jobs besides, and stopped to eat and shop in Shibuya on their way home from school. Chiaki and her best friend—a girl at her new high school who had been with her in junior high—could only afford to look, usually on the eight floors of shops in the trendy Fashion 109 Building in Shibuya. "There are so many things that I want to buy that I can't," Chiaki said.

Chiaki naturally felt like an outsider at school, which was something Mariko had been aware of for months. "I haven't told her," Chiaki said, "but I think she knows. Sometimes when I complain about school to her, she'll say, 'They have their own life and you have your own life.' "

As we were finishing, I asked Chiaki what she knew of America, curious to learn what she had absorbed from the laziness controversy. But it turned out that Chiaki, like many Japanese teenagers, was more interested in America as a kind of Pleasure Island far from academic pressures and the constrained lifestyles of Japan. "It's a free country," she said. "Compared with the United States, we are much less free. Especially in schools. You don't have the kind of entrance exams that we do. Also, your houses are much bigger, and kids my age seem more independent."

I asked where she had learned all this. "From my teacher," she said, "and from watching American movies on TV."

February arrived with a blizzard, unusual for Tokyo, that temporarily transformed the city into the kind of frosty wonderland that Mariko remembered from the winters of her youth. But it was a sodden snow, and by the next day the purposeful bustle of Tokyo had churned everything to slush. That night, as if the gods of weather were still in an uproar, a frightening earthquake awoke the Tanakas, and all of the city, to a violent shaking at four A.M. Mariko was startled out of a deep slumber to hear glasses and videotapes falling from the shelves in the living room. Tokyo had small tremors and earthquakes all the time, but this was the worst she could remember. Still, she found she was too groggy to get up and hide under the table in the living room, her normal spot during earthquakes. Fortunately, the shaking lasted only thirty seconds, and when it was over, Takeshi went upstairs to check on the children. Mariko turned on the radio and learned that the earthquake was not so severe as she had imagined, but that its epicenter was right under Tokyo Bay, less than five miles away. Its closeness explained its intensity. My husband and I were also shaken awake and were immediately terrified as windows rattled and plants and books fell noisily from shelves. Moments later, a prerecorded announcement could be heard over our neighborhood loudspeaker, telling everyone not to worry. We wondered how anyone could feel reassured by a disembodied voice saying that all was well. How did the voice know?

Mariko lay quietly in the dark for the first half hour after the quake, listening to radio reports that damage had been slight. Earthquakes had always scared her, especially as a child, when she had kept a bundle of extra clothes near her pillow to grab just in case. The worst earthquake in Tokyo had been in 1923, when half the city was destroyed, and Mariko, like everyone else, lived in fear of the next big one. "If I die by myself I'll be very lonely," she told me afterward. "But if I die with everybody else I won't care."

Mariko knew she had been slow to rouse during the earthquake because she was still so exhausted from tending daily to her parents in the hospital. "I have no time for myself," she complained. "I decided a long time ago that I would take care of my parents in their old age, so this is my duty. But if I really think about my life right now, I'll get very depressed."

In this kind of mood, she found she couldn't help but be irritated by her mother. "I'm not mad that she became sick," Mariko said. "And I still want her to have as good a life as she can. But she has been very indulged. The woman in the bed next to her is paralyzed on her right side, but she still manages to use a wheelchair by using her left leg and hand. And she can go to the bathroom. She tries hard not to drop her food, she opens the bag for her medicine, and she can peel an orange. She goes to the bathroom after meals by herself. She brushes her teeth, puts on skin lotion, and combs her hair. She's so independent. My mother never tries to do any of those things. But even before this hospital stay I was upset with her. Without my father she can't do anything. I was always telling her that he needed more freedom."

Mariko's father was due home on February 7, three weeks after he checked in. It was a long stay—in the United States, an operation such as his would usually be an outpatient procedure—but the Japanese remain in hospitals for weeks or even months longer than Americans. (In Japan the hospital stay for a new mother after a normal birth is seven to ten days; in the United States it is often only twenty-four hours.) Mariko's mother also had only a short time remaining in her month-long hospital stay. She would be home the following week, on February 15.

Nearly a month after George Bush's calamitous visit to Tokyo, public discussion among politicians and Japan's ruling elite was still returning to the episode. Poor Mr. Bush, people said. How unfortunate, how embarrassing, and yet how interesting it was that the president of the United States should be felled on the very occasion of his condescending lectures about opening Japanese markets to shoddy American goods produced by—how to put it?—an undisciplined workforce.

It was in this climate that Prime Minister Miyazawa, who had so recently cradled George Bush's head in his lap, set off yet another firestorm by offering a casual comment in the parliament that Americans "may lack a work ethic." After the earlier well-publicized remarks about lazy and illiterate workers in the United States, Miyazawa's remark was like throwing kerosene on a smoldering bonfire. The White House responded indignantly, and perhaps pathetically, that the American work ethic had produced "the greatest prosperity in the world." The Japanese media then had a field day covering every outburst from fuming Americans. Readers learned that a Texas car dealership was opening its television commercials with footage of Pearl Harbor, and that a Connecticut builder had put up a highway sign challenging any Japanese to work with him for a week. "We will see who is lazy," the sign said. Opinion polls showed that Americans were making a conscious effort to avoid buying Japanese products.

Mariko was still submerged in the care of her ailing parents, but Takeshi followed the protests from the United States with fascination. The latest flare-up in the war of words between the two countries seemed worse than usual to him, although he suspected that ordinary Americans were not paying much attention to it. In his mind, the controversy was confined to a few politicians and an excitable press, as always. A few days later he was convinced of his theory when the Japanese government, in an attempt to placate the United States, released a full transcript of Miyazawa's remarks, showing that he had been merely thinking out loud in response to a question. What he said, Takeshi thought, was much less incendiary in context than the press had reported.

The latest furor had started when a senior member of Parliament mentioned in a speech the popular Japanese canard that Americans did not buy cars made on Friday or Monday because of shoddy workmanship on those particular days. Prime Minister Miyazawa chimed in with a disastrous non sequitur, musing on the famous corporate takeovers and leveraged buyouts of Wall Street in the 1980s as a binge that merely shifted huge sums of money around. "I have long felt that this might involve something like a lack of a work ethic," Miyazawa said. The prime minister did not spare his own country, warning that Japan had its own problem with artificially inflated stock and real estate prices. "It is very important to build things of value with the sweat of our brows," he said. "This may sound like a sermon, but I have said what I feel."

Most Americans probably would have endorsed Miyazawa's measured criticism had it come from one of their own. But after the Bush trip, nobody wanted to hear another patronizing lecture from the Japanese. Japan, for its part, was fed up with years of American criticism about the need to deregulate its economy and open itself up to American products. It seemed to me the remarks of Miyazawa and the earlier comments about lazy and uneducated American workers reflected the mood of a nation that had dropped its guard and blurted out what it felt was the truth. The whole episode showed Americans something they perhaps had not realized—just what a low opinion the Japanese really had of them. As I watched these events unfold, I realized I needed to talk to Takeshi again, this time about the controversy. He was frankly relieved that I didn't want to see him at the office to ask more painful questions about his marriage and the family. Then, too, I knew from Mariko that his mood was better because his job situation had improved, and that he was working on a new plant and warehouse for a large bakery south of Yokohama.

Sachiko and I met him early in the evening after work as he eased into the first of numerous glasses of whiskey. Mariko's parents were still in the hospital, so Mariko had set up the *kotatsu* for us in her mother's more spacious room. Sachiko, Takeshi, and I assembled ourselves around it while Mariko, to my amazement, positioned herself in the kitchen, emerging from time to time to wait on Takeshi like a geisha. Mariko had put a bottle of Suntory whiskey, a bowl of ice, and a glass for him on the table, and throughout our conversation she ferried to him a delicious dinner, course by course. I especially remember grated white radish with tiny dried fish, followed by Chinese cabbage with squid. Takeshi sat cross-legged on the floor and dined like a pasha, never moving from his spot as Kiri-chan, the family cat, jumped hungrily in his lap, meowing for food. Takeshi gently stroked her head and hand-fed her a few fish—a nightly ritual, he said, adding that the cat preferred his lap because Mariko moved around too much. I realized I had never spent any real time with Takeshi and Mariko at the house, and now it was bizarre for me to see Mariko going through the motions of being such a traditional Japanese wife. Sachiko and I did not eat—we told Mariko we had plans to go out later, which we did, but we also did not want to put Mariko in a position of having to wait on us too.

I asked Takeshi first about his work. It was going better, he said, mentioning the project near Yokohama. Then he moved on to the subject of the allegedly slothful U.S. labor force. When I asked his opinion of the parliament member who had called Americans lazy and largely illiterate, Takeshi responded that he shouldn't have said what he said. "But all Japanese salarimen think the way he does," he added. "If the workers really insist on their rights, it's very hard for management to carry out its job. Maybe American workers insist on their rights too much."

Takeshi was right about one thing: the Japanese did believe that Americans are lazy, according to most opinion polls. Even Sachiko, an admirer of many things about America, admitted to me after the laziness remark that although it was a stupid thing to say, the substance made sense to her. "I hate to say it, but we all agree," she said.

The press tried to illuminate the issue, but in Japan it got bogged down in an unrelated question of whose workers were more productive. Worker productivity is measured by dividing the monetary value of goods produced by the number workers, and by that standard Americans can legitimately claim that their productivity is higher. Anyone who lives in Japan, for example, knows that while Japanese productivity in the manufacture of cars, consumer electronics, and machinery is remarkable, other industries are grossly inefficient. Japanese farmers, for instance, grow their crops on small, inefficient plots of land and have long had to be pampered by government subsidies and high tariffs or outright bans on imported food. They may work hard, but they are nowhere near as productive as American farmers.

Most statistics show, however, that Japanese workers do work longer hours than their American counterparts—three hundred hours more in a year, on average, according to one survey. But as the debate about who works harder raged on, it seemed to me the biggest difference between Japan and the United States was each society's attitude toward work itself. This was a lesson I learned not only from the Tanakas but from other Japanese couples we knew; often the husbands did not join us, even on weekends, because they were at company golf games, hot-springs visits, or other mandatory outings considered part of their professional life. In America, people go to work and then come home to their real lives. In Japan, the office is real life and home is a way station. When I used to go to offices in Tokyo, I was always amazed by the salarimen who sat at desks reshuffling the same papers, and by the O.L.s who prepared endless charts and graphs when they weren't making tea or accompanying people to the elevator.

I knew that Takeshi had spent the last four months at his office watching television and reading books, behavior that did not exactly conform with the stereotypical image of the nation of worker ants. Admittedly Takeshi's relaxed schedule was not his fault, and it had been the policy of his superiors to keep him idle. But to Takeshi that time showed his commitment to work even though nothing productive was involved. I also knew that "work" for Takeshi, as for all other salarimen in Japan, included drinking and shmoozing with his colleagues after office hours.

Whenever I met Americans in Tokyo who worked for Japanese firms, the most striking complaint I heard was that the Japanese wasted time. "In New York, people try to work superfast and efficiently during the workday, and then they go home," Christopher Shortell of the Mitsubishi Corporation's insurance department told me. "But in Japan, they drag things out. In meetings, it's not like, 'Here's the agenda; let's get this done.' " Even the Japan Productivity Center, which conducted many of the surveys on the subject, has found that Americans work "more intensely" than Japanese workers, who spread their work out over time. There has been a lot of talk in Japan about reducing working hours to make workers more efficient, but I suspect nothing will happen. Long hours are part of the machismo of the Japanese corporate warrior, who, like the samurai of old, is too caught up in his martyrdom to change.

The only real movement opposing the long hours has come with the focus on *karoshi*, or death from overwork. In the 1980s, a growing number of widows whose relatively young husbands had died suddenly of heart attacks began demanding compensation from the government under Japan's labor laws, claiming their husbands had been killed by the stress and long hours of their jobs. In all but a few cases the government rejected the claims, and I have to admit I saw its point of view. Salarimen drink and smoke heavily, and research shows that most *karoshi* victims exhibited such risk factors as narrowed arteries, high blood pressure, or high cholesterol. To me the Japanese attitude toward *karoshi* was significant because a widow with a *karoshi* claim was rebelling against the fundamental values of Japan, and her action represented another fraying of the edges in a rigid society.

As our talk proceeded, Takeshi was nursing another drink and tucking into a dish of fried carrots and bean sprouts, freshly made and served by the ever-compliant Mariko. It occurred to me then that I knew few people who worked as hard as she did. Now Takeshi turned to me. "I want to ask you one question," he said. "How can Chrysler's president make so much money even if the company doesn't make a profit? This is a very weak part of America."

I started to tell him it was a good question and a lot of Americans agreed with him. He listened briefly but then started complaining about Lee Iacocca of Chrysler.

"Even when he returned to the United States, he was still criticizing us," Takeshi said, dismissively. "What a joke."

Then he had another question for me. "Will you please define 'work ethic'?"

Put on the spot and grateful that I was not answering a question on an exam, I muddled through a vague explanation that hard work had long been an important part of America's identity, and that many Americans believed if you worked hard, your dreams could come true. Who knows what Sachiko did with that in translation, but Takeshi seemed satisfied. Now I took the ball back into my court and asked what he thought of Miyazawa's remark about the United States lacking a work ethic.

"He just said it very casually," Takeshi answered. "He thought he was speaking just to the Japanese—to us, to the family. Then overnight it went out all over the world. But these guys are politicians, and they must be careful about what they say. Maybe we all agree with these gentlemen, but these gentlemen represent Japan. They shouldn't say these things out loud."

"Americans are really mad about it," I said.

"I don't care if Americans think their country is the leader of the world," he said petulantly. "I still think that Americans are a little bit conceited. Americans should relax a little. It's no longer the era for someone to be the leader and someone else to follow. We'd rather have balance."

The whiskey seemed to be having an effect.

"Should Japan be the world's leader?" I asked.

"No," Takeshi answered decisively. "But we are working hard. We are making efforts. Of course you are much bigger, but probably workers in the United States work only fifty percent as hard as Japanese workers." There it was, what he really thought, three whiskeys in. "By working doubly hard we are almost catching up with you. We have to make twice as much effort to do it.

"I was born after World War II," he continued. "We aspired for a long time to be like America. But we don't anymore. I think your life is entirely different from ours. We are beginning to understand that America is not always the best. We have begun to understand that what is good for you is not always good for us."

11

MARIKO'S SECRET

Mariko's street in early spring

FEBRUARY AND MARCH

If the camera approaches you, don't feel self-conscious," a hip-looking man in an expensive sweater told the audience for one of Japan's most popular comedy shows. "And don't tell the person sitting next to you that you're on camera." He scanned the crowd slyly and grinned. "Now," he said, "do any of you *not* want to be on camera because you're skipping school?"

It was near noon, a mild Thursday in mid-February, and the audience of mostly young women giggled nervously. A lot were teenagers who no doubt were cutting class, but only one person, a young man, raised his hand. *You Can Laugh*, the live show starring Tamori, Japan's omnipresent funny guy in dark glasses, would be on the air in five minutes, and the audience still had to learn how to shout, "WOOOOOOOOO," and wave fists one row at a time for the big opening shot. There was a timid run-through, then another. "That's awful!" the warm-up man teased. "I give up. You're a mess." He disappeared as the show's frisky theme song boomed into the studio. Red, green, and blue lights flashed onstage. Tamori bounded out in a pair of oversized sunglasses, instead of his trademark dark aviators—a lame attempt at getting a laugh, but it worked. "WOOOOOOOOO!" yelled the delighted audience, waving their fists. Tamori, flashing the best-known gap-toothed grin in Japan, bounced around the cheesy pink, melon, aqua, and lime-green set. He was an intense, coiled figure with slicked-back hair and a slight build nicely encased in his Italian-inspired double-breasted dark suit. The show seemed to be off to a promising start.

In the middle of the audience, standing out in the sea of cable-knit sweaters and ponytails, was one aberrant, sheepish trio of women feeling considerably older than the rest of the crowd— Mariko, Sachiko, and me. Coming to the show with Mariko had been Sachiko's idea. I knew Mariko loved *You Can Laugh* and watched Tamori every day she was home. Tamori's face was everywhere in Japan—on billboards, in magazine ads, and on four different television shows on three different networks—and I decided to find out more about why Tamori appealed to Mariko and millions of others. A few weeks before the show, I had followed my curiosity and interviewed Tamori with Sachiko. He turned out to be charming, acerbic, hip, and slightly inane, and it was then that Sachiko and I asked to see his noontime show as part of the live studio audience. Sachiko thought it would be fun to go with Mariko, who was ready for some comic relief from the chaos of caring for her sick parents.

That was the sequence of events that had led the three of us to a Shinjuku television studio on Thursday, February 13. Tamori welcomed his first guest, the actor and singer Bito Isao, who plugged his performance in a Japanese stage production of *The Sound of Music*. Isao sat next to Tamori's desk and in a gesture meant to show off his humble roots—a universal show-business tradition, it turns out—offered the host a pair of socks and some sushi, both from shops in his neighborhood. Tamori then gave his guest a stack of telegrams. "They're all congratulating you on your appearance here," he said, grinning.

You Can Laugh, the most popular daytime show in Japan, was an endearingly mindless mixture of talk and jokes about the banalities of daily life and interviews showcasing the entertainment industry. It was both a wittier and sillier version, if that is possible, of Regis & Kathie Lee, with a little David Letterman thrown in. Tamori's popularity was so huge that one of Japan's top-rated shows was a Sunday-evening special consisting simply of *You Can Laugh* highlights from the previous week. Not bad for a dropout of Waseda University's philosophy department.

Tamori was forty-six, born one week after the war ended but was conceived when his father was away from home in the military. The timing raised certain questions in his mind. "I thought I looked like one of the neighbors," he told me, laughing. "I investigated later, and I discovered that my father was nearby, and was able to go back and forth." Tamori had been an insurance salesman, a coffee-shop owner, and a bowling-alley manager before getting his big break in 1976, when he was spotted in a bar in Shinjuku doing a stand-up routine about four people—an American, a Korean, a Vietnamese, and a Chinese—fighting over a game of mah-jongg. The man who discovered him was a cartoonist who himself appeared on television, and he asked Tamori to come with him as a guest on a show. From then on Tamori—whose professional name was an anagram of his family name, Morita—took off.

Much of Tamori's humor consisted in his mugging reactions to guests, but he also satirized the uptight practices of Japanese families and society, poking fun at the unpleasant scent of gift packs of pickles or the agonizing over spending just the right amount of cash for a wedding gift. After a decade on the air, *You Can Laugh* had become a favorite drop-by for the famous, the nearly famous, and the undiscovered, all of whom Tamori made fun of. "A tongue-tied guest is great for me," he said. "I make the guest more nervous. I tell him, 'This show is being watched by twenty million people.'" There had been a few American guests as well, notably Dustin Hoffman and Arnold Schwarzenegger. "Foreigners are very funny to the Japanese," said Tamori. He rarely used political humor, although George Bush's recent collapse in Tokyo had given him some ideas. "We were thinking about making fun of him," he said. "But not now—a little later."

Onstage, Tamori was through with welcoming his guest, the actor Isao, and was now listening to a long anecdote Isao evidently had prepared for the show. Recently, Isao said, he and his daughter caught an intruder in their home on a Saturday night. This was quite something, and the audience became still.

"My sixteen-year-old daughter came back from cram school a little after eleven," Isao recounted. He then proceeded to go on in excruciating detail: "She came into the living room and said, 'Were you upstairs?' That's when I noticed a light on the second floor. I went up and checked, and then I also noticed the door to the roof was open. I felt a little funny, so I got a *shinai*"—a bamboo sword used in Kendo, or Japanese fencing—"and went into my bedroom."

"Were you excited?" Tamori asked.

"I didn't see anyone," Isao continued. "But my daughter was right behind me, and she saw him first. He was lying beside the bed! I said, 'What are you doing?' And he said, 'I'm not doing anything.'"

At this point, Tamori got up and acted out the role of the intruder, first struggling with Isao and then falling down as Isao explained how his daughter hit the thief with the *shinai*. Tamori pretended to yell in pain. Isao said he managed to call the police and in the struggle he also gave the intruder a bloody nose. The intruder then asked for a tissue.

"A tissue?" Tamori repeated, his jaw dropped. "So—he liked cleanliness!" The audience laughed.

The police were at the house in four minutes but, Isao recalled, it felt like twenty. "Now I can talk calmly, but I was excited," he said, adding that at the police station, "I was shaking so much I couldn't write my name."

The audience listened to every word, clearly regarding the story as anything but comic. Mariko leaned forward, absorbed. For all his antics, Tamori had managed to create an oddly intimate atmosphere, as if we were all guests in his home, listening to a friend. I could see how shows like these bind the Japanese together just as they do in the United States. Tamori was a good listener. He lived in the world of the celebrity, it was true, but he was unpretentious and small-town on the air. Mariko put it well. "The people on that show talk about very ordinary life," she said. "So I feel very close to them."

After a break for a commercial, *You Can Laugh* resumed with a *Dating Game* segment. On one side of the stage was a gaunt young woman in a purple suit with long black hair and a tired manner. She was the bachelorette, so to speak. In typical fashion, Tamori told the woman she had nice legs, but not in an especially leering way. Then the woman told the audience a little about herself, revealing that she had been sixteen years old and her husband seventeen when the two were married. The audience gasped in a chorus, shocked at their young age. "I was pregnant the first year," the woman said. She was divorced when she was twenty-two. Her child, she said, was now ten.

"Why did you get divorced?" Tamori asked.

"We didn't get along," she said, covering her mouth with her hand and giggling.

Three bachelors then came out onstage, out of sight of the bachelorette. They wore jeans, seemed to be college students, and probably were unaware that they were younger than their potential beloved. Tamori looked them over, trying to lighten things up. "I never expected such short men," he said, before eliciting brief life stories. Bachelor B, for example, was in his third year at Waseda University and assured everyone that he studied every day.

Then it was time for the bachelorette to ask each potential date a question. She was obviously taking things seriously, and her queries were all the same: "When you come and see me for a date and my child is coming down from the second floor, what would you say?"

Bachelor A responded helpfully: "I'd say, 'What a good kid.' I wanted to be an elementary school teacher."

Bachelor B was not so promising: "I don't like children so much," he said. "So I'd ignore the child."

Bachelor C, on the other hand: "I work part-time putting on children's shows," he said. "I love children."

Not surprisingly, the bachelorette picked C, and the audience voted them $150 for a date.

After another commercial break, Tamori bantered with a new guest about the embarrassment of having to summon the hotel bellboy to adjust the television set during an adult video. There were jokes about the etiquette at funerals and about a priest with bad eyesight, which inspired Tamori to a riff in which he gave a blessing to an orange. The show concluded with all the guests running around trying to catch balloons with butterfly nets. I had to admit that the audience got its money's worth.

Off the set, during our interview a few weeks earlier, Tamori had been slightly more subdued but essentially no different from the prankster I saw onstage. We met not far from his studio, at the Tokyo Hilton, where Tamori and his retinue of half a dozen aides took possession of a secluded corner in the lobby bar. After the usual polite preliminaries, I opened by asking him to talk about Japanese tastes in humor. "In Japan, everyone is told it's not polite to tell jokes," Tamori responded agreeably. "So you could say that we don't actually have a sense of humor." From my experience, I knew that any foreigner planning to give a speech in Japan is urged not to tell jokes, and a politician or corporate executive who told a self-deprecating story to loosen up the crowd would be seen as not a serious person. Japanese comedy, such as it is, is confined to Japanese comedians.

And yet, Tamori said, "the Japanese fundamentally love humor. Superficially, they're reserved. But then the reserved people go to the bars and they become crazy." I mentioned that the Japanese always seem to worry about embarrassing themselves, and that getting caught with your pants down is a staple of Japanese comedy.

"Sometimes I really embarrass the guests," Tamori said. "The audience really enjoys it, but there are a lot of calls complaining about it. And there are also a lot of complaints whenever we use food. They say, 'There are many poor people all over the world. How can you use food for that fun?'" Eight years before, he glopped squid sauce on top of an ice-cream parfait, and he still remembers the flood of criticism. Tamori eventually stopped using food in his gags, except for the occasional pie in the face.

"I myself think the Japanese have a sense of humor," he said. "But when I get these complaints, I feel sorry for the Japanese. Maybe they don't have a sense of humor after all." He paused and laughed. "I change my opinion every three minutes."

After the *You Can Laugh* taping, Mariko, Sachiko, and I decided to have lunch together. Sachiko knew there was a good Chinese restaurant in the Tokyo Hilton—Sachiko said Chinese was the best buy for lunch in expensive hotels because a big bowl of noodles was only ten dollars—so we headed there. As we ordered, I noticed we were entirely surrounded by Japanese women. Sachiko said one particularly large group of ladies was probably a flower-arranging club out for lunch together. Over the noodles, the three of us decided that while the show might not have been the best *You Can Laugh* ever, it had been fun. We also agreed that the *Dating Game* segment had misfired.

"It wasn't funny," I said. "It was poignant."

"Yes," Mariko said. "Maybe Tamori regretted it."

Mariko and Sachiko agreed that the bachelorette was not, well, the ideal date. "It was a mismatch," Mariko said of the couple. "I didn't agree with the match, but I voted them money anyway. I would have felt guilty not to."

"The woman looked a little cheap to me," Sachiko said, as usual not mincing words.

Mariko agreed. "How can a person choose that kind of life?" she asked. "When you're sixteen years old you should be studying." Neither she nor Sachiko seemed willing to consider the possibility that the woman had not had many advantages in life. In the United States, her early marriage would have been excused, or at least seen in the context of a possibly troubled upbringing; in Japan, where children are believed to be born on an equal footing, her problems were viewed by Mariko and Sachiko as clearly her own responsibility. "She never had a chance to have a good time," Mariko said disapprovingly.

The day after the television show, Mariko's father came home from the hospital. Although his recovery from the removal of the tumor in his bladder had gone well, his doctors had kept him a week longer than planned, an entire month in all, probably to make sure he was strong enough to be discharged. His homecoming coincided with Mariko's forty-fifth birthday, on Friday, February 14. Sachiko and I arranged to have pizza delivered for the whole family, at the astonishing cost of nearly a hundred dollars, so Mariko would at least have a break from the kitchen on a difficult day. Mariko's birthday also marked the first anniversary of my initial meeting with her. The past twelve months, I reflected, had slipped by like so many pages flying off the calendar in a movie scene. By my timetable, my "year in the life" of the Tanaka family was now over. Theoretically, I should have respected the anniversary by bringing my interviews to a close and then turned to the task of writing my book. But ending things now seemed unnecessarily abrupt. Mariko and Sachiko had become an integral part of my life in Japan, and I was not ready to give them up. I sensed they also were reluctant to let go. Mariko, I knew, had always looked forward to our visits as an opportunity to let off steam and relax. On the other hand, I also knew that keeping up the interviews indefinitely would tax everyone's patience. When to stop? Fortunately—or unfortunately, depending on my mood on a given day—*The New York Times* made my decision for me. Around this time my husband, Steve, agreed to return to New York as the paper's deputy foreign editor, starting in early May, when we would have spent a little more than three years in Japan. The timetable of our return would give me another two and a half months to tie up loose ends and complete our project. In retrospect, I think stopping the interviews while I still lived in Japan would have seemed a little like abandonment to Mariko, and also to me. When I asked Mariko if the extra months of interviews were okay with her, she readily said yes.

But the fact was that she had less free time than ever, and the next month would not be a good one for her. Her convalescing father still needed attention, and in another two weeks Mariko's mother would be back as well. Mariko was hoping to start meter reading again on April 1. She was already overwhelmed and exhausted. How on earth would she manage a job? Then, of course, things got even worse. On February 17, three days after her father's return home, a nasty winter flu that was closing schools and emptying offices all over Tokyo hit Mariko, too. When her fever reached 102, she pulled out her futon and went to bed for two days. She had a splitting headache, aching muscles, and a strange, worrisome pain in her left side.

The only bright spot in her life was that Takeshi seemed to have taken a turn for the better. His construction project for the warehouse bakery south of Yokohama was still going well, and he was even drinking less. For the past month he had not come home later than ten-thirty in the evening, and even if he did have a few drinks on the way, he didn't forget what had happened to him. Mariko could also see that he was genuinely concerned about her parents. Remarkably, he was helping out at home and did the dishes after dinner without complaining. One night he actually told Mariko to go to bed early.

On the second day of Mariko's fever, there was another monthly meeting of the Ichomachi PTA's action committee. Once again, Bellmark was on the agenda, left over from the last meeting in December. Mariko was too sick to go, but I asked if Sachiko and I could show up anyway. Mariko made a call to clear my attendance with the action committee, but warned us that they were less than enthusiastic about the idea. We could go, she said, but they were mystified and suspicious about why we would want to be there without her. "I told them you're not just interested in me," she said. "I told them you're interested in the school, too."

With every expectation of a chilly reception at the meeting, Sachiko and I arrived around two in the afternoon, said hello to Mrs. Mori, then slunk to two desks in the back of the room. On top of each were snacks that had been distributed for the meeting—a miniature chocolate pie and a rice cracker, both in cellophane wrappers. Suddenly, a well-dressed action committee member appeared before us and officiously removed the treats from our desks. "There are only enough snacks for the members," she informed us in a businesslike tone. Then she put the two chocolate pies and two rice crackers back in a big cardboard box and walked briskly away. Sachiko and I stared at each other. In a notably polite country, we had just been subjected to a gesture of spectacular rudeness. But before we had a chance to say anything, yet another action committee member appeared before us and with a smile gave the snacks back.

What was going on here? Was coming to the meeting without Mariko so very offensive? Or did the woman who confiscated our sweets have some sort of vendetta against Mariko? Was the woman who returned the sweets on Mariko's side, or was she simply a bystander who could not stand the embarrassment of her colleague's action? Perhaps it was Mariko's longstanding directness that had offended at least some of the good women of the Ichomachi PTA. That, anyway, was Sachiko's theory. "Back when our kids were in kindergarten, Mariko used to be very direct with me," Sachiko reminded me. "She'd say things like, 'You didn't do enough for the class picnic.' It always made me uncomfortable." I could only marvel once again at the invisible minefields that underlie normal discourse in Japan.

The meeting started as usual at two-fifteen. "I hope everybody can be frank today," Mrs. Mori began sweetly, as if contemplating the immense task before her. She was dressed in a red sheath, more suitable, I thought, for a cocktail party, but then, this was Tokyo, where it was impossible to be overdressed. There were thirty-five women in attendance, a good turnout, but I was sorry to see that the turbaned Mrs. Sato was not among them, which substantially diminished the chances of fireworks. Mrs. Mori mentioned that this would be her last meeting as chairwoman—the new PTA would take over in April, at the start of the new school year—and she asked if the presence of Sachiko and me would be acceptable to the rest of the members. A round of faint applause seemed to mean that we passed—barely.

The Ichomachi Elementary School principal was first on the agenda, and he began by mentioning a potential kidnapper who had tried unsuccessfully to lure several elementary students into his car over the past few weeks in different parts of the ward. Such things did happen in Japan, although they were unusual, and stories about this particular case had run in the newspapers. The mothers were indeed on the alert. "We have no special news about the kidnapper," the principal said. "Mothers are making lots of efforts to patrol, and I want you to continue patrolling within your territory." He briefly mentioned the flu, the same bug that had felled Mariko and was still affecting the school, although, he said, the peak had passed. Some schools had been closed in the ward, but Ichomachi remained open.

After the principal's statement came the usual committee and class reports. One class had a rice cake party, another was going to have a miso soup party but didn't, and so on. Next came elaborate discussion, continued from the last meeting, about whether the students should continue *shudan toko*, or walking to school in groups. The mothers repeated familiar arguments on both sides of the issue, which was still unresolved at two forty-five, when everyone broke for tea and snacks. Sachiko and I, given our close call, were very grateful to have our chocolate pies.

A few minutes later, Mrs. Sato walked in, outrageously late and seemingly proud of it. Maybe now the meeting would get interesting. But the discussion of the walking-together system had taken on a new urgency with news of the kidnapper, so it continued post-snack for another half hour, leaving little time for the Bellmark issue to be addressed. Finally everyone voted to keep up the walking-together system for the first two months of each semester.

It was now three-fifteen and time at last for Bellmark. The issue, as the PTA had left it, was still at an impasse between those who favored using the Bellmark emblems to buy a new unicycle and those opposed. Faced with Mrs. Sato's objections to Bellmark as a consumer rip-off and her insistence that the ward, not the PTA, should take responsibility for buying unicycles, the action committee board had asked the class representative to take informal surveys of opinion. Today the representatives were to present their findings. Democracy and consensus-building Japanese-style churned slowly forward; I was hoping that tapping the sentiments of the parents at the grass-roots level would finally produce a decision.

Wrong. The soundings from the hinterlands turned out to be completely muddled. Although a few mothers did report a decisive point of view—two said their classes were in favor of continuing Bellmark and another characterized sentiment as "unenthusiastic"—most others conscientiously repeated the full spectrum of opinion, steadfastly refusing to say which view predominated. Some reports failed to address the issue at all and instead answered completely unrelated questions. A mother from a first-grade class, for example, went on about how opinion was divided over whether the stamps should be collected by the children or the mothers. A representative from one of the fifth-grade classes suggested that a questionnaire be sent to everyone in the school to determine what people wanted to buy—not exactly something that would speed up the process.

Toward the end of the exhaustive class reports, Mrs. Sato spoke up. "I discovered a file about Bellmark," she announced, declaring that she had been doing homework to buttress her point of view. She had even gone to the Board of Education to get what she considered dramatic evidence that Bellmark prizes should not be a substitute for government funding. "The file said that Bellmark started in 1955," she reported, adding that it was designed to help companies sell their products. "Then in 1967, the Education Ministry said that if you were to buy something for the children, you should use official money." Her point was well taken but clearly exasperating to many in the room, and there was a flood of comments from other PTA members, indicating to me that this particular issue had been around for years, if not decades.

"Every year we discuss the same thing," complained one mother, who said the Bellmark problem was allowed to linger because the action committee had more important things to do.

But Mrs. Sato pressed her point, insistent that PTA members would be violating Education Ministry edicts if they used Bellmark stamps to buy the unicycle. "We should talk about the regulations for Bellmark established by the Education Ministry," Mrs. Sato said, now becoming a bit shrill as she repeated that what the PTA wanted to do was somehow a violation of these "historical regulations."

At this point the school principal tried to interject a note of calm by beseeching everyone not to be so negative. "No one has a positive attitude," he said wearily. "The attitude is, 'Oh, are we talking about Bellmark again?' "

As Mrs. Sato stood her ground, one mother accused her of taking a position that was too inflexible. It was too much to expect that all the school's needs could be met by the official budget, she pointed out. "I don't think it's so bad to take advantage of Bellmark to do something for our children," she said.

At last, I thought, a voice of reason. The room fell silent. In the sudden void, Mrs. Mori conferred with one of her deputies.

"Do you really have a file from the Board of Education?" the deputy skeptically asked Mrs. Sato. With her turban held high, Mrs. Sato sat there, not answering. Brilliant tactician that she was, she then went in for the kill. "I think this discussion should be continued at the next meeting," she said. "We should not decide today."

It was now three-fifty. School was out. Classical music, something by Brahms, sounded over the loudspeaker. "Sayonara," a recorded voice said. "School is over. Everybody please go home." My sentiments exactly.

But the Bellmark debate continued. Eventually, Mrs. Sato said she wouldn't mind if the collection of Bellmark stamps continued for another year, but she was adamant that the stamps not be used to buy things for the students. Instead, she suggested, the PTA should buy something for itself, like a mimeograph machine. After her suggestion another mother ventured out on a limb and actually said that there did seem to be a consensus to continue the program. "This is all very emotional," she said. "If there are one hundred people, there are one hundred opinions. But in today's case, more people have said they want to continue." I thought these comments would help bring the meeting to a natural conclusion, but I was wrong again. The discussion was still going in circles at four, when I had to leave for another interview. Later, I learned that the meeting went on until almost five. The women of the Ichomachi PTA at last decided that the Bellmark program would continue, and that a unicycle would be bought. Mrs. Sato lost, having successfully stalled the issue for almost six months. If it was not exactly a victory, she could still take solace in the fact that there was always next year.

It took Mariko a week to get over the worst of her flu, and by then I had caught it, and Sachiko did too. With everyone sick, the three of us did not get together again until the end of February, on a warm, sunny day that seemed to promise the coming of spring. Mariko, however, was hardly cheerful. Her mother had come home from the hospital two days before, and although her father was helping out, Mariko was exhausted from overseeing their care and from the lingering effects of her flu. "I remember when I really had confidence about my body," she said. "I can't understand why in this short time my feelings have changed so much." The pain in her left side had been so bad that she had gone to see an orthopedic surgeon, who took an X-ray and declared her healthy but tired. Mariko also went to see her gynecologist for her annual breast exam and Pap smear, and while she was there she asked the doctor, a woman, about the pain in her side. The doctor said she sometimes had the same thing, and told Mariko not to work so hard.

Mariko knew in her heart that the real cause of her aches and pains was depression. "I can't find any value in my life right now," she told us that day. "I know that depression can cause this kind of pain. If you're working hard, you don't notice it, but now I have the time to feel it." She thought a moment. "Actually, it seems like I have time, but I don't," she said. "I can't use my time the way I want. I have to stay at home. I have no stimulation."

I had never heard the normally cheerful Mariko talk in such a downcast way, and both Sachiko and I quickly assured her that her feelings were normal. "I've experienced this kind of stagnation a few times in my life," Mariko said. "Time passes, and I feel I haven't done anything important."

It was hardly surprising that Mariko was depressed. I would have been too. After a year getting to know what it was like to be a Japanese housewife, I came to the unsurprising conclusion that in many ways she was no different from her counterparts in any other society. Although Mariko thought of herself as a mother and wife first, and treated her work outside the home as secondary, it was obvious to me how much her meter reading and her job at the travel office gave her an identity and lifted her spirits. "If I gave up work, I'd be very depressed," she said. But now she was wholly caught up in the lives of others. Although her father was able to fix her mother's meals and change her diapers, Mariko saw that he was more feeble after his surgery. After all, he was nearly eighty. Mariko felt guilty that she had let him take on so much of her mother's care over the years. Wasn't it really her responsibility, as the daughter? In view of his illness and her own lingering weakness, she wasn't sure she really could return to meter reading on April 1. She would just have to see how her situation progressed and how quickly her energy returned. Until then, she felt, it was her duty to be in the house with her parents, if only for the psychological comfort they would draw from her presence. "My father and mother feel more secure to have me here," she said. "And the children do, too."

As a result, Mariko was a little like an exile in her own home, a half-busy shut-in whose humdrum days made her feel sleepy and dull. She still got up at six-thirty, when she fixed breakfast and box lunches for her husband and children. And after they left she cleaned the house, did the laundry, and glanced at the headlines in the *Mainichi*. But at noon she watched *You Can Laugh* and then the ladies' talk show *Tetsuko's Room*, starring Tetsuko Kuroyanagi, one of the most popular television personalities in Japan. That took her up to two in the afternoon, when she studied a book to prepare for a test to get a license as a travel agent. Opening her own travel business was still a dream of hers, though seemingly less attainable than ever. At four she took a short nap, then left for Marufuji to shop for groceries. She came home, made dinner, and served it to the kids and, if he was home, Takeshi. Either she or Takeshi did the dishes, and then Mariko took a hot soak in a deep bath. By ten o'clock, even though her day had hardly been full, she felt completely worn out.

I think part of Mariko's problem was that she was looking around at her life, as people do in middle age, and asking herself if this was what she had meant it to be. It was a Japanese life, a woman's life, no worse and no better than so many others, a life spent largely in reaction to children, to a husband, to sick parents. Even on a good day Mariko knew how hard it was to get out in front of her life, to do the few things she wanted to do, to feel a sense of accomplishment, to have fun. But now in her quiet house, in the dark of a Tokyo winter, when dusk came at three-thirty and the black of night at five, she felt swallowed up. Her children were getting older and would soon be gone, just in time, it seemed, for her to turn around and be a parent to her parents, who, in the nation with the longest life expectancy in the world, might well live another twenty years. By then, Mariko would be sixty-five.

"Sometimes the three fingers go numb in my left hand," she said. "My joints are painful. And my periods these past few years have only come every two months." She was complaining so much that I wondered if she was worried that her aches and pains might be symptoms of some dire disease. "I don't think it's serious," she said, but I didn't completely believe her. "But I don't feel I can return to the days when I was so happy. I feel I'm trapped. This episode with my father has made me realize how much more of this is down the road."

She mentioned her husband's hospitalization for diabetes two years before. "He controls it by diet," she said casually. At that same time, she said, her mother was also in the hospital with high blood pressure. And her father was ill at home. "So the three together were sick," Mariko said. "But I never got depressed, even though that time was worse. I was younger then, and stronger."

In March, as the weather warmed, Mariko's natural buoyancy slowly returned. Her father was growing stronger every day, and better able to care for her mother. Mariko's own health had improved as well—her left side no longer hurt—and her other aches and pains were fading away. On March 4 she went to her first samisen lesson since her father's illness, two months earlier, and found that the familiar music invigorated her. "I feel much better," she told me afterward. The routine was a godsend, and the troubles of the winter seemed to be receding.

When Sachiko and I went to see her the following afternoon, a sodden Wednesday, we found her contentedly slicing wedges of fresh grapefruit to eat with our tea. A steady rain had brought a chill to the air, but the *kotatsu* was on and the house was cozy. Shunsuke was home from school, absorbed in roasting *mochi* cakes left over from New Year's. I watched as he browned them on the grate on top of a space heater, then dipped them in soy sauce and wolfed them down. Sachiko and I took our usual places in this domestic scene, happy for the comforts of hot tea and companionship. I had no burning questions to ask Mariko that day, and no real agenda to pursue. Maybe it was the sleepy weather, but in truth I think that the prospect of leaving Japan had made me lazy. I had my "year in the life," and anything beyond that was welcome but peripheral. Or so I thought.

On this day I let the conversation drift, from Shunsuke's three tests at school that morning—"disasters," he said—to Midori Ito, Japan's big hope in women's figure skating in the Olympics. We talked about how the young Miss Ito, the amazing athlete, had bowed and apologized to her country for falling on a jump she normally never missed, and then losing the gold medal to Kristi Yamaguchi, an American of Japanese heritage. Mariko had watched every minute of the spectacle. "I really wanted her to win," she said, suggesting that Ito deserved the gold because she was clearly the best at jumping.

We also talked that day about the recent killing of two Japanese in the United States, one, a university president, in his Boston hotel room, the other, a businessman, at his home in California. "I'd feel uncomfortable now to go on vacation in the United States," Mariko said. She viewed the murders as another sign of America's downslide and of its resentment toward Japan.

I saw Mariko again the following week, and, as before, the conversation was pleasant, but I felt I had nowhere to go with it. Hoping to change the pace, I asked if I could see Mariko's high school graduation album. Nearly a year before, when I had first met her, she had told me about her high school days. But her recollections of the class of 1965 had been perfunctory. Now I was hoping that the old photographs would draw out some memories.

Mariko happily showed me the big book, which looked no different from a graduation album from any American high school. Inside the front cover was a picture taken from the top of the school of a pink-tinged Mount Fuji, a sight more common in those days before pollution smudged Tokyo's skies. In the formal picture of Mariko's class there were neat, somber rows of fifty-four students, not one of them smiling, with an equally serious teacher in front. After this were informal "snaps," as Mariko called them, of more cheerful groups of friends, including the one of Mariko and three other girls and four boys, one of them Takeshi, under the caption "*Smah-to tatchi, ii tatchi*"—"Smart feeling, good feeling."

"This photo is unreliable," Mariko said, pointing to another picture. "These two girls were good friends, but these two weren't." She pointed to another. "And in this picture, nobody is a friend," she said, characteristically blunt. Then came pages of afterschool activities: the Baseball Club, the Art Club, the Girls' Basketball Club, the Flower-Arranging Club, the Acting Club, the Literature Club, the Tea Ceremony Club, the Cooking Club. Mariko recalled that in a Culture Club production of a famous Japanese folktale, she had played the part of an old lady who helps with the upbringing of a beautiful princess from the moon. "The girl who played the princess," Mariko recalled, "had the face of a porcelain doll." Mariko was also on her school's Sports Day committee. "So was he," she said, pointing to a picture and mentioning a man's name, a classmate's, that I hadn't heard before. "I loved him, but he loved somebody else. He was still very sweet to me, though. Now he lives in the United States, or at least I think someone told me that."

She paused.

"I also loved someone after I got married," she suddenly said.

I looked at her. So did Sachiko. There was a slight silence.

"Why are you telling me this now?" I asked.

She gave me a look—of impatience, of exasperation, of pride.

"You never asked," she said.

. . .

That was certainly true. Never had it occurred to me that Mariko, my typical Japanese housewife, would have been so daring, so irresponsible—so enterprising, really—as to have an affair. She seemed far too grounded in her family for that. Of course affairs among Japanese married women are hardly rare. But Mariko had never even hinted at an affair in our months of talking, and all her complaints about Takeshi's girlfriend had led me astray. And yet, as I looked back over our year together, I found new meaning in something she had told me that past fall about the temptations facing Takeshi. "If I see an attractive man, I feel the same way," she had said. "But the difference is whether I'll take any action." I was pleased, of course, that she had confided in me, but the new information was sobering to me as a journalist. First, I was chastened to realize how much I had fit Mariko into my own perceptions of what a Japanese housewife should be. Second, I was left to wonder with a new intensity about what else I didn't know, and never would, about Mariko's life.

Mariko, her initial confession over, was in a mood to talk. The man, she began, was a friend of Takeshi's who used to come by the house for visits. He was single, and after one or two years they began an affair. That was eight years earlier, when Ken-chan was two. The affair lasted three years, finally ending when the man decided to marry someone else. Mariko asked me not to mention any other details about him. Although she was certain that Takeshi knew—and she was grateful that he had never confronted her, then or later—the man's family did not know, and she did not want to hurt them by identifying him.

"I didn't feel guilty to have this man as a lover," she said, thoughtfully smoking her usual cigarette at the head of the table. "But it wasn't fun at all. It was a very, very hard time. Parts of it were enjoyable, but mostly it was bitter and painful. Whenever I wanted to see him, I couldn't." Sometimes, she said, they managed to sneak time during the day—the man was self-employed, Ken-chan was already in nursery school, and Mariko's working hours were flexible—but she declined to tell me where they met. In the evenings the man sometimes came to Mariko's old house to visit the whole family, and then stayed so late that Takeshi would get tired and go upstairs to bed. Mariko was left to entertain him alone, sometimes until two or three in the morning. "We ate, we played samisen, we talked," she said. He was strikingly different from Takeshi. "He had so many qualities that my husband didn't have," Mariko said. "He was very positive and very active. He liked chal-lenges." With all the intensity, and anxiety, Mariko lost twenty pounds. "I was told by so many people around that time how attractive I was," she said.

There were moments, she admitted, when she thought about walking out of the marriage. "I did think sometimes that I would leave everything here," she said. "I sometimes used to wish that I could throw everything away for just a short time—my kids, my husband, my job." But the idea terrified her. "It would have been like throwing my whole history away—my parents, my children, my husband, my life," she said. "All my memories would have been gone." And yet, she said, "even if I loved this man, I knew I'd never get divorced. He had his business, and I had three chil-dren." I asked why she could not have left her husband, taken her children, and married him, American-style. "If I had been single, I just would have gone to him," she said. "It would have been simple." But to Mariko a jerry-built family of stepfather and stepchildren was unthinkable. "My children were not his chil-dren," she said. "And my husband loves our children." The idea of her children's calling someone else Daddy was horrifying. "Mothers have to sacrifice," she said. "Sometimes that means we have to kill our own true emotions. But I feel a great responsibil-ity for raising these children."

Her relationship with Takeshi at the time, she recalled, was "nothing." It consisted, she said, "of conversations about minimum information we needed to exchange—like, 'Somebody called and please call him back.' Or, 'We received this kind of letter,' or, 'Sports Day is October 10.' " Even Takeshi knew something was wrong. A woman who worked at the neighborhood bar, a friend of the family, told Mariko that Takeshi had told her how lonely he was.

"When I look back on those days, it seems I couldn't even see my own family," Mariko said. "I played the minimum role as a mother and as a wife. It was very foolish, trying to coordinate my time for that man. It was like I was being controlled. I don't like to be controlled, and I don't want to do it again." Later she told me that she had made a mess of her homemade Japanese pickles, made from Chinese cabbage, of which she was normally quite proud. "They tasted bad," she said. "To me this meant that my mind wasn't with my family."

After three years, when the man turned forty and began thinking about settling down and having children, the affair ended. The man was introduced to another woman at an arranged meeting, an *omiai*, in January and proposed to her the following month. Mariko had known all along that this day would come, but she was devastated nonetheless. The wedding was set for October. "We met one day in September," Mariko recalled. "Of course we had known in February that we had to say good-bye. But that day he said, 'Maybe I will be able to love the woman I am marrying instead of you.' I told him that would be good for him." They talked again on the morning of his wedding. "It was a weekday and I was going to work," Mariko said. "He called, for nothing, and I didn't feel anything. I just said, 'Have a nice honeymoon.' "

At this point I asked how she and Takeshi had been faring more recently. "He's changing," Mariko said. "He's improving." It was the most positive thing I had ever heard her say about him, and it seemed, for now, to be true. Takeshi was drinking less and helping out more at home, a transformation so dramatic that Mariko was now ascribing all sorts of remarkable qualities to him. "Sometimes I think he thinks more about the marriage and our family than I do," she said. When she was seeing the other man, she added, "maybe he wanted to divorce me, but he really thinks the family is important. So he just put up with it."

I suggested to Mariko that her marriage seemed to be an inevitable series of ups and downs, a kind of endurance contest with rewards at the end. "At first I wanted to be under my husband's umbrella," Mariko said, without directly responding to what I had said. "There was the beauty of making things for him. I enjoyed the idea of being controlled by the man I loved. But I've really changed after three children. That's why I'm so puzzled about marriage. It seems like I've become a real mother. I'm more interested in being a mother than a wife. A husband is just the person who brings the money home."

Mariko had talked for two hours, and now it was time to go. On the way home I thought about everything she had told me, reflecting that a major mystery in my mind had been solved. Never had I understood the supposedly passive acceptance of the typically distant Japanese marriage, the kind so many people in Japan described as the norm. Couples had low expectations of marriage, everyone said. Marriage was for children and security, not romance. Women found intimacy with women friends in the neighborhood, men with colleagues at the office. Extramarital sex was commonplace, with the emphasis on sex, not love. These comments, however accurate, always suggested to me that the Japanese were too practical for the messy passions of life, that they were seemingly as efficient in love as in work. And yet I knew Mariko had needs and longings, like anyone else. The question in my mind, given her relationship with Takeshi, was what had she done with those needs? Now I knew at least part of the answer. Here was one Japanese woman who had lost her heart, who had exposed herself, who had been fallible, who had been human.

As I thought about Mariko on the way home, I realized I had started out trying to learn what it is like to be a Japanese housewife and had ended up seeing how kindred people really are, and how every life, no matter how plain its surface, is a drama of roiling emotion underneath. People fall in love, marriages fail, loved ones get sick and die, babies arrive to make it all more bearable. I had two feelings about Mariko as I left her house that day. The first was sadness in knowing that she had felt she had to walk away from a man she truly loved and who seemed to love her. But I was glad that she had experienced what seemed to have been truly intimate love and companionship. As she told me her story, I could also see that the passage of time had healed the rawest wounds, and had given her perspective and distance. "It was very foolish, trying to coordinate my time for that man. . . . I don't like to be controlled, and I don't want to do it again. . . ." But if she no longer felt so vulnerable, I could imagine the kind of turmoil she had gone through at the time, and how she must have crawled little by little out of a terrible black depth on her own. I remembered then something that one of her closest friends had told me, about how Mariko once cried all night with her over a bottle of sake. When I had asked the friend the cause of the tears, she just smiled. "It's Mariko's secret," she said.

The next week I picked up where we had left off and asked Mariko why she had not felt guilty about what she had done. "I was very self-centered at the time," she said. "I only thought about myself. There was no room for me to think about other people. My heart was completely with the other man. Whenever I had to talk to my husband, the conversation never went well. And when I first met the man, it was always exciting. That's why I didn't feel guilty at all. But then he started visiting us all the time, and we used to sit down exactly like this. That's when I started feeling guilty. I was always thinking about things from his point of view, and not my husband's."

Mariko insisted that her affair was not a reaction to her husband's, although she admitted that had had its effect. "When I found out that my husband had a girlfriend, I had to think differently about him," she said. "Why was he so moved by this girl? And then this man came into my life." A little later, she added: "I was really attracted to him, but it had nothing to do with retaliation and revenge."

I asked if Takeshi's affair fundamentally changed the way she looked at him. "I was very jealous," Mariko said. "I can't say I changed the way I felt about him, but I was very jealous. And even before this girl came, ever since I married, I was very, very uncertain that my husband really loved me." Soon after her marriage, she recalled, Takeshi told her that he had saved her from spinsterhood. Worse, he casually referred to their marriage as just a *nariyuki,* a kind of fated and convenient turn of events. In Mariko's mind, Takeshi had never really pursued her.

"In this marriage, I never had the experience of having an exciting date," she said. "I never got a telephone call from him when he said, 'I need you, I need you,' or, 'I can't live without you.' He's never said it. And he's never said, 'I love you.' " She thought a moment. "Actually," she amended, "in the last two or three years, he has said it."

I asked her again why she now thought she had married him. "I was twenty-four, and maybe I was feeling old," she said. "And I really wanted to escape from my brother. My husband was very nice to him, and that made me happy." She brightened. "So maybe he really loved me at that point. But it wasn't a sweet atmosphere."

"Did you love him?" I asked.

"Yes," she said emphatically. "He had a sweet character. And he still does."

12

A JAPANESE LIFE

Mariko and the other mothers watching the high school football game

APRIL

By the end of March the cherry trees were in blossom again, bringing a poetic pink veil and the usual inebriates to Tokyo's parks. A year before, I had gone to Chiaki's junior high school graduation, and it was astonishing to me how quickly the months had passed. As always, the season was a time of taking stock. For Mariko, the blossoms that year were a sign of rejuvenation, a final closing of her winter troubles. "If there is a heaven and a hell," she told me, "when I'm in the middle of the cherry blossoms, and when the wind is warm, I feel like I'm in heaven." But to me the blossoms were a melancholy reminder that I was facing my last spring in Japan. In a month my family and I would be packing up to start another life in New York City, which Mariko and Sachiko viewed as little better than Sarajevo. To be honest, I was a little uneasy about living in

New York after three peaceful years in Japan, although I tried to tell myself that I had fallen prey to the overplayed stories about crime in America and would be cured of my fears when I got back home.

But it was with a great wistfulness that my family and I went to the cherry blossom festivities in our neighborhood park that spring, and ate yakitori and roasted corn and fried noodles under the otherworldly pink mist. As I looked around at the crowds, I realized how much I would miss this three-year interlude in our lives. There is a dramatic, emotional finality in leaving a foreign country, much more so than in an ordinary move. Japan, like India before it, had become a character writ large in my life, and Mariko and Sachiko had taken their place among the people I felt closest to. I had seen them constantly for fourteen months and had enjoyed with them a surprising intimacy drawn from our shared enterprise. We were partners and compatriots, and now I was breaking up our trio. Although I never felt as intensely about Japan as I did about the raucous, all-consuming India, Japan was absorbing, it was comfortable, it was safe, it was home. If India was a passionate affair, Japan was a peaceful marriage. My daughter had been born in Japan, had gone to the neighborhood nursery school, and had played on the swings under these cherry trees. It was going to be very painful for us to leave.

Mariko's life would go on without me, which, absurdly, made me feel a little left out. Even now, as one school year was ending and another one beginning, Mariko's calendar was filled with meetings, mothers' events, and other start-up activities of the season. That month she had been to no fewer than three parties—a Japan Travel Bureau office party, a dinner organized by mothers at a local restaurant for Ken-chan's fourth-grade teacher, and another dinner for Chiaki's fifth- and sixth-grade teacher. (Elementary school teachers in Japan frequently stay with a class for more than one academic year.) Chiaki was about to enter eleventh grade, but the mothers still had an annual get-together with the teacher who had taught their children five years before. I was amazed to hear that Mariko belonged to four mothers' groups that organized such activities. The groups met only once a year, and naturally their talk was confined to pleasantries about children and school. But keeping up the ties was a remarkable tribute to the respect that teachers command in Japanese society, and to the mothers' devotion to maintaining continuity in their children's lives.

Mariko had also become the mother in charge of Ken-chan's baseball team, which meant she had to show up at games every Sunday morning to provide snacks and moral support for the boys. And of course the ladies of the Ichomachi PTA were gearing up for what would no doubt be another disputatious year. There had been a meeting in the school auditorium to choose the new members of the action committee, and, not surprisingly, no one wanted to serve. Even Mariko begged off, saying that she was the baseball mother, and that her parents were ill; being Mariko, however, she offered her help on big projects. Finally, the women decided to choose the new action committee members by lottery, which, predictably, provoked a time-consuming discussion. Mariko, for one, observed that putting the names of mothers not in attendance into a hat was useless, since their absence indicated they were probably working and wouldn't be able to serve if their names were drawn. But by this time, two mothers had volunteered, and at the meeting's end five more had succumbed to peer pressure and signed up. At one point a mother actually suggested that they abolish the PTA altogether, which, according to Mariko, annoyed everyone. "The PTA is a place for parents to talk," she said. "And children grow through the community activities we do. They don't grow only through school."

PTA irritants aside, these early spring days were a happy time for Mariko, who knew her relaxed mood would end soon enough, on April 1, when she at last went back to work. As usual, Takeshi complained that Mariko was having too much fun, and he began to revert to his old behavior, after his brief period of being helpful during her parents' hospitalization that winter. "Remember when he changed a little after my father's illness?" Mariko said. "Well, now he's discovered that I'm enjoying myself because I'm not working. He's changed back. The atmosphere is—'I am king.' A month ago, I made his lunch, of course, but he did the wrapping of the food. But this morning he said, 'You're just wasting your time these days. Why don't you wrap it up?' He has become very arrogant again. Two days ago, he told me, 'Why don't you put away the futons?' What he meant was that since I'm at home, my job is putting away the futons. Like a servant."

By mid-April, with just two weeks left in Japan, I realized I needed to follow up the gingko trees story one last time by meeting with Mr. Tanizaki, the unofficial mayor of Ichomachi. I had dropped the issue in December but still wondered why such a canny politician had supported something so unpopular as laying waste to a beautiful stand of trees. The Ichomachi shrine did not seem to be an especially powerful force in the community. It was a small, charming neighborhood shrine, and a rather broke one at that.

In an attempt to unravel the mystery, Sachiko and I first paid a call on Mr. Mori, the shrine priest, who was married so unhappily to the PTA president. I have no idea whether Mrs. Mori ever told Mr. Mori the substance of her startling confessions to me, but I suspect not. On the day we met with her husband she demurely served tea, her face set, like a Noh mask, in one of those enigmatic smiles expected of Japanese women when they are performing their subservient roles. Sachiko and I smiled emptily back at her, silent partners in her secret.

Mr. Mori dressed for the interview in the everyday but quite spectacular clothes of his profession, a white robe and a pair of deep purple culotte-like silk trousers. As we sipped our tea, he told us that the annual income and the yearly operating expenses of the shrine were about eighty thousand dollars each. "But every year there are losses, and we have to borrow money," he said sadly. "We've been operating at a deficit for the past ten years."

The parking lot, he said, was vital to the future of the shrine, which was old and in desperate need of repair. He explained that the decision to cut the trees was "more or less" made by the shrine's board of directors, which was composed of twelve prominent neighborhood citizens, most of them old, all of them men. As for which board member first came up with the idea of the parking lot, he was vague.

"There are people responsible, but I can't say anything more," Mr. Mori said. He held out little hope that there would be a quick solution to the problem of what to do with the felled trees. "The parking lot will happen eventually," he said. "But for the time being, it's like a cease-fire."

When Sachiko and I went to see Mr. Tanizaki, he was no more illuminating about the mystery of the cut trees. He received us as before in his kitchen, where he outlined much of what we already knew. "The shrine needed a way to generate income," he said. "They decided to build a parking lot, and in order for that to happen, they had to cut down the trees. If there had been a way to have a parking lot without cutting the trees, that would have been best. But there wasn't." He spoke evenly and amiably as we sat at his kitchen table, with a touch of regret in his voice, but there was little conviction or passion in his account. Then he turned to the stalemate over what to do next. The trees, he said with a sigh, were still lying where they had been felled eleven months before. The administration of the ward, it seemed, had yet to give permission to allow large trucks onto a pedestrian path near the shrine so they could pick up the trees and cart them away. With a tone of resignation, Mr. Tanizaki explained that he had sought permission for the trucks to come in the year before, but the ward bureaucrats replied that he would first have to get the "understanding" of the people who had objected to cutting the trees in the first place. So democracy had asserted its claims after all. Mr. Tanizaki told us that he had in fact asked Mr. Mori to hold a meeting with the tree huggers, but Mr. Mori, according to Mr. Tanizaki, never did. "So it's still pending," he said. "The shrine really isn't making any effort to persuade the neighborhood people. The people are very much against the parking lot, and the shrine is frightened."

Mr. Tanizaki appeared to be caught in a true dilemma. On one hand, he seemed sincere when he said that ways needed to be found to ensure the shrine's survival. "The most important thing is to maintain the shrine," he said. "The shrine is considered to be the god of the village. We are under its protection." On the other hand, he showed more than a trace of irritation when he said that the shrine had perhaps arrogantly ignored the wishes of the local community in doing what it did. He seemed to be waiting for the priest and the shrine's board of directors to realize they had to listen to the neighborhood if they wanted to complete their project.

Mr. Tanizaki's comments all sounded reasonable, but I left his kitchen with the feeling that there was something missing. Both Mrs. Sato and Mariko had told me they also were uncertain why Mr. Tanizaki had not taken a stronger position in favor of saving the trees. Sachiko felt it too, and had an idea how to unravel the mystery. "You have to talk to my father," she said. "He'll explain everything." Her suggestion seemed unlikely to lead anywhere. Sachiko's father was a retired businessman, and he lived in Kiryu, a small town outside of Tokyo. Although he had close ties to the Liberal Democratic Party, I couldn't imagine what he had to offer on the gingko trees. But Sachiko had for a long time wanted me to meet him and to see her hometown. What could it hurt?

A few days later we were in Sachiko's family home, a large, luxurious Japanese house in the hills above Kiryu, listening as her father, a shrewd, seventy-five-year-old businessman with long-standing and deep ties to the political powers in his community, spun out his theories of the gingko trees. I had given him the details I knew, and he, savoring the possibilities, rose to the occasion. "We know that Mr. Tanizaki has to face reelection to the ward council," Sachiko's father began. "So it's not in his political interest to be on the side of the shrine. There must be some reason why he is. Now, the priest alone would not have made the decision about cutting the trees. Probably he went to the shrine board, discussed the shrine's financial problems, and asked for help. Perhaps someone said, 'How about a parking lot?' After that, the board may have consulted Mr. Tanizaki and asked, 'What should we do?' Probably the board has always historically supported him. After all, he has more power than they do. Now, Mr. Tanizaki may have himself suggested the parking lot at this point, or he may have simply agreed with the parking lot idea and told them he would help with approvals from the ward council. Maybe he said he would be happy to handle the tree issue himself. And maybe he even told the shrine he would buy the trees from them. Because I think he may have plans to sell them somewhere. Gingkos are very good for furniture. Priests generally don't have a mind for business, but Mr. Tanizaki owns a fuel company, so he has lots of connections with lumber companies."

Startled, I asked Sachiko's father how much money could be made from the trees.

"Well, it takes five or ten years for a tree to dry," he said. "After that, trees of that size are very valuable in Japan. And gingkos are very straight when you cut them for lumber. In ten years, I would guess, you could get five or six million yen per tree." I quickly did the math, and came up with the astonishing sum, for all of the trees, of two million dollars.

"Is this just a theory or are you sure this is what happened?" I asked.

"One hundred percent sure," Sachiko's father said, chuckling. "Mr. Tanizaki doesn't think he's done something wrong. He doesn't feel guilty."

He then spun out an even more fanciful theory on what a truly brilliant politician would have done when told by the shrine board that they were prepared to cut down the trees. Mr. Tanizaki, he said, should have taken the issue to the community, spread the word that the trees were in peril, and helped the shrine raise money to solve its financial troubles. Then Mr. Tanizaki would have been beloved by the shrine leaders as well as popular in the community—and the trees would have been saved.

"If that's what Mr. Tanizaki had done, he would have had a chance to be the mayor of the whole ward," Sachiko's father said. "But Mr. Tanizaki is getting old. Maybe he's given up on his reelection. Maybe the money is more important." He savored the idea. "If I met him, I could tell in one glance what he had done," he said with a mischievous smile.

Sachiko's father's conjecture was seductive because it explained everything with a neat conspiracy theory. Certainly it is true that politics is a lucrative calling in Japan. But it was also possible that Mr. Tanizaki was telling the absolute truth when he said he believed that cutting down the trees for the parking lot was the only way to save the shrine. Once they were down, perhaps he was inclined to wash his hands of them, at least until the shrine was ready to make some sort of gesture to the people in the neighborhood, like Mrs. Sato and even Mariko, whose youthful memories of the shady byways of the gingko trees had been so violated.

"How can I find out what really happened?" I asked Sachiko's father.

He smiled. "It's impossible," he said.

. . .

Over the next two weeks, I tied up loose ends in a series of "lasts": a last dinner with Mariko, a last lunch at her house, a last talk with Takeshi, my last (though it was also my first) chance to see Shunsuke play football.

His game was at nine on a breezy, unseasonably humid Sunday morning, an odd time, I thought. On the other hand, football is a recently imported sport, growing in popularity but not yet part of the social fabric of Japan. The game between two rival high schools drew no crowds, cheerleaders, or marching bands. Instead a few friends and mothers collected along the sidelines of a muddy, ragged football field. As usual, there wasn't a father in sight, which I found strange and irritating. Why couldn't at least one Japanese father have roused himself on a Sunday morning to cheer on his son?

Sachiko had stayed home, rebelling at the eleventh hour against this last excursion to a banal event. So I stood around in the mud with Mariko and the other mothers, all dressed as if for an elegant lunch in blazers, silk scarves, stockings, pumps, and pearls. They seemed puzzled by what was occurring on the field, so I asked Mariko if she knew anything about football.

"I can't understand it at all," she said cheerfully, in English. "Very difficult. *Zen, zen*—not at all." Eager to be of help, I told the mothers that a touchdown was worth six points, which they seemed to find interesting.

At halftime I asked if they knew the score, but nobody did. The mothers cheered when Shunsuke's team moved the ball forward, but then the team got pushed back to its own ten-yard line. After a blocked punt, they got pushed back farther into the end zone. Later, when the opposing quarterback was barreling down the field, Mariko was unable to control herself. "Slow down!" she shouted. Shunsuke was mortified, and the game turned into a rout for his team.

The following week brought us into late April. Mariko, Sachiko, and I took ourselves out for a good-bye dinner at Il Forno, the restaurant in Roppongi where Sachiko and I had talked to Shunsuke in January. On a beautiful spring evening we reminisced about the year, surveyed the stylish crowd, and drank too much Italian wine. Sachiko flirted with one of the waiters, and Mariko gave me an audiotape of her *Kanjincho* performance at Gas Hall. As we ate, I asked Mariko to tell me if she could think of one important thing that I had not asked her that year, but rather than answering, she went off on a different tack. "You know what I've discovered?" she said. "I'm really Japanese." I laughed, but she was serious. "After all the interviews with you," she said, "I learned that whenever we talked about cars, or about pesticides on food, I always took the Japanese side. But when we were just talking, Elisabeth and Mariko, it didn't matter."

It was not just that Mariko sided with Japan in the trade wars, or considered American imported oranges too dangerous to eat. She always had a consistent Japanese perspective on social issues as well, from accepting the limitations of her marriage to tolerating her husband's drinking to caring for her parents in their old age. In her world, her choices made sense. "There is more than one way to do things," she said. "For example, marriage." I knew she had inferred from the tone of my questions during the year that I thought she should consider ending the marriage, and it was true there had been many times when I thought that Mariko should have left Takeshi and never looked back. Now I was sorry I had let my feelings show so much, particularly since I had come around to the view that despite all her talk, Mariko would never divorce Takeshi, and probably should not. Takeshi cared for her in his fashion; it was Mariko, after all, whom he had turned to in his despair the past fall, when he had told her in the middle of the night that he didn't feel like living. More important, I understood the restraints on Mariko when it came to divorce, and that ending her marriage would very nearly destroy her.

"There are other considerations in a marriage, like children," Sachiko said, chiming in with Mariko. "It's not always such a terrible thing to stay in an unhappy marriage."

"Yes, yes, yes," Mariko said.

A week later, Sachiko and I met Takeshi at a neighborhood *izakaya*, a kind of pub, which served a delicious mix of Japanese and Western food. As "Yesterday" by the Beatles played in the background, we took our seats and ordered beer and a shrimp salad to start. Takeshi, no doubt relieved that this was the last time he would have to deal with me, seemed relaxed and relatively happy. I asked how work was going. "It's been a busy week," Takeshi said, explaining that a government inspector had come to look over one of his projects, and that at another of his projects, the bakery warehouse, he was installing steel frames. By and large, he said, work was a lot better. "But I'll never find it enjoyable," he said.

I switched over to the subject of his marriage and Mariko. In the past, I had always been hesitant to push him too hard on personal matters, afraid that my questions would scare him off or make him mad enough to put a stop to my interviews with Mariko. Tonight I had no desire to embarrass Takeshi with any final invasion of his privacy, but I was interested in the larger question of his relationship with Mariko, even if it was something he was loath to discuss. I began by asking if he could describe the ideal Japanese wife.

"A quiet woman," he said. "Someone with conservative views. And someone who can cook well and clean well."

"What are 'conservative views'?" I asked.

"It means a wife who sees the husband's position as higher than her own. She respects the husband."

"Is Mariko like that?" I asked.

He smiled. "Hmmmmm," he said. "Half."

"Why did you marry her?" I asked.

"I started working in my company, and I was so busy," he said. "I didn't have time to get to know girls at all. But I had known her very well. Both of us were twenty-four at the time."

Takeshi went on to explain that he had first proposed to Mariko in a casual way four years before their marriage. After that the two had just drifted along, although he assumed Mariko was waiting for him to fulfill his commitment when the time was right. "In those days, twenty-four for a woman was the limit to get married," he recalled. "I didn't want to keep her waiting any longer than that."

He ordered a second beer. "She didn't seem to have any boyfriend," he said. "So it seemed like it might be a good idea to get married."

"Did you love her?" I asked.

"I don't know about that," he said, laughing. "Again, I didn't know a lot of women. I always felt it was a lot of trouble having a girlfriend. Even calling a girl was very troubling."

I pressed him, asking if there was anything special he saw in Mariko.

"I just happened to see her around the neighborhood," he said. "Since I'd known her since junior high, I didn't have to have a pose. I could talk to her very casually, like a friend instead of a woman."

"Has your marriage been what you expected?" I asked.

"Yes," he said thoughtfully. "I've really enjoyed it. The first ten years especially. And since the kids have grown up, now I feel that it's very natural that she's around me."

Takeshi's answer truly surprised me, and I studied his face as he sat across the table from Sachiko and me. He had finished his second beer and was ordering a bottle of sake, and I wondered if even this small amount of alcohol was having its effect. But he seemed sober, and in the restaurant's subdued light he was quite attractive, a wiry, angular man who seemed such a contrast to the round edges of his wife. Smiling, I asked what it was that he liked about marriage.

"I've never thought about that kind of thing," he said. "It wasn't a big love, and I just got into it somehow without thinking consciously. Since I've been with her twenty years, you can imagine. I really think everybody has the same kind of feeling after being with a woman for twenty years. I don't get excited with her, and when I look back over twenty years, it seems like there were no big or crucial events."

I asked about the birth of his elder son, Shunsuke, in 1974. But Takeshi, like many Japanese men, did not accompany Mariko to the hospital, let alone the delivery room, and visited her only once during her stay of several days. "It seems like I'm evil," he sighed. "In those days there were so many men who left work to see their wives in the hospital. But I didn't want to be like that. And even if I went, I would have felt stupid waiting in the waiting room for the baby to come. There was nothing I could do."

We veered back to his marriage. "I really enjoy it, without the big love," Takeshi said, more gently than I would have expected.

"Have you ever had a really big love?" I asked carefully, curious to see if he would mention the woman in the bar who had upset Mariko years before.

"No," he said. "But it's possible to believe in it. I wish I could have had a big love." Perhaps there had been no woman in the bar, I reflected. Perhaps there had been, and Takeshi was not telling the truth. Or perhaps the woman had been only a friend, and Mariko had overreacted. Or perhaps the woman in the bar had been a passing fancy, a minor distraction who made him feel young at a time when his wife was wrapped up in the demands of their children. More interesting to me was Takeshi's wistfulness in missing out on a "big love." Although I knew how much comments like that hurt Mariko—and she had heard plenty of them during her two decades of marriage to Takeshi—I was struck nonetheless by Takeshi's longings, his honesty, and his limited hopes.

I asked about Chiaki, curious how he felt about the daughter who seemed so distant from him. "She's a little bit of a strange girl," he said thoughtfully. "So she will grow up to be very independent." But Shunsuke, he said, "will take a very, very ordinary way of life. He has inherited my character, which I didn't want. He's too ordinary, without a sense of adventure." Ken-chan, he said, "is very stubborn and very lively."

Winding down, I asked Takeshi if, at the age of forty-five, he liked the way his life had turned out. Of course I already knew the answer. "No," he said. "I don't work at the things I like. But I don't really know what kind of work I want." He told me then that his dream had always been to build dams. "But I didn't realize that dream," he said. "It's my fault. I didn't find work with a company that does that kind of construction." He once had a chance to work for such a company, he told me, but his boss at Nippon Electric convinced him to stay. "I was so weak that I couldn't break through that kind of persuasion," Takeshi said, as morose as ever.

We had been over this ground before, and while I was sympathetic, I didn't want my last interview with Takeshi to wander into the self-pity I had heard from him in the past. He had always been interesting and honest, I thought, on larger questions, such as what the Japanese really think of the United States. Now we began talking about the Gulf War, and America's role in the world. "America is the world's policeman," he said disapprovingly, adding that the United Nations was too influenced by the United States, Britain, and France. He went on to say that Japan should forgo a seat on the United Nations Security Council. "For the time being, Japan doesn't need it," he said. "Germany doesn't either."

I asked if he thought Japan was a democracy. "Yes," he said. "Pretty much. Eighty percent—coming to be." Then he talked with a kind of pride about the lack of welfare in Japan. I didn't bother to ask about the government assistance that had made it possible for his in-laws to spend so much time in the hospital. Our dinner was now nearly over, and it seemed a good time to change the subject. After a year of interviews, I asked, had Mariko changed?

"No," he said. "Nothing has changed. Seriously speaking, you made a mistake to select Mariko as a model. She's not a typical housewife. And Sachiko-san is living in the neighborhood, so I don't want you to know my story." I had always suspected this—that while I might have been safe as a listener to his confessions, Sachiko was too close for comfort.

"But you wouldn't have told me anything anyway," I said.

"Yes," he said reflectively. "That's true."

"Why do you say that Mariko is not a typical housewife?" I asked.

"She's a very mysterious person. I don't understand her." Takeshi paused for a moment, thinking. He had downed most of the sake at this point and was having trouble maintaining a coherent train of thought. "But you were right to choose her," he finally said. "Japan is full of Marikos."

If so, there are a lot of Takeshis too—men in midlife crises and imperfect marriages with unfulfilled dreams. Takeshi was restless and dissatisfied but not profoundly unhappy. I don't think he ever expected much from his marriage, certainly not great intimacy. Three healthy children and a wife he felt comfortable with were blessings enough. At the beginning of the year, I had asked if he thought his family was typical. Yes, he told me, it's a good family. When I asked why, his answer was telling: "Because nothing bad has happened to us." Like Mariko, Takeshi saw all the newspaper and magazine articles about Japanese marriages breaking up when the children were grown, but it didn't seem to be what he wanted. He wanted constancy, he wanted comfort, he wanted the security of knowing that Mariko would take care of him and the children and her parents and that nothing would change. But how different, really, was this from so many tired, twenty-year marriages in the West? If it was not what Takeshi had imagined in his youth, it was what he had been dealt, and he would follow along. For me, this last dinner with Takeshi was a poignant moment. For a year I had viewed him almost entirely through Mariko's eyes, and had been irritated by his drinking, his inertia, his criticisms of his wife, and his avoidance of me. I don't think Mariko's perceptions were wrong, but on this night I saw him much more on his own, as a person more vulnerable and sympathetic than I had ever imagined. I had always known that Mariko was the strong one, but tonight, as Takeshi pondered his life across the table from me, I realized for the first time how much more he needed her than she needed him.

The last time Sachiko and I went to Mariko's was for lunch on April 30, when she prepared an exquisite spring feast for the three of us. Arranged on her table were sautéed lotus roots, grilled salmon, deep-fried sweet potatoes with black sesame seeds, bamboo shoots with seaweed, an octopus-and-cucumber salad, rice, a clear soup, and Mariko's pickled Chinese cabbage, quite tasty this time, all served in delicate little Japanese bowls and baskets seasonally decorated with tender maple and lilac leaves. Mariko had outdone herself, and Sachiko and I cooed over the elegant dishes. The week before I had given Mariko a big new color television set, my gift to the family after a year of interviews, and now it was on, bringing to our lunch live coverage of the funeral of a famous twenty-six-year-old Japanese actor who had died, authorities suspected, of a drug overdose. A steady rain was falling, and we watched as crowds of fans, mostly young women, lined up with umbrellas to pay their respects. The delectable lunch aside, it was a gloomy day, and we talked a lot about the funeral. Mariko said it all reminded her of her younger brother, who was on her mind again. The day before, April 29, had been the eighth anniversary of his death, although this year the family had not marked the date with any special observance.

Over the next two days Steve and I frantically closed down the house, said good-bye to our neighbors, and moved for our last two nights in Japan into the Imperial Hotel. Our plane left on Sunday, May 3, and at noon that day, as we were about to board the airport bus, Mariko and Ken-chan and Sachiko and her son, Yota, arrived to see us off. A few friends from Steve's office had come by too, forming a small curbside contingent. In the midst of it all I said a hurried good-bye to Mariko, feeling a jumble of emotions—genuine sadness that our time together was over, relief that fourteen months of reporting had come to an end, and puzzlement over what Mariko really was in my life. Subject? Friend? A stranger with whom I had traveled "a great distance"? Oddly, I felt the intimacy I had reached with Mariko had gone as far as I wanted. I could disrupt and dissect her family for only so long. My leaving, I think, had brought out the last secrets she was prepared to share. Where would we have gone from there? I had become less of a blank slate in her life and more, really, of an ally, and I sensed that further confessions would have made Mariko, and me, uncomfortable. As we parted we may have hugged each other, but I honestly cannot remember what happened in the tumult of leaving. The Japanese are not huggers, and it doesn't sound like Mariko anyway. I got on the bus with Steve and Madeleine, and Sachiko and Yota followed behind in the RX-7, with our dog in the backseat. They waved at us periodically during the hour-and-a-half ride to the airport, and at Narita they helped us get both the dog and our luggage safely on the plane. Unlike Mariko and me, Sachiko and I had a shared language and a common sensibility. She had introduced me to Mariko and in fourteen months had become my friend and accomplice in trying to penetrate Mariko's thinking. She had also been nothing less than a lifeline for me in Japan. We had a tearful good-bye just outside customs, promising each other we would call, write, and visit. Fourteen hours later I was in New York, my days in Japan brought to an abrupt end.

As I thought about Mariko during those first weeks back home, I knew I had hardly been a detached observer in her life. In the past, I had always tried to keep a professional distance from my subjects, but this time I had become hopelessly intertwined in Mariko's life, and she in mine. What could I do? Mariko so welcomed me at her family celebrations that after a time I felt it was only decent to ask her and the kids to a Halloween party I had for the neighborhood children, or to our annual Christmas party. When my aunt and my ninety-year-old grandmother visited Tokyo, Mariko invited them to hear her play the samisen at a local community center, so of course I included her when I had friends over to my house to meet them for dinner a few days later. I know Mariko enjoyed the exposure to a bit of America, but she gave a much greater gift in making me feel a part of ordinary life in Japan, from PTA meetings to neighborhood festivals to meter reading to the wit of the comic Tamori. But I know that my presence changed "ordinary life" for her and that she will always associate 1991 and 1992 with me. I cannot claim that what I have reported here is the naked, objective truth, but it was an authentic experience, and I learned more from it than from anything else I did in Japan.

From my experience with Mariko and her family, I came to understand at the most fundamental level why the family is the lifeblood of Japan, critical to its identity, social order, and economic success. Of course Americans themselves believe that stable families help create secure children, brighter students, and even a more competent workforce. Americans also make enormous sacrifices for their children and try to raise them to be "good citizens" in their communities and the larger world. But I don't think that most parents in the United States feel the overwhelming responsibility to their society that the Japanese feel, to turn out the best children they can. "In Japan, when you're a wife and mother, and

contributing to a family, you feel you're doing a lot for society,"
Mariko told me during our last dinner together. "Maybe this is
why we don't have so many drug-addicted young boys." Her comment, patronizing as it was to the United States, proved to me once
again why motherhood is such a serious occupation in Japan.
Motherhood brought a powerful sense of purpose to Mariko's life,
and conferred on her a status unknown to most mothers in the
United States.

And yet, as I learned from the Tanakas, a stable, successful
Japanese family is not necessarily composed of personally happy
individuals who have forged loving relationships. In Mariko's
family the oldest and the youngest generations hardly spoke to
each other. Her husband kept a cool distance from his children.
And her marriage, if judged by an American ideal, was hardly a
success. As she told me that spring, "I wanted to live with a man
I really loved. I wanted to devote my whole life to him. I wanted
him to be my lover, my best friend, a good father. I wanted two
heartbeats into one. I wanted everything." But these were the
desires of one individual. By the time I left Japan, I could see that
Mariko not only had made an uneasy peace with the shortcomings of her husband but had decided, at least for the present, that
the needs of her family were greater than her own. In a larger
sense, she seemed to feel instinctively that Japan itself, the great
family of families, was more important too. As the news anchor
Hiroshi Kume told me, "The country comes first, and the people
come later. I don't like this way of thinking, but the Japanese
really do seem subordinate to Japan."

I still don't know what it is about the Japanese that makes them
so bound to the group. Is it a characteristic that arises from some
odd but rich wellspring of culture or from particular incentives in
the Japanese system? The debate continues among American and
Japanese scholars today. On one side are the traditional historians
of the era of World War II and after, notably Edwin Reischauer and

Ruth Benedict, the author of *The Chrysanthemum and the Sword*, still brilliant today, who argue that Japan, a deeply homogeneous nation, is held together by natural bonds of harmony and family. On the other side are the revisionists, notably Karel van Wolferen, who see "harmony" as an ideology covering up the oppressiveness of a system that rewards conformity and punishes dissent. (Some leaders on the left in Japan call their nation one of "benevolent fascism," a system that threatens to cast people out if they don't keep in line.) Although I came to see the merits of both points of view, I learned from Mariko that it is the rewards of participation rather than the penalties of dissent that keep the nation together. True, Mrs. Sato was ostracized because of her strident opposition to Bellmark, the cutting of the gingko trees, and the Japanese establishment in general. But I also saw the powerful sense of belonging that Mariko experienced as a woman playing her role in her society, as samisen student, as festival goer, as PTA mother. And yet it is a peculiar mixture, this system of exclusion and inclusion. The author and critic Donald Richie once called it in a conversation with me the "social coercion necessary for harmony"—a delicate boundary line I have tried to define in this book.

Toward the end of the year, I asked Mariko if she ever felt coerced by her society. "Of course," she said, shrugging, as if it were obvious. She seemed to understand that we are all coerced to some degree by the expectations of the people around us, and that coercion is not necessarily enslavement. In her society, there were no obvious oppressors, but there were limitations on what was possible in life. Mariko was a member of the middle class, but she lived in a small house with antiquated plumbing and no central heating, could not afford to go to restaurants with her family, was compelled to enroll her children in an education system that put them on a forced march through childhood, and had no real way, if she ever wanted it, to combine motherhood and a full-time career. By middle-class American standards, she was trapped. By her standards, she may have been trapped, but she was trapped in a cozy, comfortable place that had other rewards—order, for example, and cleanliness and predictability and civility and safety. Mariko never felt uneasy on city streets after dark, and thought it was perfectly natural that six-year-olds should take the subways to school.

As I prepared to leave Japan, I often wondered if it would continue to be so cohesive, and if Mariko's children would feel, as adults, that same sense of belonging. "My children have not yet lived up to my expectations," Mariko admitted to me shortly before I left. "I really expect them to be people who will be independent and achieve. But with Shunsuke, I really have complaints. It seems he doesn't put any effort into what he does." Certainly Shunsuke, and Chiaki too, reflected the pressures on the Japanese family when they envisioned futures for themselves that rejected the lives of their parents. In a postwar era of workaholic, absentee fathers, Shunsuke was determined to run his own business, keep his own hours, and have more leisure time. Chiaki, a witness to her mother's exhaustion in raising three children and holding down two part-time jobs, insisted she would not marry at all. These plans may have been only the dreams of youth, and I don't know if the two will really follow through. But it is significant that they were questioning the bedrock Japanese values of hard work and sacrifice for family, and seemed ready to put their own needs first. In its own quiet way, their attitude amounted to a revolution. Two generations earlier, such thoughts would never have occurred to their grandmother Ito. A generation later, in a sign of change, their mother not only thought about these matters but struggled daily between the need to fulfill her own wants and her obligations to others. To what stage would her children evolve? "After this year," Mariko told me, "I've been thinking that I should do more things for myself. But then my husband will say I'm selfish." Perhaps Mariko was caught at a kind of crossroads in the evolution of modern Japanese society, a bridge between the generation of her mother and that of her children. Or perhaps she was simply feeling pulled in all directions, like any woman of the late twentieth century, and had decided, like most of us, that the family was the most important thing in her life.

Hers was not, after all, an unimportant life. As I look back on it now, I can see that it was a life of small successes and modest hopes and the grand accomplishments of children, a life full of resolve and connectedness, a life that brought nothing less than life to the people around her. What more could Mariko want? What more could any of us want? It was a Japanese life, yes, but it was also any life, lived by a good soul who day after day pushed forward against the wind, finding purpose and pleasures and a sense that she belonged where she was, at home in Japan.

ACKNOWLEDGMENTS

It is a great pleasure to thank the special people who helped me with this book. First, I am indebted to Mariko and her family, for their great patience and open hearts, and to Sachiko Kamazuka, who taught me what was important in Japan, and who made me laugh. The Shibamotos—Kumiko, Shinzo, Hanako, and Hiroko—were not directly involved in the book but were such stellar neighbors and good friends that I like to think of them as my other family in Japan.

I would like to thank my colleagues in the Tokyo bureau of *The Washington Post*, Tom Reid, Paul Blustein, Fred Hiatt, Pooh Shapiro, Shigehiko Togo, and Yasuko Maruta. I also owe much to Hiroshi Ishikawa, Fumio Kitamura, Midori Hanabusa, and Megumi Arai at the Foreign Press Center. Also thanks to Akira Saito of *The Yomiuri Shimbun*, Namiko Suzuki, Mitsuko Takahashi, Henry Scott Stokes, Rachel Swanger, Carla Rapoport, Katie Hall, Kumiko Makihara, Nobuyuki Nakahara, Sam Jameson, James Bailey, Yukio Okamoto, Suwako Endoh, Murray and Jenny Sayle, Emily Shibata Sato, Karl Schoenberger and Susan Moffat, the Ozawas—Shizuko, Toshiro, Sachiko, and Yuto—and especially Jim Sterngold and Ellen Rudolph, and David Sanger and Sherill Leonard.

I am grateful to my editors at *The Washington Post*, Mary Hadar, Ellen Edwards, Bob Kaiser, Len Downie, and Ben Bradlee. At Times Books, Peter Osnos was once again an enthusiastic editor and understanding friend who planted the idea for this book in my mind and then kept me inspired. Also thanks to Peter Smith and Darrell Jonas of Times Books; my copy editor, Virginia Avery; Robbin Schiff; and Naomi Osnos. Amanda Urban, my agent and friend, gave me the gifts of her curiosity, her excitement, and her belief in the book. I am particularly grateful to Wayne Furman and the New York Public Library for providing me with a desk in the fertile atmosphere of the Frederick Lewis Allen room, where part of this book was written. Many thanks to the others who helped and encouraged along the way—Susan Chira and Michael Shapiro, Les and Noriko Pockell, Michele Slung, Lorraine Shanley and David Sneider, Meryl Gordon and Walter Shapiro, Mimi Gerbst, Cathy and Walter Isaacson, Dan Yergin and Angela Stent, Dr. Michael Weisman, Lisa Weisman, Lynn Weisman, Adela Gumahin, and most especially Geraldine Baum for her friendship and 4:30 P.M. wake-up calls.

My mother, Gunhild Rose, was as always my greatest supporter, and made my work on parts of this book possible just before the birth of my second child. I am also indebted to the rest of my family for their love and encouragement—my father, Ted Bumiller; my stepmother, Ruth Ann Bumiller; my stepfather, John Rose; my sisters and stepbrothers; my mother-in-law, Etta Weisman; my late father-in-law, Joseph Weisman; and my ninety-four-year-old grandmother, Elizabeth Bumiller.

Last, I would like to thank my children, Madeleine and Teddy, without whom this book would have been finished a year earlier, but who were irresistible distractions from the work at hand. Most of all, I want to thank my husband, Steve, who took me to Japan and then lived through this book, and who kept me going with his wit, patience, and love.

—Elisabeth Bumiller
Bronxville, N.Y.
July 1995

SELECTED BIBLIOGRAPHY

Beasley, W. G. *The Modern History of Japan.* Tokyo: Charles E. Tuttle, 1973.

Benedict, Ruth. *The Chrysanthemum and the Sword: Patterns of Japanese Culture.* New York: New American Library, 1974.

Bernstein, Gail Lee. *Haruko's World.* Palo Alto, Calif.: Stanford University Press, 1983.

Buruma, Ian. *A Japanese Mirror.* London: Penguin Books, 1985.

Carr-Gregg, Charlotte. *Japanese Prisoners of War in Revolt.* St. Lucia, Queensland: University of Queensland Press, 1978.

Condon, Jane. *A Half Step Behind.* New York: Dodd, Mead & Co., 1985.

Eichelberger, Robert L. *Our Jungle Road to Tokyo.* New York: Viking, 1950.

Field, Norma. *In the Realm of a Dying Emperor: A Portrait of Japan at Century's End.* New York: Pantheon, 1991.

Furuki, Yoshiko. *The White Plum: A Biography of Ume Tsuda.* New York: Weatherhill, 1991.

Gordon, Harry. *Die Like the Carp.* Stanmore, New South Wales, Australia: Cassell Australia, 1978.

Hall, John Whitney. *Japan: From Prehistory to Modern Times.* Tokyo: Charles E. Tuttle, 1989.

Ienaga, Saburo. *The Pacific War, 1931–1945: A Critical Perspective on Japan's Role in World War II.* New York: Pantheon, 1978.

Iwao, Sumiko. *The Japanese Woman: Traditional Image and Changing Reality.* New York: The Free Press, 1993.

MacArthur, Douglas. *Reminiscences.* Toronto: McGraw, 1964.

Manchester, William. *American Caesar: Douglas MacArthur*

1880–1964. New York: Dell, 1979.

Nakane, Chie. *Japanese Society.* Tokyo: Charles E. Tuttle, 1970.

Pharr, Susan. "Status Conflict: The Rebellion of the Tea Pourers." In Krauss, Ellis S., Thomas P. Rohlen, and Patricia G. Steinhoff, *Conflict in Japan.* Honolulu: The University of Hawaii Press, 1984.

Reischauer, Edwin O. *The Japanese.* Cambridge: Harvard University Press, 1977.

Rohlen, Thomas P. *Japan's High Schools.* Berkeley: University of California Press, 1983.

Seidensticker, Edward. *Tokyo Rising: The City Since the Great Earthquake.* New York: Alfred A. Knopf, 1990.

———. *Low City, High City: Tokyo from Edo to the Earthquake.* Tokyo: Charles E. Tuttle, 1989.

Toland, John. *The Rising Sun: The Decline and Fall of the Japanese Empire.* New York: Random House, 1970.

van Wolferen, Karel. *The Enigma of Japanese Power: People and Politics in a Stateless Nation.* New York: Alfred A. Knopf, 1989.

Vogel, Ezra. *Japan's New Middle Class.* Berkeley: University of California Press, 1963.

Waley, Paul. *Tokyo: City of Stories.* New York: Weatherhill, 1991.

White, Merry. *The Japanese Educational Challenge: A Commitment to Children.* New York: The Free Press, 1987.

Whiting, Robert. *You Gotta Have Wa.* New York: MacMillan, 1989.

INDEX

abortion, 80
Adenauer, Konrad, 164
Ainu, 237–38
alcoholism
    definition of, 98, 99
    diseases associated with, 100
    See also drinking
All-Japan Sobriety Association, 98
Amaterasu (sun goddess), 24
America. *See* United States
American Caesar (Manchester), 46
American Revolution, 166–68
ancestors, worship of, 107
Arakawa River incident, 91–92, 97, 247
Asakusa area (Tokyo), 66–72, 133–40
Asano, Yuko, 250–51
automobiles, American, 254, 261–62, 277
Azabu High School, 152–53
Azabu Middle School, 171–72

baby-sitters, 82–83, 230
Bando, Mariko, 85
baseball, 129–30, 157, 262
Bellmark issue, 229, 231–36, 240, 294, 296–99
Benedict, Ruth, 26, 330

bento (packed lunches), 27
Bernstein, Gail Lee, 11
birth control, 80
Bon (Festival of the Dead), 104–5
Buddhism, 104, 105, 107–8, 154, 224
Buddhist temples, 187–88, 189–90, 250, 251
bullying (*ijime*), 32–33, 36
Bush, George, 131, 253–54, 261, 276–77, 288

Carr-Gregg, Charlotte, 48–49
cars, American, 254, 261–62, 277
cherry blossoms, 31–32, 233, 245, 311, 312
children, Japanese
    alone at home, 82–83
    and favoritism, 18
    first, 18
    help with, 82–83
    men's role in birth of, 323
    See also specific person
Christmas, 224, 247
The Chrysanthemum and the Sword (Benedict), 26, 330
Chupiren (women's group), 80
Clean Government Party (Komeito), 109, 242, 243

Common Sense (Paine), 167
communism, 134, 242–43
concentration camps, 161–63
concert, samisen, 223, 224–28
Confucianism, 24, 107, 154
consumer electronics, 55
corporations
    and employee picnics, 32
    and religion, 108
    as surrogate families, 26
corruption, political, 132
cost of living, 123–25
cram schools (*juku*), 12, 18, 20–21,
        154–56, 157, 168–78
Crichton, Michael, 11
Croissant magazine, 140, 220–21

death
    from overwork (*karoshi*), 281
    and funeral customs, 61–62
Declaration of Independence, 167
democracy
    and the gingko tree affair, 316
    Japan as a, 54, 155, 324
    and local politics, 193
    and the PTA meetings, 228–31,
        235, 296–97
    seeds of American, high school
        lecture on, 167
    Takeshi's views about, 324
Die Like the Carp (Gordon), 48
diversity, dissent
    in Japanese society, 128, 237,
        238–39, 244, 329–30
    See also "resisters"
divorce, 8, 306, 320–21

doctors, 256–57
Doi, Takako, 74
Dreamy Trip (TV), 119
drinking, 96–102, 186, 190. *See also*
        Tanaka, Takeshi (husband),
        drinking of

earthquake, 274–75
economy
    and the consumer electronics
        industry, 55
    and cost of living, 17
    and expansion of the cartels, 39
    and Japanese self-confidence, 7
    and politics, 132–33
    and the standard of living,
        133
    in the Taisho Era, 39
    and Takeshi's job frustrations,
        200
    and working women, 78
education
    during the American Occupation,
        155–56
    as a challenge, 178
    characteristics of Japanese, 150–52
    and college workloads, 173
    cram schools as a parallel system
        of, 170
    criticisms of, 153–54, 165
    and dropouts, 33
    funding of, 152
    as highly valued, 154–56
    as homogeneous, 151
    lessons for Americans from Japa-
        nese, 178

and the Meiji Restoration, 26

and mother-child relations, 4

as nationalistic, 155

results of Japanese, 150

and rote learning, 143, 152, 153–54

and the "school refusal syndrome," 177

and social class, 83, 156

and student exchanges, 152–53, 155

and the visit to Ken-chan's school, 141–50

of women, 73–74, 80

See also cram schools (*juku*); schools

effort, attitudes toward, 35, 37, 178

Eichelberger, Robert, 44, 45

elder brother, Mariko's

birth of, 38

and caring for parents, 38

Mariko's relationship with, 38, 55, 248, 254–55

marriage of, 60

and the New Year's holidays, 248

visit by, 255

elderly

care of the, 257–58, 258–61, 301

See also Ito (Mariko's mother); Saburo (Mariko's father)

employee picnics (*hanami*), 32

English, teaching of, 158–59

The Enigma of Japanese Power (van Wolferen), 11

Enoki, Misako, 80

family

comparison of Japanese and American, 7–8

and Confucianism, 24

corporation as surrogate, 26

erosion of the, 27

fathers' lack of participation in life of, 8, 26, 34, 76–77, 81, 329

grocery shopping for the, 122–25

importance of the, 331

as lifeblood of Japan, 328–29

mothers' role in, 26–27, 81–82

power of heads of households in, 25–26

preparing meals for the, 119–22

stress on the, 27

and Sunday outings, 102

See also Tanaka family

Father's Day, 95–96

fathers. *See* men/fathers

feminism, 72–85, 221–22

Festival of the Dead (Bon), 104–5

Field, Norma, 238

finances

and feminism, 79

See also Tanaka family: finances of the

"flushing response," 100

folk religions, 107

food

and preparing family meals, 119–22

shopping for, 122–25

Westernization of, 121

See also lunches

food cooperatives, 194–95
football, 262, 319–20
foreigners, as amusing to Japanese, 288
Il Forno (restaurant), 261, 320
Fujiwara family, 25
Fukushima, Mizuho, 221
Furuki, Yoshiko, 155
Futaba girls' school, 176

Gakushuin University, 172
geisha, 227, 228
Gempei War, 25
generational issues, 36, 37, 209, 260, 272–73, 301–2, 328–29, 331–32
gifts, 223–24, 267, 270
gingko tree affair
    and Mr. Mori, 314–15, 316
    neighborhood reaction to the, 22–23, 110
    and politics, 22–23, 236, 237, 242–43, 244–45
    Sato's views of the, 232, 241–43
    and social class, 237
    as a symbol, 22–23
    and the Tanizaki interview, 314, 315–18
"Gochisosama-deshita," singing of, 147
Gorbachev, Mikhail S., 131
Gordon, Harry, 48
grocery shopping, 122–25

Hall, John Whitney, 24
hanami (employee picnics), 32

Hara, Toshio, 134
Harajuku shopping district (Tokyo), 102–3, 250
Haruko's World (Bernstein), 11
health
    and doctors, 256–57
    insurance, 257
    teaching about, 160–61
    See also specific person
Heian Era, 25
hierarchy, Japanese attitude toward, 26
high school
    Mariko in, 56–58, 303
    Takeshi in, 57–58
    See also education; schools
Higuchi, Keiko, 221
Higuchi, Yoshito, 171
Hiroko (high school classmate of Mariko's), 56, 57
Hokkaido
    Mrs. Sato's home in, 240
    Tanaka family's vacation to, 125–29
homes
    architecture of, 186
    "broken," 151
    children alone in, 82–83
    cost of, 94
    furnishings of, 15–16
    guests in Japanese, 9, 81
    heating in, 15
    and household help, 81–82
    land for, 185
    ownership of, 17
    rental of, 127

of Tanaka family, 14–16, 127,
185
working women's responsibilities in, 74, 81–82, 85
See also family
honeymoons, 42
Hosokawa, Morihiro, 109, 162
hospitals, 257, 275–76
humor
Japanese taste in, 290–91
See also You Can Laugh

Iacocca, Lee, 282
Ichomachi area
description of, 13–14
districts of the, 185
festival in the, 184–91
in Mariko's youth, 54
politics in the, 191–97
Tanaka family's roots in the,
184–85
ward council meetings for the,
193–97
See also gingko tree affair;
Ichomachi Elementary School
Ichomachi Elementary School
and potential kidnapper, 295–96
PTA of the, 228–36, 294–99, 313
visit to the, 141–50
Ichomachi High School, 36
Ichomachi shrine, 110, 184, 189–90,
228, 237, 314. *See also* gingko
tree affair
ie (three-generation family),
25–26
ijime (bullying), 32–33, 36

illegal immigrants, 95
Imperial Palace, outing to the,
103–4
In the Realm of a Dying Emperor
(Field), 238
individualism, in Japan, 11–12,
23–24, 26, 329–30. *See also*
diversity, dissent
Isao, Bito, 286–89
"*Itadakimasu*," singing of,
146–47
Itami, Juzo, 136–37
Ito (Mariko's mother)
birth of, 39
care of, 36–37, 256, 257–61,
264–65, 269, 275–76, 293, 299,
300–301, 302
childhood/youth of, 39–41
courtship/marriage of, 38, 40,
41–42
education of, 40
and the elder son's visit, 255
and the Ichomachi festival, 188
interview with, 38–53
living arrangements of, 36
Mariko's relationship with,
36–37, 56, 57, 275–76,
300–301
and the New Year's holidays,
248
in postwar Japan, 51–53
and religion, 108, 109
and Saburo's health/hospitaliza-
tion, 256, 257–61, 269
in World War II, 42, 51, 52
Ito, Midori, 303

Ito, Mr. (cram school teacher), 169
Iwao, Sumiko, 77–78

Japan
American Occupation of, 26–27, 50, 53–54, 155, 156, 230
American products in, 10, 123–24, 254, 266
birthrate in, 27
Bush's visit to, 253–54
crossroads of cultural change in, 331–32
democracy in, 54, 155, 324
diversity/dissent in, 128, 237, 238–39, 244, 329–330
earthquakes in, 274–75
family as lifeblood of, 328–329
fear of discord in, 234
hierarchy in, 26, 156
homogeneity of, 128, 150–51, 329–30
individual in, 11–12, 23–24, 26, 329–30
and killing of Japanese vacationers in U.S., 303
national self-confidence of, 7
"outsiders" in, 8–9
punctuality in, 126
social history of, 23–27
U.S. relations with, 253–55, 265–66, 276–83, 303
workaholic culture of, 128
Japan Travel Bureau, 17, 58, 269, 312
The Japanese Educational Challenge (White), 178

Japanese Prisoners of War in Revolt (Carr-Gregg), 48–49
The Japanese Woman (Iwao), 77–78
Japan's High Schools (Rohlen), 152, 154, 168
Japan's New Middle Class (Vogel), 11

Kaifu, Toshiki, 74, 131
Kamazuka, Sachiko (interpreter)
car of, 12–13
and choice of the Tanaka family as subject, 12
and cram schools, 20–21, 172, 177
education of, 13
health of, 299
on loneliness, 133
and Mariko's birthday, 292
and Mariko's depression, 300
and Mariko's first interview, 12, 15–16
Mariko's relationship with, 21
and the *nanakaiki*, 62, 63
and the New Year's holidays, 249, 250, 251
outings with, 112, 114
personality of, 13, 21
and religion, 106
and the Sanja Matsuri, 66, 68, 69
and Takeshi's China trip, 256
Takeshi's feelings about, 325
See also specific interview or visit

Kamazuka, Yota, 112, 169, 186, 327

Kan (pop star), 250

Kanemaru, Shin, 137

kanji (Chinese characters), learning, 143, 145–46

Kanjincho, or *The Subscription Scroll* (Kabuki play), 88–89, 225

Karaki, Masako, 173, 174–76

karaoke, 113–15, 139, 225

karoshi (death from overwork), 281

Kato, Hidetoshi, 173

Kato, Shuiichi, 154

Kayama, Yuzo, 114

Keio University, 174–75

Keisei High School, 171

kidnappers, 295–96

Kikuchi, Koiichi, 70, 135–39

kimono, 226, 227

kindergarteners, cram schools for, 173–76

Kobayashi, Yutaka, 152–53

Kohaku Utagassen (television program), 249–51

Kojima, Eiichi, 161–68, 211

Komeito (Clean Government Party), 109, 242, 243

Koshien Stadium (Osaka), 129–30

Kume, Hiroshi, 329

Kurihama Hospital, 100

Kuroyanagi, Tetsuko, 301

Kyoto University, 80

leave-taking

and the Il Forno good-bye dinner, 320

and the last day, 326–28

and lunch at Mariko's, 326

preparations for, 293

Liberal Democratic Party, 109, 131–32, 132–33, 192, 193, 243

Lotus Sutra, 109

lunches, making, 27

MacArthur, Douglas, 44, 45, 46, 50, 53, 144

Mahmud, Arshad, 186, 189, 190

maids, live-in, 41, 81–82, 83

Manchester, William, 46

Mariko. *See* Tanaka, Mariko

marital relations

and birth of children, 323–24

and birthdays, 29

and care of Mariko's parents, 265

children's views of parents', 272

and customary forms of address, 204

and expectations of marriage, 325–26

and Father's Day, 95–96

and intimacy, 310, 320–21

and Mariko's affair, 305–7

and Mariko's independence, 66

and Mariko's subservience/deference, 20, 86

Mariko's views of, 329

and the samisen lessons, 86, 224–25, 226–27, 228

and the Sanja Matsuri, 89

and separate existences, 72–73, 125

marital relations (*cont.*)
  and Takeshi's drinking, 28–29,
    91–93, 95, 96–97, 129, 133,
    200, 205, 247–48, 266–67,
    294, 307
  and Takeshi's job, 200
  and Takeshi's personality, 307–8,
    313–14
  and Takeshi's views of Mariko,
    204, 313–14, 321–22
  Takeshi's views of, 321–23
  See also marriage
marriage
  acceptance of distant, 308
  arranged, 40–41
  Chiaki's attitudes about, 208–9
  expectations of, 8, 308, 325–26
  and honeymoons, 42
  of the Moris, 245–46
  problems in, 255
  reasons for, 75–76, 310, 321–22
  Takeshi's views about, 310,
    325–26
  See also marital relations
Masakado monument, 108
media, and feminism, 80
Meiji Era, 26, 67, 155
Meiji Jingu, 250
men/fathers
  as absent from the home, 8, 26,
    34, 76–77, 81, 319, 329
  "new" Japanese, 29
  trips of, 255
  women as freer than, 76–77, 205
meter reading, water, 179–84
middle-age crisis, 301

mikoshi (portable shrines)
  and the Ichomachi festival, 184,
    187, 189, 190
  and the Sanja Matsuri, 65–66,
    67, 69–71, 139–40
Ministry of Education, 176–77, 297,
  298
Ministry of Finance, 201, 202
Mitsui & Co., 108
Miyazawa, Kiichi, 7, 254, 276–77,
  282
mizuko jizo (round-faced dolls),
  188
Mori, Mr., and the gingko trees,
  314–15, 316
Mori, Yoko, 228–29, 235–36,
  243–47, 294, 295, 298, 314
Morikawa, Reiko, 82
Moriyama, Mayumi, 74–75, 83–84
Moroki Kai cram school, 173–74
motherhood
  as primary duty of Japanese
    women, 6, 75–76
  as a serious occupation, 328–29
mothers
  as active in schools, 148, 151–52
  and cram schools, 176
  responsibilities of, 122
  role in family of, 26–27

nanakaiki (anniversary of death),
  61–62
Nanking massacre, 162
national health insurance, 257
national self-confidence, 7
New Year's holidays, 248–52, 254–55

Nichinoken cram schools, 171
Nichiren Buddhism, 109
Night and Fog (film), 161
Nippon Electric, 59, 93–94, 201–5.
    See also Tanaka, Takeshi (hus-
    band), job of
nursing homes, 38, 259–60

office ladies (O.L.s), 12, 74, 84, 209,
    280
    and *Tokyo Love Story*, 116–19
Oga, Takeshi, 171
Okada, Yoshihiro, 71
"One Flower," 143, 144–45
Ota, Tooru, 117–18

pachinko parlors (pinball gambling
    dens), 35–36
Paine, Thomas, 167
Pearl Harbor, fiftieth anniversary
    of, 211, 255
Persian Gulf War, 212
Pharr, Susan, 84
"The Pitiful Elephants," 143–44
politics
    and corruption, 132
    and the economy, 132–33
    and the gingko tree affair, 236,
        237, 242–43, 244–45
    and the Gorbachev coup, 131
    local, 191–97
    Mariko's views about, 131–33
    and religion, 108–9
    women in, 74–75, 194–95
    women's views of, 131–33
    and the *yakuza*, 136–37

private schools, 154, 156
professional careers, for women, 81,
    83–85
protests, in Japanese society, 232,
    234, 238, 330
PTA, Ichomachi Elementary
    School, 228–36, 294–99, 313

Reischauer, Edwin, 329–30
religion
    and corporations, 108
    folk, 107
    and the Ichomachi shrine,
        110
    of Mariko, 104–7
    "new," 108–9
    and politics, 108–9
    and seasonal religious festivals,
        107
    and superstition, 107–8
    See also Buddhism; Confucian-
        ism; Shintoism; Soka Gakkai
"resisters," 237–38, 244. *See also*
    diversity, dissent
restaurants, going to, 28
Richie, Donald, 330
Rissho Kose Kai, 108–9
Rohlen, Thomas, 152, 154, 156,
    168
Roppongi district (Tokyo), 261

Saburo (Mariko's father)
    care of, 293, 299, 300–301, 302
    as caring for wife, 36, 37
    courtship/marriage of, 38,
        40–42

Saburo (Mariko's father) (*cont.*)
  drinking of, 37, 53
  and the elder son's visit, 255
  as a father, 56, 60
  health of, 256–61, 264–65,
      267–70, 276, 292
  and the Ichomachi festival, 188
  interview with, 38–53
  living arrangements of, 36, 37
  Mariko's relationship with, 37,
      268–69, 300–301
  and naming of Mariko, 4, 52
  in postwar Japan, 51–53
  Takeshi's relationship with, 270
  in World War II, 4, 42–49, 50–52,
      255
Sakamoto, Harumi, 85
Sakauchi, Koichi, 177–78
Sakurauchi, Yoshio, 265
samisen
  and the concert, 223, 224–28
  lessons, Mariko's, 25, 86–89, 302
samurai, 25, 155
Sanja Matsuri, 65–72, 89, 139, 184
Sansom, George, 25
Sato, Yumiko
  and the Bellmark issue, 232–33,
      234–35, 236, 238, 239–40, 295,
      296, 297–98, 299
  causes espoused by, 239–40
  and the gingko tree affair, 236,
      237, 241–43, 316, 318
  husband's support of, 240
  interview with, 238–43
  as a "resister," 237–38, 330
Sayle, Murray, 136

school lunches, 16, 27–28, 146
"school refusal syndrome," 177
schools
  ambiance of, 142–43, 160
  bullying in, 32–33, 36
  friendships from, 255
  mothers as active in, 148,
      151–52
  public perception of, 170
  and the school year, 151
  and sports/extracurricular activi-
      ties, 160
  students walking to, 230, 296
  See also cram schools;
      education; private schools;
      specific school
seasonal religious festivals, 107
Seikatsu Clubs, 194
Sensei (teacher)
  in Ken-chan's school, 141–50
  and the samisen lessons, 87, 89
sex
  extramarital, 92, 305–310
  teenage, 262–63
sex tours, 256
sexual harassment, 73, 80–81
Shigemori, Kenji, 98
Shikoku, vacation on, 129
Shimada, Aya, 172–73
Shimada, Hideko, 172–73
Shimomura, Mitsuko, 98
Shinjuku Lib Center, 80
Shintoism, 105, 107, 224, 242–43,
      250
Shortell, Christopher, 281
shrine festival, 6

shudan toko (students walking to
school in groups), 230, 296
"soaplands," 127
social class
Chiaki's views about, 273–74
and cram schools, 177
and education, 83, 156
and the elder brother's marriage,
248
and the gingko tree affair, 237
institutionalization of, 25
and working women, 83
Socialist Party, 74–75, 131–32, 164,
195, 243
Soka Gakkai, 106–7, 236, 242, 245
Sony, 55
sports/extracurricular activities,
160. *See also* baseball;
football
student exchanges, 152–53, 155
student riots, 80
The Subscription Scroll, or *Kanjincho* (Kabuki play), 88–89, 225
Sugino, Kohjiro, 98–99
Sun line, 24
Sunday outings, 102
Suzuki, Honami, 118–19
Suzuki, Namiko, 76

Taisho Era, 39
Takahashi-gumi, 70, 133–39
Takeshita, Noboru, 132
Tamori, 259, 285–91
Tanaka, Chiaki (daughter)
age of, 17
aspirations of, 21, 208–9, 271, 331
birth of, 60
boyfriend of, 34, 206, 208, 273
and cram school, 171–72
education of, 178, 181
graduation of, 28, 31, 32–36
and the Hokkaido vacation, 126,
127
interviews with, 208–210,
270–74
jobs of, 271
Mariko's relationship with, 18,
34, 37, 127, 206, 208–9, 258,
263, 271, 274, 331
on marriage, 209
and the New Year's holidays,
250
on parents' relationship, 272
prayers for, 106
and sibling relationships, 210,
263, 272
and social class issues, 273–74
sports activities of, 207
and Takeshi's drinking, 92
Takeshi's relationship with,
272–73, 324
and *Tokyo Love Story,* 116–17
typical day of, 172
on the United States, 274
Tanaka family
finances of the, 17, 127, 226–27,
260, 269
Hokkaido vacation of the, 125–28
outings by the, 102–4
power balances in the, 263
roots in the Ichomachi area of
the, 184–85

Tanaka family (*cont.*)
    Takeshi's views on Mariko's role
      in, 205
    as a typical Japanese family, 325
Tanaka, Ken-chan (younger son)
    age of, 17
    on America, 207
    aspirations of, 207
    and baseball, 313
    birth of, 60
    Chiaki's views about, 272
    education of, 18, 21
    and the Hokkaido vacation, 126
    and the Ichomachi festival, 188,
      189, 191
    interview with, 207
    Mariko's relationship with, 208,
      263
    and the New Year's holidays, 250
    outings with, 102–4, 111–13
    in school, 141–50
    school lunches of, 16, 27
    Takeshi's relationship with, 129,
      207, 324
Tanaka, Mariko
    affair of, 305–310
    aspirations for children of, 331
    aspirations of, 301
    birth of, 4, 52
    birthday of, 27, 29, 292–93
    childhood/youth of, 54–57
    communicating with, 20, 21–22
    community activities of, 28
    courtship/marriage of, 57–59
    and cultural change in Japan,
      331–32

    depression of, 299–301
    education of, 156
    feelings of liberation of, 72–73
    health of, 293–94, 299–300, 302
    high school years of, 56–58,
      303–4
    independence of, 220–22
    jobs of, 17, 58, 59, 179–84, 300,
      313
    meaning of name of, 4, 52
    as a mother, 60, 306–7, 308
    physical appearance of, 15
    and privacy, desire for, 5–6, 22
    reasons for agreeing to be inter-
      viewed, 19, 22
    reasons for marriage, 310
    Shunsuke's views of, 263–64
    as a traditional Japanese woman,
      222, 320–21, 331–32
    typical day of, 301
    as a typical housewife, 6, 325
Tanaka, Megumi, 85
Tanaka, Mitsu, 80
Tanaka, Shunsuke (older son)
    age of, 17
    aspirations of, 157–58, 210–11,
      331–32
    birth of, 60, 323
    Chiaki's views about, 272
    cooking by, 303
    and cram school, 171
    education of, 18, 156, 157–58,
      181, 211
    and football, 206–7, 319–20
    girlfriend of, 158, 205–6, 262–63
    on his parents, 263–64

and the Hokkaido vacation, 126
interviews with, 207, 208,
    210–12, 261–64
Mariko's relationship with,
    157–58, 208, 263, 331
and the New Year's holidays, 250
personality of, 258
prayers for, 106
and sibling relationships, 210,
    263
and Takeshi's drinking, 92
Takeshi's relationship with, 319,
    323
on the Tanaka family, 263–64
on the United States, 254,
    261–62
Tanaka, Takeshi (husband)
affair of, 92, 305, 310
aspirations of, 204–5, 325–26
attitude toward book of, 20,
    185–86
children's views of, 263–64,
    272–73
China trip of, 255, 256, 258
cooking for family, 96
courtship/marriage of, 57–59
and the earthquake, 274–75
drinking of, 28–29, 91–93, 95,
    96–97, 129, 133, 200, 205,
    247–48, 266–67, 294, 307–8
education of, 57, 58, 156
as a father, 92, 128, 207, 263–64,
    272–73, 319, 323
and Father's Day, 96
health of, 58, 257, 302
in high school, 57–58

and the Hokkaido vacation, 127
and the Ichomachi festival, 186,
    191
interviews with, 185–86,
    200–205, 278–83, 321–26
job of, 17, 18, 59, 93–96, 199–200,
    247, 265, 278, 321, 324
and job vs. family, 203–4
life assessment of, 324
lunches for, 27
and Mariko's affair, 305
and Mariko's family, 60, 259–60,
    261, 270, 294
Mariko's secrets from, 86–87
on marriage, 310, 321–23, 325–26
and the *nanakaiki*, 61, 62
and the New Year's holidays,
    248, 250, 252, 255
personality of, 181, 294, 307–8,
    313–14
on politics, 253, 254, 265, 277,
    279–83, 324
and the Sanja Matsuri, 66, 70,
    72, 89
and sports, 130
as a trapped man, 205
trips of, 255
vulnerability of, 326
on who runs the Tanaka family,
    205
See also marital relations;
    Tanaka family
Tanioka, Kuniko, 221
Tanizaki, Yukio
and the gingko tree affair, 243,
    314, 315–18

Tanizaki, Yukio (*cont.*)
  and the Ichomachi festival,
    191–92
  and Ichomachi politics, 191–97,
    315–18
Taoism, 107
tea, serving, 84
teacher(s)
  of cram schools, 169
  interview with Ken-chan's,
    147–48
  parties for, 312–313
  salaries of, 147, 169
  samisen, 225, 226
  as a source of knowledge about
    U.S., 274
  See also Sensei; *specific person*
teenage sex, 262–63
television
  and *Dreamy Trip*, 119
  and the New Year's holidays,
    249–50, 250–51
  and school discussion topics, 147
  as a source of learning, 254, 274
  and *Tokyo Love Story*, 115–19
  and the visit to the studio, 7,
    285–92
Tetsuko's Room (television pro-
    gram), 301
three-*k* job, 94–95
Tokugawa Shogunate, 25, 26, 67, 155
Tokyo Hilton, lunch at the,
    291–92
Tokyo, Japan
  in the 1960s, 55
  Bumiller's impressions of, 8–10

postwar, 49–50
  in *Tokyo Love Story*, 118
Tokyo Love Story (television pro-
    gram), 115–19
Tokyo University, 83, 171
Toshimaen (water park), 111–13
True Story Age, Kijuchi story in,
    137
Tsuda College, 155
Tsuda, Ume, 155
Tsujimoto, Yoshiko, 222

Ueno, Chizuko, 79
United States
  and American products in
    Japan, 10, 123–24, 254,
    261–62, 266
  and the American Revolution,
    166–68
  and Bush's visit to Japan, 253–54
  Chiaki's views about the, 274
  comparison of drinking in Japan
    and the, 96–101
  Japanese relations with, 253–55,
    265–66, 276–83, 303
  Ken-chan's views of, 207
  killing of Japanese vacationers in,
    303
  Shunsuke's views about the, 254,
    261–62
  sources of Japanese knowledge
    about, 254, 274
  Takeshi's views about the, 254,
    265–66, 277, 278–83, 324
  work ethic in the, 7, 266, 276–78,
    279–83

vacations, 125–29

van Wolferen, Karel, 11, 330

Vienna, Austria, 197

Vogel, Ezra, 11

ward council meetings (Ichomachi area), 193–97

Waseda Commercial High School, 156–68, 262

Waseda Koto Gakuen, 157

Waseda University, 157, 287, 290

Weisman, Madeleine, 68, 69, 112, 113, 186, 312, 327

Weisman, Steve, 68, 69, 112, 186, 187, 190, 293, 327

Weizsacker, Richard von, 162

White, Merry, 178

The White Plum (Furuki), 155

Whiting, Robert, 130

Woman Mob Fighter (film), 136–37

women

  attitudes about men of, 76–78, 205

  changes since World War II concerning, 73

  education of, 73–74, 80, 83, 155

  as freer than men, 76–78, 205

  independence of, 220–22

  and politics, 74–75, 131–33, 194–95

  professional careers for, 81, 83–85

  as single parents, 81

  statistics about, 73–74

  typical pattern of life for, 76–77

  and the ward council, 193–95

  yakuza view of, 138

  See also feminism; mothers; PTA; women's movement; working women

women's movement, 6, 72–85

work ethic, in the U.S., 7, 266, 276–78, 279–83

working women

  and the economy, 78

  and education, 83

  home as primary responsibility of, 74–75, 76, 81

  and politics, 194–95

  and professional jobs, 74–75

  and PTA meetings, 229

  and serving tea, 84

  and social class, 84

  statistics about, 73–74

  and supportive husbands, 83–84

world history, teaching about, 161–68, 211–12

World War II

  American knowledge of Japanese society during, 26

  blame for, 53–54

  Ito in, 42

  legacy of the, 38–39, 244

  Saburo as a soldier during, 4, 42–50, 51–52, 255

  teaching about, 141–42, 143–44, 161–63, 164, 211–12

yakuza (Japanese mobsters), 6, 70–71, 133–39

Yamaguchi, Kristi, 303

Yanagisawa, Yumiko Jansson, 81

Yano Research Institute, 170
You Can Laugh (television program), 259, 285–92, 301
You Gotta Have Wa (Whiting), 130
younger brother, Mariko's
  accident of, 55–56
  birth of, 55
  death of, 61
  drinking/violence of, 56, 57,
    59–61, 97, 109, 247–48
  and the Festival of the Dead,
    104–5
  Mariko's marriage as an escape
    from, 59–60

Mariko's relationship with, 55,
    61, 326–27
marriage of, 60
memorial service for, 61–62,
    104–5
and religion, 108, 109
Saburo's relationship with, 56,
    60
Takeshi's relationship with,
    60
Yushima Tenjin shrine, 106

Zenchu (agricultural cooperative),
    123